The **VEGETARIAN TIMES** Cookbook

The VEGETARIAN

COLLIER BOOKS · Macmillan Publishing Company · New York

TIMES Cookbook

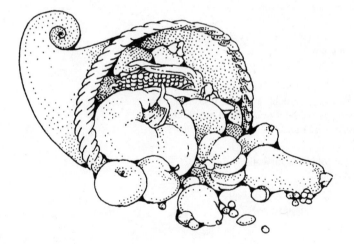

by the Editors of VEGETARIAN TIMES
WITH HERBERT T. LEAVY

Macmillan Publishing Company
866 Third Avenue, New York, N.Y. 10022
Collier Macmillan Canada, Inc.

Library of Congress Cataloging in Publication Data
Main entry under title:
The Vegetarian times cookbook.
 Includes index.
 1. Vegetarian cookery. I. Leavy, Herbert T.
II. Vegetarian times.
TX837.V427 1984   641.5′636   84-12119
ISBN 0-02-010370-0 (pbk.)

**Macmillan books are available at special discounts
for bulk purchases for sales promotions, premiums,
fund-raising, or educational use. For details, contact:**

**Special Sales Director
Macmillan Publishing Company
866 Third Avenue
New York, N.Y. 10022**

First Collier Books Edition 1984

10 9 8 7 6 5 4 3 2

Designed by Jack Meserole

Printed in the United States of America

CONTENTS

RECIPES

ACKNOWLEDGMENTS

We wish to thank the staff of *Vegetarian Times* for their excellent cooperation in compiling the recipes and other materials for this book. From approximately 1,500 recipes at our disposal, we selected what we believe to be a superb collection, reflecting the magazine's high standards. Special thanks to Bill Schnirring, the publisher, and Victoria Moran and Paul Obis, the editors. Splendid editorial assistance came from Lillian Borgeson on the introductory chapters, and Janet Schuy provided valuable editing and typing services for the 400 recipes chosen. Cooking advice from Mary Kuefner, as well as recipe testing, gave us peace of mind and some fine meals.

Herbert T. Leavy

Recipe Acknowledgments

All of the recipes were published in *Vegetarian Times*. A number of them were originally published in books, and we would like to mention these, their original authors, and the books in which they appeared. We appreciate the publishers' cooperation in allowing *Vegetarian Times* to use these recipes in the magazine and in this book. They are listed here by the chapter in which they appear:

Appetizers: Spiced Tofu Marinade from *The What to Do with Tofu*

Cookbooklet by Grow-cery, 6526 Landsdowne Avenue, Philadelphia, PA. Lentil Pâté and Soya Pâté from Martha Rose Shulman, author of *The Vegetarian Feast,* Harper & Row, New York, NY.

Beverages: Cranberry Glog, Cranberry Tea Punch, Avocado Aperitif, Basic Nogs, Fruit Flip, and White Lightning from *The Non-Drinker's Drink Book* by Gail Schioler. Single copies may be ordered (for $10.95 plus $1.00 postage and handling) from the publisher, Personal Library, Suite 439, 17 Queen Street East, Toronto, Ontario, Canada M5C IP9.

Soups: Quick Borscht from *The American Heart Association Cookbook,* published by David McKay Publishing Co., New York, NY. Garlic Soup from *The Airola Diet and Cookbook* by Dr. Paavo Airola, published at $12.95 by Health Plus Publishers, P.O. Box 22001, Phoenix, AZ 85028.

Salads: Tabouli Salad I from *Ten Talents* by Rosalie and Frank Hurd, Box 86A, Rt. 1, Chisholm, MN 55719. Cold Bean Salad from *Cookbook for People Who Love Animals* by World of God, Inc. Both books are available from North American Vegan Society, Box H, Malaga, NJ 08328. Information on salads and Middle Eastern Pasta Salad, Sook Choo Na Mool, and Oriental Salad Dressing from *A World of Salads* by Rosalie Swedlin, published at $9.95 by Holt, Rinehart & Winston, New York, NY.

Main Dishes—Fast Foods and Stews: Vegetarian Stew from Frances Sheridan Goulart, author of *Eating to Win,* published at $8.95 by Stein & Day, Briarcliff Manor, NY 10510. Whole Wheat Macaroni Casserole, Brown Rice and Carrot Casserole, Bean Burgers, and Lentil Casserole from *The Airola Diet and Cookbook* (see listing under *Soups* above). Vegetable Stew from *The Moosewood Cookbook* by Mollie Katzen, published by Ten Speed Press, Box 7123, Berkeley, CA. Mushroom Stew from *Vegetarian Epicure, Book II* by Anna Thomas, published by Alfred A. Knopf, New York, NY.

Main Dishes—Tofu and Soy: Scrambled Tofu from *More Vegan Recipes* by Freya Dinshah, published by North American Vegan Society, Box H, Malaga, NJ 08328. Soy Nut Meat from *Ten Talents* (see listing under *Salads* above). Un-Salmon Loaf from *Eat for Strength and Not for Drunkenness* by Agatha M. Thrash, M.D., published by Yuchi Pines Institute, Health Education Materials Dept., Rt. 1, Box 273, Seale, AL 36875. Pan-Fried Tofu and Fried Tofu with Vegetables from Debbi Hubbell. Scotch Eggs from *The Vegetarian Gourmet Cookbook* by Paul Southey, published by Van Nostrand Reinhold, New York, NY. Scheherezade Casserole from *The Moosewood Cookbook* (see listing under *Main Dishes—Fast Foods and Stews* above). Soy Burgers reprinted by permission from *Laurel's Kitchen: A Handbook for Vegetarian Cookery & Nutrition* by Laurel Robertson, Carol Flinders, and Bronwen Godfrey, copyright 1976, Nilgiri Press, Petaluma, CA 94953.

Breads: Apple Bran Muffins from *The Best of Jenny's Kitchen* by Jennifer "Jenny" Raymond, published at $6.95 by SunRay Press, P.O. Box 335, Littleriver, CA 95456.

Condiments: Homemade Ketchup from *Laurel's Kitchen* (see listing under *Main Dishes—Tofu and Soy* above). Information on condiments from Clare Barrett Obis. Nutritional Yeast Gravy adapted from *The Book of Miso* by William Shurtleff and Akiko Aoyagi, published by Ballantine Books, New York, NY. Cashew Nut Cream and Cashew Milk Gravy from *Ten Talents* (see listing under *Salads* above).

Desserts: Soy Coffee Cake from *The Soybean Cookbook* by Dorothea van Gundy Jones, published by Arco Publishing Co., New York, NY. Peanut Butter Cookies from *Cookbook for People Who Love Animals* (see listing under *Salads* above). Carob Apple Brownies from *More Vegan Recipes* (see listing under *Main Dishes—Tofu and Soy* above). Inspiration from the world of soy dishes also came from *The Vegetarian Gourmet Cookbook* (see listing under *Main Dishes—Tofu and Soy* above), *The Vegetarian Feast* (see listing under *Appetizers* above), *The Moosewood Cookbook* (see listing under *Main Dishes—Fast Foods and Stews* above), and *The Book of Tofu* by William Shurtleff and Akiko Aoyagi, published by Autumn Press, Brookline, MA (available from Ballantine Books, New York, NY). Caroballs I, Carobana Cupcakes, Soya-Carob Squares, and Sugarless Carob Cookies from Ellen Sue Spivack, author of *Beginner's Guide for Meatless Casseroles,* published by Ross Books, Berkeley, CA. Country Life Tofu Cheesecake from Josette Wahl. Carob Icing from *XXIII World Vegetarian Congress Cook Book* by Freya Dinshah, published by North American Vegan Society, Malaga, NJ 08328. Fudgesicles from *The Cookbook for People Who Love Animals* (see listing under *Salads* above).

Lunch Spreads: Peanut Butter Spread from *Foods for Healthy Kids* by Dr. Lendon Smith, published by Berkley, New York, NY.

Holiday Menus: Elegant Stuffed Pumpkin, Cream of Pumpkin Soup, Pumpkin Sauce, Pumpkin Butter, Tofu Pumpkin Pie, and

Pumpkin-Rice Pudding (inspired by a Carol Flinders recipe) from Martha Wagner, co-author of *The Soy of Cooking: A Tofu and Tempeh Recipe Book,* published at $3.95 by White Crane Publications, P.O. Box 3081-V, Eugene, OR 97403. Marinated Beets, Noodle Soup, Tossed Salad, Stuffed Squash, Gluten Gravy with Seitan, Seitan, Cranberry Applesauce, Candied Sweet Potatoes, and Pureed Chestnuts from Eunice Farmilant, author of *The Natural Foods Sweet Tooth Cookbook,* published by Jove Books, New York, NY. Wheat Gluten from Cornelia Aihara, author of *The Do of Cooking,* published by the George Ohsawa Macrobiotic Foundation, Boston, MA.

If any sources for recipes or other information were inadvertently overlooked, it was totally unintentional, and we sincerely apologize.

INTRODUCTION

About ten years ago the U.S. Senate Select Committee on Nutrition, chaired by George McGovern, issued a report on the dietary status of America. The report suggested that Americans cut back their consumption of animal fats, refined carbohydrates, and salt.

At the time, these guidelines were seen as radical by many in the food industry. The notion that Americans were eating too much animal fat threatened the meat industry; a call for cutting back on salt shook up the movers and shakers of the canned foods industry; and a call for less sugar was sour news for just about everybody else in the processed food industry.

The repercussions were enormous. Lobbyists from the food interests demanded a fair shake and the infamous McGovern Report was trimmed. What emerged was a watered-down version that the food industry found easier to accept. Nevertheless, the controversy fueled the debate over America's eating habits that had been sitting on the back burner for nearly a century.

While various health and healing properties have always been attributed to certain foods, America's "dietary reform" was begun during the last century by a handful of crusaders who were concerned about the kinds of foods Americans were eating. Among these health crusaders were Presbyterian minister Sylvester Graham, inventor of the graham cracker; John Harvey Kellogg; and C. W.

Post. Both Post and Kellogg founded cereal companies to provide Americans with an alternative breakfast food to replace the gruel and porridges which were then commonly eaten.

Later, at the turn of the century, dietary reformers included the likes of Horace Fletcher, who concluded that because we had thirty-two teeth, we should chew our food thirty-two times, and Bernard MacFadden. Most of these early health crusaders were colorful characters whose calls for dietary reform were usually mixed with fire and brimstone messages of temperance and a warning that dietary and sexual excesses would most assuredly lead a person to eternal damnation.

During the early part of this century, science captured the imagination and its magic spread to food. In 1911 the idea that there might be something called a *vitamin* was first proposed, and in 1913 vitamin A was one of the first vitamins to be discovered at the University of Wisconsin and at Yale. In the following decades, science identified other vitamins and later, proteins, amino acids, and various micronutrients.

For a time, the allure of science was pandemic: the country was caught up in a scientific hysteria of sorts, and with good reason. Science offered a rational explanation for the unexplainable. It held the promise of reducing food spoilage, eliminating communicable diseases, and along with industry, made inventions such as the refrigerator possible.

In the Roaring Twenties, the country was prosperous, life was good, and the future seemed limitless. In these optimistic times there seemed little need for dietary reform. The freewheeling times of the twenties changed after the stock market crash and for many, getting *anything* to eat presented enough of a problem.

Then World War II started and the effort to win taxed the best scientific minds as there developed a need for new medicines and methods of food preservation to feed the distant and seafaring troops.

By the late forties, so many advances had been made in modern medicine and nutritional science that anything that questioned it was viewed as cultish or unpatriotic. During the late forties and early fifties a number of natural health proponents actually suffered persecution by the FDA and the AMA, which branded those offering alternative paths as quacks.

These campaigns came to be viewed as excessive, and eventually, public sentiment caused the government to moderate its campaign against health "quackery," but not before the Basic Four Food Groups were established in 1956.

The Basic Four was a dietary pattern established to provide Americans with an easy-to-follow guideline for meeting their nutritional needs. Today, the Basic Four is the cornerstone of modern nutritional education. The Basic Four Food Groups consist of a milk group; a meat group; a bread and cereals group; and a vegetable-fruit group.

Not surprisingly, since nutrition was seldom taught in depth in school, many people never considered the origin of the Basic Four. Yet, because it has been institutionalized and is now a fundamental precept in nutritional thinking, few bother to question its authority. It should be noted, however, that prior to the Basic Four there was a Basic Seven and before that, a Basic Twelve. And, other countries today use other nutritional standards. In the Philippines, for example, the Basic Six is the standard.

Obviously, a "Basic" seven, twelve, or six would suggest more dietary choices. However, the Basic Four was introduced to simplify the rules of good nutrition for Americans, and after the formulation of the Basic Four, the USDA embarked on a public nutrition program to spread the message of this new, easier approach to good diet. One of the effects was a rise in meat-eating in the late fifties that continued until the publication of the McGovern Report in 1976.

In the mid-fifties and early sixties, a new group of self-styled health promoters arrived on the scene, telling people that they had to get back to natural foods.

The messages were varied and even to this day some of the theories contradict each other, but early latter-day health proponents like J. I. Rodale and Adelle Davis were saying, essentially, that something was wrong with the American diet. Both Rodale and Davis were strong proponents of supplements, arguing that food was now devitalized and reasoning that people could replace the missing elements with supplemental vitamins, minerals, and other ingredients.

Again, the FDA intervened, charging quackery and even jailing health food store owners for practicing medicine without a license.

Adelle Davis later died of cancer and Rodale suffered a heart attack, but for a new generation of Americans the idea was planted that maybe something was missing from food: maybe our diet of white bread, pot roast, and canned beans wasn't so good after all.

In the mid-sixties the idea caught on and the so-called health food movement went along for the ride during the turbulent sixties and early seventies. Like most things during those times, it underwent change and passed through various fads, including wheat germ and protein powders.

Gradually, "health foods" gave rise to "natural foods," the distinction being that rather than supplement your diet, one could return to the source of good nutrition.

Take rice, for example. As it comes from the plant, most rice is brown. But in the milling process the rice is stripped of its outer hull and polished to give it a nice, white appearance. This greatly increases its shelf life, but in the process, much of the real nutritive value of the rice is lost: the fiber, which is present in the outer hull, is lost and so are eighteen or so identifiable vitamins. Large food companies replace four of the eighteen vitamins and call the rice enriched or fortified, but it still doesn't have its fiber or the fourteen other vitamins still missing. Some early proponents of supplementation would urge people to take supplemental vitamins and fiber tablets, but in contrast, advocates of natural foods would argue that it would be much easier to simply eat the rice the way it is harvested. Why bother with milling it?

The position of the supplementalists has changed and today most people who favor supplements recommend them "just to be sure" you are getting adequate nutrition or to replace drug therapy in the treatment of certain disorders.

In any event, the health foods and natural foods exist, for the most part, side by side in many health food stores.

The natural foods movement that began during the late 1960s and early 1970s in many ways paralleled and was a part of the anti-establishment scene of that era. During these times, to belong to a food co-op and to buy from small and organic farmers was to make a social and political statement. This sort of dietary social consciousness reached its height in 1972 with the publication of Frances Moore Lappé's epic book, *Diet for a Small Planet*. In it, Lappé outlines the wastefulness of meat and urges that people adopt a meatless diet as a means of reducing world hunger. "Think globally, act locally" took root.

When the Vietnam War ended in 1973, the fever of social activism subsided. But a return to a better diet and healthier living fit in well with what many people turned to: for those turning to fitness, better diet was a natural; for people following a religion a simple diet was often mandated; and for the "back to the land" crowd, growing your own also meant eating your own. There were, in short, many reasons to continue eating better. And besides, the food of the seventies probably *was* worse than the food of fifty years earlier. The earth was full of pesticides, the soil was being depleted of nutrients, and all manner of chemicals were being injected daily into our foods to give them more shelf life, make them more appealing to the eye, and make them more convenient.

There were *lots* of reasons to eat better, and people started demanding better foods: foods that were less refined and that had fewer unnatural ingredients.

Just as public awareness about many issues had been raised by the mid-seventies and just as many once radical ideas seemed now to warrant thoughtful consideration, the issue of food and nutrition took on the air of respectability.

All consumers now seemed to be truly concerned about the ingredients that were finding their way into our food supply. And, people began to question whether a diet so high in salt, animal fats, and refined carbohydrates was really so good. Scientists at leading institutions and policy makers with vision also began to wonder, and soon health and nutritional awareness became serious consumer issues.

In the late 1970s and early 1980s more "official" reports about diet and health were issued from leading universities, consumer organizations, policy groups, and health organizations.

In the last few years very large and influential organizations such as the American Cancer Society (ACS) have officially recognized the link between diet and health. Finally, in early 1984, the U.S. Department of Health and Human Services (HHS) came around to officially recognizing this relationship.

The statements coming from the ACS and HHS reflect, rather than shape, public thinking or consumer trends.

Consider, for example, that in 1973, the total gross sales of all health food stores in the U.S. were $150 million. Ten years later, that figure had jumped to $2.2 billion. During the same period, the amount of red meat eaten by Americans had fallen by nearly 15 pounds a year, a decrease of 10 percent.

Although health food store sales are often used to illustrate the interest in health by Americans, this is just one of many indicators. The whole fitness boom is another. Meanwhile, little things, like less sugar in pre-sweetened cereals, is yet another.

Everywhere we look these days the interest in health by Americans seems evident, and it is difficult to quantify.

Fortunately for vegetarians, times have never been better. The health consciousness that pervades our society makes it easier for all of us to shop and eat in restaurants.

Vegetarianism has always been equated with health, and rightly so: the diet is lower in animal fats, high in fiber, and naturally high in vitamins, minerals, and other nutrients.

A vegetarian diet is for everyone. It is completely safe, and probably better for babies, children, adults, and the elderly . . . just about any group you can think of.

For years, a great deal of emphasis was placed on teaching people *how* to follow a vegetarian diet. People wondered: Will I get enough vitamin B_{12} and enough protein? Such questions are understandable, but for the most part, answering them here would require at least a thumbnail sketch of nutrition.

I'd like to propose a simpler answer; the answer to the question How can I become a vegetarian? is that you already are.

Every person on this planet is a vegetarian by nature—or something very close to it—but not all of us vegetarians follow a meatless diet.

Meat and other animal foods are, even today, such an accepted part of the American diet, that logic has become reversed.

Well, it's the same sort of thing when it comes to eating. While there are many good reasons to stop eating meat, there are fewer reasons for starting in the first place or continuing to do so.

The way in which most of the people of the world eat supports the view that the vegetarian diet is our natural diet. Anatomically, humans resemble herbivores much more than they do carnivores. Our teeth, for example, contain large, flat surface areas, suitable for grinding grains and vegetables. Our digestive tract is long, like that of other herbivores. In contrast, meat-eating animals have short digestive tracts. Meat, when it sits around in a stomach at 100 degrees Fahrenheit or so, will degrade rather rapidly, so short intestinal tracts are useful in eliminating it quickly. Plant foods, on the other hand, do not spoil as rapidly, and the high-fiber content of these foods makes them not only safer, but probably necessary to give our diets bulk.

But the best reason I can think of for continuing to eat meat is inertia. It's tough to change old habits.

And that, really, is the purpose of this book: to make it easier for you to change your diet for the better, to get back to a more natural way of eating. But to do so deliciously and easily.

The recipes in this book came from many people who have written for *Vegetarian Times* magazine. Many of them have written cookbooks of their own. You can find their books and other good vegetarian cookbooks at bookstores, libraries, and your local health food store.

The recipes in this book are a sampling of the recipes you'll find in other fine vegetarian cookbooks.

We have selected the recipes to appeal to a wide range of tastes and talents: like a good meal, there is a little bit of something here for everybody.

If you already follow a vegetarian diet, there should be enough here to serve as a basic good cookbook to have around the house. If you presently do not follow a vegetarian diet, there should be enough here to persuade you that a meatless diet is varied and good tasting.

It has taken more than a year to cull through ten years of our magazine and pick out the best for you. We hope we've done our job.

One

WHAT TO HAVE IN THE HOUSE—
STAPLES AND FRESH FOODS

It's certainly possible to be a well-nourished vegetarian on standard supermarket fare. Your neighborhood grocer has the fresh vegetables and fruits you will need, dairy products and eggs if you choose to use them, dried beans, some whole-grain breads and cereals, and perhaps even a "health food" section. Most vegetarians find, however, that their menus get both sparkle and substance—and on bulk items like nuts and flour they can save money—by shopping at natural foods retailers or joining a food co-op.

From wherever you stock your larder, you will want to be a wise consumer. Read labels carefully: Ingredients are listed in order of prominence, but manufacturers can be very clever. If you are cutting down on sugar, for example, you would probably buy the loaf of bread that has sugar fifth or lower on the ingredients list. But if other caloric sweeteners—honey, molasses, corn syrup, rice syrup, dextrose, malt, et cetera—are included too, there is a lot more sugar in that bread than you would think at first glance.

Vegetables and Fruits

Fresh produce is wonderful: vitamin-packed, colorful, tasty, the boon of waist-watchers, and no labels to decipher. The dark leafy greens are nature's nutritional powerhouses. Vary your salads with romaine, escarole, and endive (iceberg lettuce is something of a nutritional pauper). Learn to enjoy the stronger cooked greens—collards, kale, mustard—as well; they are chock full of calcium, iron, vitamin A, and even protein. Try to buy produce that is locally grown and in season when you can. That means a plentiful array, low prices, and produce at its peak of flavor and nutrition (see the charts on pages 17–22).

If you are paying premium prices for organic fruits and vegetables, be sure they are what they claim to be. The term "organic" refers to food grown without chemical fertilizers or pesticides. Since some disreputable farmers and merchants have marketed ordinary produce as organic, be sure that the market or health-food store you are dealing with has an impeccable reputation. Beyond that, you can expect organically grown vegetables to be smaller and less regular in size and shape, more flavorful, and maybe a little "buggier" than the agribusiness products. Or you could plant your own organic garden and eat self-satisfaction along with your sweet corn.

Fresh vegetables should be cooked in a tightly covered saucepan in as little water as is necessary to make them tender but not mushy. Many leafy greens are best cooked in just the water that adheres to them after washing. Steaming vegetables and quickly stir-frying them Oriental-style are excellent ways to retain satisfying crispness and most of the nutrients. And remember the delight of munching healthful vegetables raw, as salads or as elegant *crudités* with dip. (Fruits, of course, are the yummiest raw deal around, the dessert of Eden and of many health-conscious vegetarians.)

Frozen produce is a convenient second choice to fresh. In some cases, when vegetables are picked and "flash frozen" the same day, their nutrient content is higher when they get to your table than the fresh variety that has suffered early harvesting, long transport, and an extended supermarket stay. When you buy frozen vegetables, avoid any package that has ice on the outside; the odds are that it has thawed and been refrozen. Ask the checker to sack your frozen foods together, preferably in insulated bags that retard defrosting. Get them home fast and put them away first.

Since frozen vegetables have already been partially cooked, you can quickly finish the job at home. Follow the instructions on the package (salting the water is really unnecessary). And shorten cooking time, thereby preserving nutrients, by separating frozen pieces with a fork as they cook.

Frozen, unsweetened fruit is useful for fruit salads and compotes, and when added to blender drinks gives them a wonderful frosty thickness. And it is much cheaper to satisfy a December's strawberry craving with the frozen variety than those shipped from halfway around the globe.

Dried fruits are excellent winter staples; the drying process has been used for centuries to preserve foods with almost no nutrient losses. Dried dates, figs, apricots, et cetera, are extremely sweet but can be reconstituted by soaking in water overnight to "plump them up" to more of their original state. When shopping, look for those that are unsulphured. Sulphur dioxide is added to most commercially available dried fruits to preserve their color, but it is a questionable additive to which some people respond with severe allergic reactions. Unsulphured fruits do not look as pretty, but in your mouth it is taste over beauty every time!

Dried vegetables can be used as they come in stews and sauces just as long as you increase the cooking liquid accordingly. Add an extra cup of water for every cup used in vegetable stews, 2 extra cups for every cup used in soups. After adding the dried vegetables, bring the mixture to a boil, cover the pot, reduce to a simmer, and cook for 10 to 20 minutes. Or reconstitute dry vegetables by steeping them: Put them in a saucepan, cover them with boiling water, and put a tight-fitting lid on the pan. Keep the water hot but not boiling until most of the vegetables are rehydrated. Save any unabsorbed liquid for soup stock.

A can opener should be the least used gadget in your kitchen. Canned fruits have traditionally been limp and lifeless and are usually packed in sugary syrup. The canned-in-juice varieties are a vast improvement and can be useful when fresh fruit is unavailable. Canned vegetables are often soggy shadows of their former selves, overcooked in the canning process and usually heavily salted. Fresh raw peas, for example, have nearly ten times more sodium than fresh peas, ounce for ounce.

Legumes

This category covers dried beans, peas, lentils, and peanuts. These simple foods have long been unappreciated by many, but they form the center of a good vegetarian diet. They are rich in protein, B vitamins, and numerous minerals, contain virtually no fat, and have that stick-to-the-ribs quality that allows them to easily play the main dish role. The versatile legumes (also called pulses) can be used in soups like navy bean and split pea; in ethnic dishes such as chili, hummus (garbanzo dip), and lentil pilaf; and in vegetarian specialties such as loaves, burgers, and casseroles.

Whether you buy them in one-pound supermarket packages or in health-store bulk, look for legumes of consistent color and size, having smooth, unwrinkled skins and a minimum of dirt and defects. Stored tightly covered in a cool dry place, they will last just about forever. (Dried peas of a strain thought to be extinct were found upon excavation of King Tut's tomb. They were sprouted, grew, and are no longer extinct.)

All legumes except split peas, lentils, and peanuts should be soaked in water before cooking—up to 6 hours at room temperature or refrigerated overnight. Toss out any beans that float to the top during soaking, then cook the rest in ample water. (You can use the soaking water if you have washed the beans first.) Cooking times vary from 40 minutes to 3 hours depending upon the bean at hand, although pressure cooking shortens this considerably. If you use salt, add it at the last minute since it retards the tenderizing process. You will know the beans are done when they are easy to pierce with a fork and seem tender but firm. That is the time to add not just salt but the numerous other flavorings from molasses to vinegar that legumes take to so well.

Typically, 1 cup of dried pulses will yield 2 to 2½ cups cooked. This is the opposite of meat which shrinks on cooking, so the economic benefits of beaning up on legumes are obvious.

Grains and Pasta

Let's pretend: A pickpocket steals your wallet containing $40. His conscience then bothers him that you are left broke, so he slips $6 back to you. Would you feel enriched? Of course not. You would feel robbed of $34. Yet the millers of grain act out a similar scenario every day: Up to forty nutrients are stripped from whole grains in the refinement process, yet by adding back half a dozen or so of these, the resultant product is said to be "enriched."

Of all the grains used in America, only oats, in their familiar "rolled" form, have been widely available as a cereal whose nutrients have managed to survive conventional processing. But the whole-grain situation is changing. The grains, their flours, and breads and pastas made from them can now be purchased in both health-food stores and some standard markets. Be aware that "flour" or "wheat flour" means the refined type; look for that word "whole" on the ingredients list.

When buying any whole-grain foods, be sure the store selling them has a rapid turnover of such products because their shelf life is shorter than that of the denatured variety. Keep the breads and flours refrigerated (measure flour and bring it to room temperature before using in baked goods). Whole grains themselves may be stored in jars like legumes. It is when the grain is crushed to be made into flour that its oily germ is exposed to air and to the danger of rancidity.

Whole-grain cereals are easy to cook—just stir into boiling water (typically 2½ cups of water to each cup of cereal). They can then be used in numerous ways: as breakfast food with fruit or a little butter and honey; as a bed for savory beans or stir-fried vegetables; and as a base for meatless loaves or burgers. It is also quite simple to make pasta from whole-wheat flour. To 1½ cups of flour, add 2 eggs (or 1 egg and 2 teaspoons of oil) and blend with a fork. Knead the dough until it is easy to work and use a rolling pin to roll it out on a floured board. When it is as thin as you want it, let the dough "rest" for about an hour. It will be dry but not brittle and ready to cut into thin strips or any other shape you want. Let the pasta rest for another hour or two before cooking. (Homemade pasta will keep a long time in your freezer, but don't thaw it before cooking.) Ready-made whole-wheat spaghetti and lasagna are fairly widely marketed, and health-food stores even stock pastas made from soy, corn, and other flours.

Nuts and Seeds

These are the original munchies: self-contained, natural, and snacking-good. They contain concentrated nourishment—protein,

B vitamins, vitamin E, several minerals, and essential fatty acids. Their fat content makes them high in calories—excellent for hikers and athletes, to be used with a touch of moderation by the rest of us. But use them; they are extremely versatile in cooking and baking, and they add flavor and crunch to hundreds of recipes.

When buying nuts in their shells, stock up in the autumn and early winter when they are fresh and abundant. In a cool dry place, they'll last until the next year's harvest. Look for clean, unblemished shells and avoid any that feel too lightweight for their size. You can expect 1 pound of unshelled nuts to produce about ½ pound of edible nutmeats.

If you think *The Nutcracker* is better as a ballet than as a kitchen implement, look for shelled nuts of firm, healthy appearance. Find out from the store how long the nuts have been out because, once shelled, they can turn rancid and attract insects. And do buy in bulk: Only a millionaire could use nuts in reasonable quantities from those high-priced 2-ounce bags. Keep nuts and seeds refrigerated where they will stay fresh four to six months; in the freezer they will last a year. If you lack refrigerator space, put them in dark-colored jars with tight covers and store them in a cabinet up to two months.

Among the virtues of nuts and seeds are:

Sproutability. Many seeds, as well as some legumes and grains, can be easily sprouted to produce a tender, high-quality mini-vegetable packed with vitamins and other nutrients. Special sprouting equipment and instructions are available in most health-food stores. You could also start by simply soaking alfalfa or sunflower seeds (or mung beans or lentils) overnight in a jar of pure water. Pour that water off (it is said to be good for plants) through the jar's mesh-topped lid or a piece of cheesecloth rubber banded to the jar top. Rinse your future sprouts twice daily so they stay slightly moist but not soggy. In a couple of days they will be ready to eat in salads or after being lightly stir-fried.

Nutbutter. It isn't limited to peanuts only. Cashews, Brazils, roasted sesame seeds, and roasted sunflower seeds can be turned into delicious spreads with the help of a food processor or grinder. Lacking these, you can use a blender, but this method may require the addition of oil or water to get a spreadable consistency. Store the butter in the refrigerator, but let it soften at room temperature a bit before spreading. If the oil separates, simply stir it back in.

The "meal" that results from grinding nuts or seeds in an electric mill or blender can substitute for part of the flour in breads and other baked goods and in sauces; it can also be added to cooked cereals. When using a blender for the job, select the highest speed and use ¼ cup of nuts or seeds each time.

"Milk." Nuts and seeds make delicious dairylike beverages. Raw cashews and blanched almonds work best. To make the milk, whiz 1 cup of nuts and 1 quart of water in your blender; add sweetener (1–2 tablespoons of honey per quart) and any of the following options: 1 tablespoon of mild oil, ⅛–¼ teaspoon of salt, or vanilla extract or carob powder to taste. Store in the refrigerator; it is perishable like cow's milk.

Sweeteners

White sugar and its brethren—brown, turbinado, and so-called raw sugar—are still highly refined sucrose and add no health-building properties to the diet. Research indicates that these substances are, in fact, "antinutrients," robbing the body's vital stores. Certain biochemists have pointed out that the degree of refinement to which sugar is subject renders it no longer a food but more of a drug, and some people do believe they are addicted to it. Even if these are extreme arguments, the fact remains that Americans consume a tremendous amount of sugar's "empty calories."

There are more natural sweeteners to keep the dessert lover in us all happy. Remember, though, that even these are highly concentrated and should be used sparingly, but it doesn't take much to make treats that are downright dynamite.

Honey has some trace minerals, about twice as much sweetening power as sugar, and comes in a variety of flavors, depending on the pollen used by the bees that made it. As a general rule, the darker the color, the sweeter the honey. When you replace sugar with honey in a standard recipe, cut the amount in half and use a little less liquid than the recipe calls for.

Molasses is one of the first products subtracted from sugar in the refining process, and in addition to sucrose it contains most of the nutrients that sugarcane has in the field before it gets to the mills: iron, calcium, thiamin, and riboflavin. Molasses has a strong flavor and is best in spicy baked goods like gingerbread, or to sweeten a blender drink.

Maple syrup is sweeter than sugar but not as sweet as honey, and it is mild enough for many uses. Its nutritional value is small, but its taste on the morning's buckwheat cakes is terrific.

Sorghum, corn, rice, and barley malt syrups are made from grain and are available at supermarkets and health-food stores. All have some nutritional value but—like all the sweets—are not to be used in sufficient quantity for those nutrients to make much of a dietary contribution. In baked goods these syrups are best used in combination with another sweetener.

Date sugar, found in natural foods shops, is granulated from whole, dried dates. Dates themselves, with their 75 percent natural sugar content, are excellent for sweetening cereals and can be blended with liquid to sweeten whatever you are baking. Using this whole food is the most wholesome way to sweeten.

Fruit juice concentrate—the familiar frozen kind or the syrup variety at your health-food store—can be used in place of other syrups. Mixing a small amount of it with club soda or sparkling water also makes an instant, natural soft drink.

Oils

Oils are abundant in such foods as nuts, seeds, and avocado. They are also present in vegetables. The essential fatty acids they provide are just that: essential. But we tend to overdo a good thing here by reliance on extracted oils. The bottled oils are taken from their plant sources via a chemical process. The health-food store has "cold-pressed oils," but even these are processed with some heat. You can't simply "squeeze" oil from an olive or corn kernel.

We have known for years that Americans' heavy consumption of saturated fats, almost entirely from animal sources, brings potential health risks, and we have learned more recently that *total* fat consumption—saturated and unsaturated, animal and vegetable—needs to be curtailed. This does not have to condemn us to boring meals, though. Simply cutting down on fat—using 1 tablespoon in a recipe that calls for 2, sautéeing in half oil/half water, collecting a few low-oil recipes for salad dressing—can keep favorite flavors intact. Here's some information about specific oils:

Safflower oil is very mild in taste; it is fine for cooking but a little too greasy to use as a dressing. It is the oil highest in polyunsaturated fats and is therefore recommended for people watching their cholesterol levels.

Corn oil has a mild flavor. It is okay for sauces and dressings and is high in polyunsaturated fats. Its high smoking point makes it a top choice for deep-frying, but that is the least healthful cooking method.

Peanut oil, like corn oil, has a high smoking point and is fine for deep-frying. Its mild flavor makes it suitable for sauces and dressings, too. It is fairly high in polyunsaturated fats.

Soy oil is high in polyunsaturated fats, but in its unrefined form it is dark in color and strong in flavor.

Olive oil has a rich, distinctive flavor. It is the oil of choice for many cooks in salad dressings and sauces.

Sunflower oil has a mild flavor and is very high in polyunsaturates. It is excellent for salad dressings but limited in cooking use.

Sesame oil, almond oil, hazelnut oil, walnut oil, and avocado oil are all high in polyunsaturates, useful for salad dressings, and characterized by a sharp or nutty flavor. Use them with other oils or for special effects.

Herbs and Spices

Herbs and spices form the most creative part of cooking and the part least susceptible to strict rules. The tips listed here will give you some general information about these intriguing ingredients, and the chart on pages 10–12 will tell you some of the uses.

· Herbs can be used fresh or dry. In most cases the dried version is concentrated and much stronger, so adjust amounts accordingly.

· Most fresh herbs have a short season and, except for parsley, are hard to find in stores, which is a good reason for growing your own. To store fresh herbs, wash, dry, and wrap them in paper toweling, and refrigerate in a plastic bag.

· To dry fresh herbs, hang them in a dry room until they are brittle enough to crumble or dry them in a shallow baking pan in a very low oven. Store dried herbs in jars with tight-fitting caps in a cool dry place (not next to the stove), and label each jar with name and date. Though dried herbs have a lot of potency per teaspoon to begin with, they start losing their seasoning power after about a year.

· To enrich the flavor of dried herbs, presoak them for a few minutes in a liquid (oil, lemon juice, soup stock, et cetera) that will be used in the recipe.

· If a taste test tells you that you have overseasoned something you are cooking, toss in a peeled raw potato to take up some of the excess flavor.

· Add herbs and spices to a long-cooking dish 15 to 30 minutes before serving. Longer cooking robs many of them of their characteristic flavor.

How to Use Herbs and Spices

allspice	Reddish-brown berry available whole and ground. Use with cooked apple dishes, pumpkins, squash, sweet potatoes, and in spicy cakes and cookies.
anise	Aromatic seed that can be used whole and ground. Adds a light licorice flavor to cakes, sweet rolls, fruit pies, and salads. Makes a strong, aromatic tea.
basil★	Use fresh or dried with eggs in green salads and with vegetables (especially tomatoes).
bay leaf★	Dried leaf can be used whole in sauces and casseroles. Remove before serving.
burnet	Float the leaves of this herb in cold beverages (like mint) or use in green salads. Has a cucumberlike flavor.
camomile	Makes strong, flavorful, aromatic tea. Good before sleep.
caraway★	Small crescent-shaped seed is used in cheeses, rye bread, pickling, and with cabbage, turnips, and onions.
cardamom	Available in whole seeds and ground. Its lemon-ginger flavor spices fruit punches, puddings, and sweet potatoes.
catnip	Makes strong tea.
cayenne	Ground hot pepper can be used in Mexican salsa and other sauces, in soups, and with eggs.
chervil★	With a taste reminiscent of both anise and parsley, its dried leaves, whole or ground, can be used in green salads and white sauces.
chive★	Long tubular leaves have a light onion flavor. Use dried or fresh and scissor-sliced. Favorite accompaniment for baked potatoes, sour cream, dips, and cottage and cream cheese.
cilantro★	Round leaves are always used fresh in Italian and Latin American salads and casseroles.
cinnamon	Available in sticks and ground. Sweet, spicy addition to baked goods, hot cocoa and cider, and custards.
cloves	Comes ground and in whole dry buds. Sweet and spicy. Used in hot beverages and sweet sauces.
coriander★	The berry of the cilantro plant. Used in baked goods.

Note: A star identifies herbs and spices that are relatively easy to grow at home.

How to Use Herbs and Spices (*Cont.*)

costmary	Its leaves make a light minty tea. Can also be used in soups, sauces, and green salads.
cumin	Available ground and as whole seed. Good in soups and spicy sauces. Provides traditional pungent aroma in Mexican and Indian fare.
dill★	Seeds are used whole in pickling spices. Ground dill and the plant's dried leaves are also good in salads and sauces.
fennel★	Whole seeds and ground stalks are both used. Try them in Italian breads and rolls. Also for tea.
fenugreek	Available in whole and ground seeds. Used in curry powder and chutneys. Also for tea.
ginger	Comes in whole and cracked roots, also ground and crystallized. Used in baking and as an exotic addition to stir-fried vegetables.
hyssop	Leaves are a minty addition to vegetable and fruit salads. Flowers can be used for tea.
lovage	Celery-flavored leaves and stalks. The seeds are used in cakes and cookies.
mace	The outer covering of the nutmeg shell is available ground and dried; tastes like a milder version of nutmeg. Used in fruit pies, puddings, and vegetable breads.
marjoram★	Available ground and dried whole leaves. Excellent in salads and sauces and with cooked green vegetables.
mint★	Available whole, crushed or ground leaves, fresh, and dried. Used in cold beverages, teas, and with beans and peas.
mustard★	Available as whole and ground seeds, also as prepared condiment. Sharp flavor enlivens sauces, dressings, and many other dishes.
nutmeg	Comes ground and as whole seeds. A favorite in many egg dishes, puddings, cooked vegetables, and spicy baked goods.
oregano★	Available ground and dried whole leaves. Its strong flavor is a good addition to tomato sauces used for pasta.
paprika	Available ground. Used as a mild garnish for eggs, cream sauces, salads, et cetera.
parsley★	You can get it fresh, dried, and in flakes. Use it with almost anything but fruits and sweets.
pepper	Dried peppercorns are available whole and ground. Next to salt, this is the world's most ubiquitous seasoning. Usable in practically all cooked and many fresh foods.
rosemary★	Needle-shaped leaves are used whole, fresh or dried, and ground.

Note: A star identifies herbs and spices that are relatively easy to grow at home.

	Slightly sweet flavor is pleasant with many cooked vegetables; use it in soups, sauces, and Italian dishes.
saffron	Available (and expensive) as whole filaments and ground. Use in Spanish breads and cakes, and in white sauces.
sage★	Gray-green leaves are available whole and ground. Use sage in salad dressing, cheese dishes, and with beans and peas.
savory★	Available as whole and ground leaves. Aromatic herb is a traditional seasoning for lentil soup and is good with tomatoes, beans, and cabbage.
tarragon★	Available whole and ground dried leaves. Use in dressings, salads, sauces, and in egg and tomato dishes.
thyme★	Gray-green leaves are used dried and ground. Light lemon flavor. Goes well with cooked and fresh tomato dishes.
turmeric	Available ground. Use in cream sauces and curry, and with rice and noodles.
vanilla	Can be used in whole-bean form and as liquid extract. Used in baked goods, puddings, custards, ice cream, sweet sauces, and nut milks.

Note: A star identifies herbs and spices that are relatively easy to grow at home.

Glossary

Note: Many of the items here may seem exotic. Unusual foods and foreign foods can add interest to a vegetarian's diet just as they can to anyone else's, but they are *not* necessary for pleasant and healthful meatless meals. Experiment with some foods that are new to you and see what you think. If you end up back with your favorite fruits, vegetables, grains, and beans, and some cheese if you like, you'll still be doing just fine.

adzuki Small, deep-red beans used in baked goods and salads; also for growing some of the best-tasting sprouts around.
agar Japanese sea vegetable used for its jelling quality. (Also known as kanten and agar-agar.)
alfalfa Grain seed that provides what is probably the most common form of "sprout." Alfalfa sprouts are very easy to grow and can be used in sandwiches, salads, soups, and as garnishes.
amaranth A grain that can be popped like corn or milled into flour

and used as a thickening agent. Seeds contain high-quality protein in large amounts. Leaves are nutritious too. Used by ancient Aztecs.

anise   Spicy seeds available whole and ground. Used in cakes, pies, salads, liqueurs, and pastry.

arame   See seaweed.

arrowroot   Starch derived from a plant root and used for thickening. In combination with soy flour (one teaspoon to ½ cup of warm water) can substitute for eggs in baking.

bean curd   See tofu.

bran   Brown outer layer of grain usually extracted in modern processing but extremely nutritious. A concentrated source of B vitamins and minerals and an important fibrous food. Found in most natural foods stores and easily added to cereals, cookies, breads, et cetera.

buckwheat groats   The three-cornered seed of the fruit of the buckwheat plant, always treated as a grain, is ground into flour and used in pancakes, biscuits, and muffins.

bulgur   Cracked wheat that has been hulled and parboiled to conserve most of the nutrients of whole wheat. It looks like cracked wheat, is used as a cereal or side dish, and can substitute for rice.

burdock root   Vegetable that grows wild in northeastern United States. Eaten when young, it is very alkaline and has an "earthy" smell and quality. Can be steamed, baked, and sautéed, and is used in soups.

carob   Also called St. John's Bread, the pods of a Mediterranean evergreen. Closely resembling chocolate in flavor, it has no caffeine but does have calcium and natural sweetness. You can buy carob in chip and powder form, either raw or roasted. When adding it to beverages, use it as a syrup by adding 1 cup of carob powder to 1 cup of water and stirring to a boil over low heat. With the addition of ¼ part honey, carob syrup can be used instead of melted semisweet chocolate in any standard recipe.

chick-pea, also called garbanzo   Beige-colored, round legume used in purees, vegetable stews, and salads.

chicory   A tap root, ground, roasted, and used as a substitute for coffee or mixed with coffee to reduce caffeine and the cost of the finished product.

cornmeal, whole   Most supermarket cornmeal has been *bolted* and *degermed*—processes that remove much of the hull and the nutritional value. Whole cornmeal retains full nourishment but is more perishable. Cornmeal comes both white and yellow; either color can be whole or degermed.

dulse   See seaweed.

fava   Flat kidney-shaped bean used in casseroles, soups, and pasta dishes.

fenugreek   The seeds of this herb are often used for sprouting. Sprouts are spicy and are used as accent and seasoning in casseroles, et cetera. The seeds may be used for tea as well.

germ   The seed of a grain product which, like bran, is usually removed in modern processing to increase its shelf life. Wheat germ and corn germ, the two types most often available, are perishable (the raw much more so than the toasted variety) and must be tightly sealed in the refrigerator. They are a good source of protein, vitamins, and minerals. They can be sprinkled on salads and desserts or added to any baked goods.

granola   A snack or cereal made by combining whole grains, honey, raisins, nuts, et cetera. Made yourself or carefully selected at a natural foods store, this can be a healthful cereal. The advertised brands, though, are overly sweetened and high in fat.

hijiki   See seaweed.

Irish moss   A sea vegetable that can be used as a jelling agent but requires refrigeration for firmness. Yields the extract carrageenin. Use Irish moss for aspics, dessert molds, and meatless bouillon.

kefir   A fermented milk popular in the Middle East and Russia. It is sweet tasting, easy to digest, and delicious when blended with fresh fruit. Also used in dips and vegetable dressings.

kelp   See seaweed.

kombu   See seaweed.

lecithin   An oily substance usually derived from soybeans (also found in egg yolk). Sold in granular and liquid form, lecithin is used as an emulsifier in some recipes and can substitute for eggs in baking. Due to antioxidant property, it has been used as a food supplement.

Marmite   Brand name for yeast extract.

masa harina This whole-grain cornmeal, soaked in lime water, is used throughout Latin America for making tortillas.

millet Tiny yellow grain boiled for breakfast and main dishes. Also used to thicken and flavor soups and sauces. The whole seed makes pleasant-tasting sprout, but almost all millet sold for cooking has had the outer husk removed and will not sprout.

miso A fermented Japanese seasoning made from a mixture of soybeans and grain plus salt, water, and mold starter. Used as a condiment, spread, or soup base. Comes in several varieties (red miso, white miso, rice miso) with subtle flavor variations.

nori See seaweed.

oats This light-brown grain, available in rolled or cut flakes, is used as cereal, as thickening, and in baked goods, pancakes, et cetera. Even the "quick" and "minute" varieties provide whole-grain nutrition.

okara This is the "pulp" that is left over when you make tofu from curdling soymilk. Can be used in salads, burgers, or as a base for natural pet food.

parsley root The root of the popular herb has the strong aroma and flavor of parsley. It can be used in soups in the way one would use celery root (celeriac).

pectin, low-methoxyl Used to make jelly without the sugar required by other pectins.

rye berries Whole rye in long thin kernels. Can be used as cooked cereal or ground for flour. Makes sweet-tasting sprout.

Savorex Brand name for yeast extract.

seaweed Sea vegetables come in a vast array but are similar in their salty "ocean-y" taste and smell and outstanding nutritional properties. All are extremely rich in minerals, and most are good protein sources. *Arame* is good in salad, sauces, and soups. The deep *dulse* can be used in salads, sandwiches, and relishes after simply soaking a few minutes in water. Mild-flavored *hijiki* is nice in stir-fries and even served alone with a dash of lemon after a 15-minute soak in water. *Kombu* can be toasted or stuffed with cheese or vegetables. *Nori* is a thin leaf used for wraps (vegetarian *sushi* is seasoned vegetables wrapped in nori). *Wakame,* more like leaf vegetables than other sea plants, is eaten raw in salad or cooked with beans or in soup. The best known sea vegetable is *kelp* which, although strong and rather "fishy" in large quantities, comes in powder form as a salty seasoning and in tablets as a natural supplement of iodine and trace minerals.

sesame seeds Available unhulled, hulled, toasted, and raw. The source of sesame oil and sesame butter (see tahini). Unhulled seeds make excellent sprouts when young.

shoyu Natural soy sauce made from aged and fermented soybeans and wheat. Quite salty, it stands in well for granular salt.

soba Japanese buckwheat noodles.

soybeans Rich in high-quality protein and called in the Orient, "honorable soybean, meat without bones." Can be prepared and eaten like any other legume, but the whole bean does require a long cooking time so the quicker-cooking soy flakes, grits, and granules are popular. Soaked beans can be blended with water, strained, and the resultant white liquid cooked and sweetened for a tasty milk. Ready-made soymilk and instant soymilk powders are sold at health-food stores. There is even soy ice cream! Soybeans can be sprouted, but the hearty sprouts, valuable for their high-protein/low-calorie ratio, must be cooked before eating. "Soynuts" are a roasted version of the beans that make a crunchy snack. (See also okara, shoyu, tamari, tempeh, tofu.)

tabouli Popular grain salad made from cracked wheat.

tahini Sesame butter. Used in Middle Eastern dishes and in a tasty salad dressing.

tamari Natural soy sauce made from soybeans and salt, aged and fermented. The term is often used in referring to shoyu.

tempeh Fermented food, usually made by exposing cultured soybeans to the mold, *rhizopus oligosporus,* it is a reliable source of vitamin B_{12} and makes a substantial main dish.

tofu (bean curd) "Soy cheese" is made from curdling soymilk. Tofu is extremely versatile since this white cake is bland by itself and adapts to whatever seasonings are used with it. It can be used in savory soups, salad dressings, dips, casseroles, stir-fries, or to make vegetable burgers. It can also be sweetened for cheesecake or yogurt. An excellent source of protein and calcium, tofu is virtually

Glossary (*Cont.*)

fat-free. Look for firm tofu to use in most recipes and the soft variety for dressings and purees.

triticale A hybrid of whole wheat and whole rye that is cooked whole or cracked for cereal or milled to make flour.

TVP "Textured vegetable protein" is available dry for reconstitution with water and used instead of meat in loaves, chili, spaghetti sauce, et cetera. This processed product is also the base for the frozen and canned "mock meats" that some vegetarians deplore ("Who wants fake meat?") but that others find most useful in the early stages of dietary change.

wakame See seaweed.

wheat This is the most widely used grain in America. Whole "wheat berries" may be cooked as cereal and also make a sweet, delicately flavored sprout. Bran, bulgur, cracked wheat, wheat germ, and flour (whole-wheat bread flour and the lighter pastry flour) are among the forms of wheat available.

yeast extract This dark savory paste is especially popular in Britain and Australia for seasoning and as a sandwich spread. It has the nutritional properties of powdered yeast (see below), and most brands are B_{12}-fortified.

yeast, nutritional Also called "yeast flakes" or "torula yeast," this powder is grown on molasses and is extremely high in protein and all the B-complex vitamins except B_{12}, which is often added. Some varieties (the old brewer's yeasts) are very bitter and strong, suitable only for nutritional supplementation in blender drinks, et cetera. Other forms are mild tasting and can be used on salads, in soups, and for making sauces, spreads, and gravies with cheeselike flavor. Smoked yeast (Bakon Yeast) is a useful seasoning for greens and split pea soup where pork is otherwise used.

How to Buy and Store Vegetables

Vegetable	Season	Signs of Quality	Storage
Artichoke	Spring	Close-growing leaves form tight globe. Uniform green color.	Will keep 4 days refrigerated in plastic bag.

How to Buy and Store Vegetables (*Cont.*)

Vegetable	Season	Signs of Quality	Storage
Asparagus	April–June	Tight, compact tips; smooth, dark-green color. White asparagus are less nutritious.	Wrap stalks in damp toweling; put in covered container or plastic bag. They'll keep for 2–3 days in refrigerator.
Beet	Summer, early Fall	Firm, round bulb, deep-red color, small to medium size with slim tap root. Young beet greens can be cooked like spinach.	Cut top off about 2 inches above the bulb. Refrigerated in plastic bag, beets will keep up to 3 weeks.
Broccoli	October–May	Dark-green, close-clustered buds. Leaves are rich in vitamin A. Can be prepared like other greens.	Will keep 3–5 days refrigerated in plastic bag.
Brussels sprouts	Fall	Bright green color, firm heads, tight leaves.	Refrigerate in plastic bag 2–4 days.
Cabbage	All year	In white and green cabbage look for tight leaves, compact head, heavy for its size, and good color—greenish white for white cabbage, purple for red cabbage. Savoy cabbage should have dark-green color and crumpled leaves.	Will keep for as long as 2 weeks refrigerated in plastic bag.
Carrot	All year	Smooth surface, tapered shape, crisp (not limp) feel, and orange color.	Cut off and discard tops. Will keep for over 2 weeks refrigerated in sealed plastic bag.

How to Buy and Store Vegetables (*Cont.*)

Vegetable	Season	Signs of Quality	Storage
Cauliflower	Fall to mid-Winter	White compact florets; hard, well-shaped head.	Refrigerate in plastic bag 3–5 days.
Celery	All year	Stiff, crisp, shiny stalks. Green celery is more nutritious than white, bleached version.	Refrigerate in plastic bag 1 week.
Celery root (celeriac)	Summer	Smallish size, crisp texture, and brown root.	Store 1 week in refrigerated bag.
Corn	May–September	Plump, even kernels squirt juice out in hard spray when pierced. Husk should be green and look moist.	Best eaten immediately but will keep for 1 or 2 days if refrigerated in husks.
Cucumber	All year	Look for unwrinkled dark-green skin; firm, heavy for size. If waxed, peel.	Will keep for 1 week refrigerated in plastic bag.
Eggplant	July–September	Smooth, tight, shiny skin; firm body; deep-purple color. Choose those light in weight for their size.	Will keep 2–4 days refrigerated in plastic bag.
Greens chicory collards dandelion endive escarole kale lettuce mustard sorrel spinach watercress	Spring, early Summer for most	Bright green leaves. Because outer leaves have more nutrients, avoid greens that have been stripped to inner leaves only.	Put into perforated plastic bag. Keep in refrigerator for up to 5 days.

How to Buy and Store Vegetables (*Cont.*)

Vegetable	Season	Signs of Quality	Storage
Kohlrabi	Summer	Firm light-green bulb with crisp green top. Member of cabbage family.	Store tops and bulbs separately in plastic bags and refrigerate. Tops will keep 2–3 days, bulbs 1–2 weeks.
Lima, green	Spring, Summer	Plump, shiny pod.	Refrigerate in shells 2–5 days.
Mushrooms	All year	Small to medium mushrooms are more flavorful than big fibrous ones. Cap should be white or light brown closed tightly around stem with no gills showing. Clean off black spores with damp cloth or special brush; do not immerse in water.	Refrigerate in closed paper bag or ventilated container for 5 days.
Okra	May–October	Small white or bright-green pod. Buy when firm and crisp	Refrigerate in perforated plastic bag 4–5 days.
Onion	All year	Hard, round shape with dry papery skin, mold-free.	Store in cool, dark, dry place in net bag. Will keep 4–6 weeks.
Onion, green (scallion)	All year	Small white bulb; crisp, dark-green stem. Use entire scallion.	Refrigerate in plastic bag for up to 1 week.
Parsnip	Fall, Winter	White, firm, well-tapered root. Peel to remove heavy wax routinely used.	Will keep for about 3 weeks refrigerated in plastic bag.
Pea, green	February–July	Bright-green pod with medium-size, uniform peas.	Refrigerate in pod, uncovered, for 2–4 days.

How to Buy and Store Vegetables (*Cont.*)

Vegetable	Season	Signs of Quality	Storage
Pepper, sweet (green or red)	May- October	Firm, crisp, unwrinkled bell, glossy color. Scrub especially well if waxed. (Outdoor birds like to eat the white seeds inside peppers.)	Refrigerate in plastic bag up to 5 days.
Potato	All year	Firm, well shaped, no discoloration. Avoid those with greenish cast to the skin. For baking or cooking whole, choose uniform sizes. Cut out "eyes" before cooking if any have developed.	Store in cool dry place, preferably with some ventilation. Will keep 1–2 months.
Radish black, red	Late Spring to early Summer	Round shape, firm to the touch. Huge red radishes are usually fibrous and flavorless.	Refrigerate in plastic bag for up to 2 weeks.
white		Icicle-shaped tap root, 3 to 4 inches long, should be firm and slender.	Refrigerate in plastic bag for up to 2 weeks.
Rutabaga	Fall, early Winter	Medium size; smooth, thick skin. Peel to remove wax.	Store in cool dry place. Will keep 1 month.
Squash, summer: pattypan	Spring, Summer	Medium size; firm, clear skin.	Will keep for up to 5 days refrigerated in plastic bag.
yellow	Spring, Summer	May be crookneck or straight. Should have light yellow skin and be fairly heavy for size.	Same as above.

Vegetable	Season	Signs of Quality	Storage
zucchini	Spring, Summer	Firm, dark-green skin.	Same as above.
Squash, winter acorn buttercup butternut chayote hubbard pumpkin spaghetti	Fall, Winter	All but chayote should have hard rind and true color—dark green for acorn, buttercup, and hubbard; beige for butternut; orange for pumpkin; yellow for spaghetti. Chayote has pale-green rind.	Will keep several months in a cool dry place.
Stringbean	May–October	Smooth, crisp pod, long and slender in shape. Should snap crisply when broken.	Refrigerate in plastic bag for 2–5 days.
Sweet potato	Fall, Winter	Smooth, firm potato of good shape; medium size.	Store in cool dry place for a week.
Tomato	All year	Plump shape; uniform color.	Refrigerate in crisper for up to 1 week.
Turnip	October–March	Tender skin, mostly white with some purple, small to medium size.	Refrigerate in plastic bag 1–2 weeks.
Yam	Fall, Winter	Tuber should be smooth and firm with brownish to reddish skin.	Store in cool dry place for 3–5 days.

Note: Vegetables should be washed just before use; the addition of 2 tablespoons of vinegar to a sink of water may help in the removal of some of the spray residue.

Two

GEARING UP—
KITCHEN EQUIPMENT

Some vegetarians are classic gourmets. From crockery to cutlery, whisks to woks, their kitchens are showplaces and every device for creative cooking is at hand. Probably more vegetarians, however, are of the "small is better" school of thought. They seek to trim the fat from their lives as well as from their diet. Just to see one of their pared-down kitchens is a delight pure and simple. There is an order to it. And objects there so express the beauty of function that food preparation gear often shares wall space with jars of beans and grains.

If you are a new vegetarian or just experimenting with meatless, whole foods meals, no additional equipment needs to be added to a reasonably well-outfitted kitchen. As time passes you will find that certain appliances and instruments are used much more frequently than others. Then, as your barbecue grill, rotisserie, and steak knives are sold at garage sales, they can be replaced with items especially useful to the vegetarian chef.

Pots and Pans

The Rolls-Royce in this department is stainless steel waterless cookware. It allows for cooking at low temperatures with virtually no liquid added, thereby preserving maximum nutrient content. It is extremely expensive but lasts a lifetime and is an investment worth making.

Other stainless steel crockery, preferably with copper or aluminum-clad bottoms, is also a smart choice. It offers good heat conduction and is easy to maintain. (When using any stainless steel, be careful to keep the burner set at medium or lower to avoid scorching.)

Cast iron is the pick of many back-to-nature cooks. It's durable and strong, and unlike any other cookware actually offers the nutritional benefit of adding iron to foods. When an acidic food like spaghetti sauce is cooked in one of these pots for 3 hours, its iron content is increased 29 times. When rice is cooked for 20 minutes in iron, its content of this vital mineral is upped 3.7 times. To care for iron pots, do not scrub them harshly. Dry them immediately after washing to prevent rust, and season them occasionally by rubbing with solid shortening and placing them in a slow oven (about 200° F) for a couple of hours.

Cookware coated with teflon or a similar nonstick surface has the advantage of enabling you to cook with little or no added fat. It is also a snap to clean. Gentle handling is necessary to keep from marring the coating. This is especially important since teflon often covers an aluminum utensil. Aluminum can be toxic to the body, and certain research has linked high systemic levels of this metal with senility and even cancer. For this reason, only spoons and spatulas expressly designed for teflon should be used with it, and uncoated aluminum pots and pans should be largely avoided. (Do not wrap baking potatoes in aluminum foil either. Rub the skins with a little oil if you like, but "naked" potatoes bake just fine.)

Copper can also create toxic substances, and although, like aluminum, it is an excellent heat conductor, it should never have direct contact with food. Tempered glass and porcelain enamel utensils are often attractive in design and, as is also true for stainless steel, transmit no taste of their own to food.

Whatever material is chosen for cookware, avoid the temptation to save money here. In this case, a price that is too low nearly always means low quality as well.

Helpful Appliances

Blender—nearly essential. You will use it for smoothies and shakes, purees and soups, nut and soy milks, sauces and gravies, dressings and dips, baby food and waffle batter.

Food Processor—handy to be sure. It can chop, slice, mix, and perform marvelously whether you need vegetables for salad or the makings for a cake. It can also perform some, but not all, of a blender's duties more efficiently. If your family is small and you do not entertain a lot, though, you can probably do the processing manually in the time you would spend cleaning your machine. In that case, consider a cone grater or "salad master." These are easy to use, cost next to nothing, and use no electricity.

Flour Mill—for fresher flour than you can buy anywhere. There are manual and automatic models, and cost varies accordingly. If your talent, hobby, and stress reducer is whole-grain baking, you would profit from this appliance that grinds those grains into flour just when you need it.

Nut Mill (alias coffee grinder)—a little electric gizmo that makes meal from nuts, seeds, and certain grains. This meal can be sprinkled on foods, used as part of the flour in baking, or added to blender drinks and baby food. The mill can also grind fresh spices like mustard, cardamom, and fennel.

Juicer—provides Mom Nature's elixirs for whatever ails you— or so the devotees of raw vegetable juice would have us believe. These juices are chock full of nutrients anyway, and carrot juice with the addition of celery, parsley, beet, spinach, or apple is a real taste treat. A variety of juicers are sold at health-food stores. Most work on the centrifugal principle and require that the pulp be cleaned out of the machine periodically during the juicing process. Some models eject it automatically, and one advertises itself as a "total juicer," giving you pulp and all. One kind makes marvelous "ice cream" from frozen bananas, and another kneads bread dough. Shop around. (Citrus juicers, powered by electricity or by you, are inexpensive and readily available at department stores.)

Microwave Oven—for quick heat-ups, defrosting, rushed evenings, and simply when you are hungry *now*. Since you will probably be using fewer convenience foods as a vegetarian, one of these modern marvels could be a real timesaver. Many concerned people are wary of them, though. Radiation leakage isn't the worry so much (quality control on these products is excellent), it is just the idea of cooking food with microwaves that disturbs them. Use your own good judgment.

Accessories and Gadgets

Cutting Board—an ample board of beautiful wood for all the vegetable chopping and bread dough kneading you will be doing.

Double Boiler—insures gentle cooking, especially for whole cereals that might otherwise scorch. An inexpensive alternative is to use an asbestos pad between the burner and an ordinary pot.

Fruit Ripener—domed lucite bowl to help fruit, unfortunately picked green in many cases, ripen without spoiling. Sold at gourmet shops, these make lovely centerpieces as they do their job.

Knives—really good ones, and a sharpener to keep them that way. You will want knives for chopping and paring, and a serrated knife for bread. If you bake a great deal, you might even consider an electric knife.

Pressure Cooker—can substantially cut the time you would otherwise spend on cooking legumes, whole grains, and certain vegetables. Most pressure cookers are aluminum, but if this is your only aluminum pot, it is probably a reasonable compromise.

Salad Spinner—dries greens and other fixings after washing for all those salads vegetarians consume.

Sprouter—for making a sure thing of growing a counter-top crop of organic munchies. Health-food stores offer several types, from a set of perforated lids for use with Mason jars to self-contained, tiered mini-gardens for raising three varieties of sprouts at once.

Tofu Settling Box—can save regular tofu users a stack of cash by making their own. A special little wooden box for the purpose is sold at health shops and comes with a beginner's supply of culture for making soybean curd.

Vegetable Scrubber—to be sure you have removed as much spray residue as possible.

Vegetable Steamer—compact "flower petal" rack that allows you to prepare vegetables by the healthful steaming method that preserves nutrients. Look for a steamer made of stainless steel.

There is plenty more, of course. You might be able to use a pasta machine, a yogurt maker, a hot-air corn popper, or even a meat grinder, now employed for ricing cooked beans and grains and making sweet pastes from dried fruits. But a kitchen full of toys is not required for making meatless meals that nourish the body and delight the psyche. Sticking to basics can, in fact, keep you more in tune with what you are doing. Food preparation can be an act of creative mindfulness in which you feel your connection with the earth from which the food comes.

A great deal of unconscious wasting occurs in kitchens, but conscious conservation can take place there instead. Using a minimum of nonbiodegradable items such as plastic wrap and aluminum foil, and even being judicious with other throwaways (paper towels, wax paper), can add to awareness. Storage containers can be reused, especially now that bulk-food stores invite customers to bring their own jars for nutbutter, oil, honey, et cetera. Biodegradable washing compounds and cleaners, notably those health-store brands made from natural vegetable substances and not tested on laboratory animals, are favored by many vegetarians. Even water, which seems so limitless, is a precious resource that the respectful cook uses with prudence.

Within these parameters, the presentation of meals to guests, family, or yourself alone becomes a daily special occasion. You feel yourself becoming a co-worker with nature. That is worth a lot.

Three

COOKING METHODS

Food preparation can be an art. A joy. A gift.

It's also a science and a skill, which, if mastered, enables the cook to enhance basic foods, both aesthetically and nutritionally. This section is a miniature manual on preparation, a reference on the cooking techniques called for in the recipes.

Baking, Roasting

When cooking by dry heat in an oven, avoid overcrowding, which inhibits air circulation and causes uneven baking. If you use two shelves at the same time, stagger the pans so air can still circulate. And get to know your oven: the temperature dial gives a reasonable indication of what's going on inside, but few are 100 percent accurate. Once you realize whether your oven is on the hot or cool side, adjust the dial accordingly. (In either case, when using Pyrex bakeware set it 25° F lower than you would otherwise.)

Barbecuing

Cooking on a grill over direct heat, usually with charcoal, isn't a major pastime for vegetarians. You can still do it, though, with corn in the husk, jacketed potatoes, and some vegetarian burgers. If nostalgia overcomes you, you can even get meatless hot dogs at health food stores. (And for campfire roasts, consider kosher marshmallows that have no animal gelatin in them.)

Blanching

This brief steaming or boiling, followed by a quick cooling in cold water, prepares vegetables and some fruits for freezing or drying. It is also used—without the ice water dunk—to facilitate the removal of the skins from nuts such as almonds and filberts.

Boiling

This method of moist cooking is probably responsible for more lost nutrients than the refining of wheat to make white bread. Almost all foods, especially vegetables, should be immersed in boiling water for only the shortest time possible, if at all. When a recipe instructs you to boil, it usually intends that you bring the liquid quickly to the boiling point, place the food in it, and as soon as the liquid bubbles again, reduce the heat to a simmer (a very slow boil at which only tiny bubbles come to the surface). Similar methods are double-boiling and steaming; usually one of these can be used as an alternative to boiling.

Braising

The traditional method of cooking vegetables in French gourmet cuisine, braising is slow cooking in a fat (usually butter) and a little liquid in a closed pot. A deep, rich flavored vegetable is the result.

Broiling

This cooking under direct heat with the use of a special rack is not recommended too often in vegetarian cookbooks, so you'll be cleaning a sticky broiler a lot less often. You will use your broiler primarily for melting cheese on sandwiches or casseroles and for top browning during the last few minutes of the heating process.

Deep-frying

The health-conscious cringe at deep-frying. It increases the fat and calorie content of any food astronomically, so it instantly sabotages one of vegetarianism's prime body benefits. Either stir-frying or sautéing often substitutes nicely, but you still may want to deep-fry occasionally such items as tempeh strips or tempura. When you do, the oil must be heated to 350° F–385° F. The food should be dry and at room temperature, then placed in a wire basket with a long handle so that it's well submerged, cooks quickly and uniformly, and is allowed to drain.

Double-boiler cooking

A double-boiler consists of two nesting pots. Water boiling in the lower one gently cooks food in the upper pot by steam. Double-boiling is ideal for delicate white sauces, soymilk, and grains such as millet that might otherwise stick or burn. A similar process involves placing smaller food containers in a larger pot of water—in the preparation of custard, for example.

Pressure-cooking

In a pressure cooker, a heating temperature as high as 250° F can be maintained under 15 pounds of pressure. This method saves time and, properly done, preserves nutrients and flavor. It can be especially useful to vegetarians in preparing legumes like soybeans or garbanzos, which otherwise take many hours of soaking and simmering. When cooking beans this way, it is important that before you close the lid, you allow the sudsy bubbles they produce to come to the top for skimming. Be sure to keep the opening in the top of the cooker free of the suds to avoid the possibility of the jiggler's exploding out. Other precautions: (1) Get a quality pressure cooker; (2) Don't fill the cooker too full; (3) Watch the flame; if the jiggler gets noisy, turn the stove down; (4) Never cook split peas or oatmeal in a pressure cooker; (5) Study the manufacturer's instructions and follow them carefully.

Sautéing

This is pan-frying in a small amount of hot oil or butter or a combination of the two. Some research has indicated that bringing vegetable oil to the high temperatures necessary for frying might render it carcinogenic. This would make butter the superior choice, despite its notorious cholesterol content. The best option of all might be "steam frying," sautéing in half fat, half water. Either way, for best results use food at room temperature and don't overcrowd the pan.

Steaming

This form of moist cooking can be accomplished with a pressure cooker, a special two-part steaming pot, or most commonly with a collapsible rack that fits in a standard saucepan. To use one, bring an inch or two of water to a boil in the saucepan; insert the rack in its expanded position and place the food on top so that it's just above the boiling water. Cover the pan tightly. Vegetables cooked in this way retain their flavor, shape and nutrients. Remove them from the heat when they're still brightly colored and just tender enough to cut with a fork.

Stir-frying

The traditional wok or any good-sized frying pan with a tight lid can be used for stir-frying. In this process, freshly minced, sliced, or shredded vegetables—sometimes with the addition of tofu, Chinese noodles, et cetera—are heated in one or two tablespoons of hot oil. They are tossed constantly until they are just tender. For slightly softer vegetables, cover the pan for a moment or two.

None of the above

Don't underestimate the good sense of sometimes skipping this business of cooking altogether. Especially in warm weather, making a meal of fruit and nuts or salad and cheese can be a treat well worth giving yourself.

Four

PRESERVING FOOD

It's a special feeling: knowing that fine fruits and vegetables, grown yourself or bought when they're lowest in cost and highest in quality, have been preserved and tucked away for use later. There are several ways to do this, some easy, some demanding.

Freezing

You'll need:

· Rigid, straight-sided containers for liquid and semiliquid foods. Choose the size that's right for one meal. The container can be of plastic, glass, or metal. Heavily waxed cardboard—such as cardboard milk containers, cut down and cleaned—should be used only if they're lined with a sealable plastic freezer bag.

· Foil, heavy plastic, laminated paper, or cellophane for nonliquid foods. Make sure you wrap the food well and seal tightly.

· Masking tape or freezer tape for sealing wrapped packages and resealing the lids of plastic containers (without tape, they're not airtight). Also gummed labels and felt-tipped pens for dating and identifying what you've frozen.

· A thermometer. Set your freezer to −10° F the night before you plan to freeze in quantity. Don't freeze more than two pounds of food per cubic foot of freezer space at any given time.

· A wire basket for blanching vegetables and a rack for steam-blanching them (see below).

Leave enough head space in rigid containers to allow for the expansion of liquid or semiliquid foods but not enough space to let air sneak in. The rule of thumb is to allow ½ inch in plastic cartons, 1 inch for glass jars.

Fresh fruits can be frozen dry and unsweetened or with a light syrup made by dissolving 1 cup of mild honey (clover is nice) in 3 cups of boiling water, then chilling. Fruits in syrup—or alternatively in unsweetened fruit juice such as apple or white grape—keep longer and generally retain their shape and texture better. Fruits that discolor during the freezing process—apples, cherries, peaches, and plums—should be sprinkled with lemon juice before being packed dry. If you freeze them in syrup, add a little lemon juice to the sweetener. Ascorbic acid powders like "Fruit Fresh" also prevent discoloration. An economical substitute is a bottle of generic vitamin C tablets: use one ground or dissolved 500 mg. tablet per quart of syrup. For fruits frozen without syrup, use one ground 500 mg. tablet for each packaged pint.

Fruits—especially berries—may also be pre-frozen in a single layer on an open tray, then put into plastic bags and sealed. Treated this way, they'll shake out as individuals instead of a block when you're ready to use them.

A few more notes about freezing fruit:

· Apples should be peeled, cored, sliced, and protected from discoloration as described above.

· Frozen whole bananas cannot be thawed and used as fresh, but very ripe ones, peeled and then frozen, are excellent for frosty blender shakes. Banana puree also freezes well.

· Cantaloupe and other melons can be frozen in cubes or balls and pre-frozen on trays.

· Cherries should be washed, stemmed, and pitted before freezing, and should be protected against discoloration.

· Peaches are best peeled, pitted, sliced, and packed in a light honey syrup with a little lemon juice.

· Pineapples should be pared carefully, their dark "eyes" removed.

Timetable for Blanching

Vegetable	Blanching Time (minutes)	Vegetable	Blanching Time (minutes)
Artichoke	8–10	Kohlrabi, sliced	3
Asparagus	3	Lima beans	1½
Beets	*	Mushrooms	†
Broccoli	4	Okra	3–4
Brussels sprouts	4	Parsnips	2
Cabbage, shredded	2	Peas, green	1½
Carrots, sliced	2½	Peppers, bell	2
Cauliflower, florets	3	Rutabaga, diced	2
Corn, kernels	4	Squash	*
Corn on the cob	6–10	Stringbeans	1½
Eggplant, sliced	4	Turnips, diced	2

*Blanch until tender.
† Sauté instead of blanching, then freeze.
Note: Add 1–2 minutes for steam-blanching.

Cut them into slices or chunks, and pack them in a light honey syrup or in their own juice.

· Plums should be washed, pitted, and protected against discoloration.

Most vegetables freeze as well as fruits do. (Celery, cucumbers, potatoes, and whole tomatoes are the exceptions.) The extra step of blanching is required, but that's a small price to pay for cashing in on your garden all year 'round. To blanch vegetables, first wash and prepare them as you would for cooking. Then select either of the following techniques:

1. The boiling water method. Put a gallon of water in a large pot and bring it to a rolling boil. Put a pound of vegetables into a wire basket or strainer and lower it into the water. Cover the pot and blanch for just the amount of time shown on the chart. Then take the vegetables out and plunge them into ice water or hold them under cold running water until they're cool all the way to their center. Then drain and pat them dry.

2. Steam blanching. Put one or two inches of water in a big pot and

put a rack over the water; bring water to a boil. Put a single layer of vegetables in a basket; put the basket on the rack and cover the pot tightly. Steam blanching takes about a minute longer per batch than blanching in water, and the batch is smaller—but as is always the case when you steam rather than boil vegetables, you'll preserve more nutrients. After steam blanching, cool the vegetables using either of the methods described above.

Drying

Most fruits and vegetables can be dried to produce a healthful snack, lightweight hiking food, or a pleasant addition to soup and casseroles. To prepare them for drying, wash and peel the fruits or vegetables and cut them into thin slices or small pieces. Blanch the foods very quickly. Fruits that discolor can be soaked in a solution of 1 tablespoon lemon juice to 1 quart of water, then drained.

Drying may be done in a solar collector drier or an electric dehydrator; follow the manufacturer's instructions. To do your drying in an oven, put the food directly on the oven racks, one layer at a time. (If the pieces are too small and yours is an electric oven, cover the racks first with cheesecloth. Do not use cheesecloth in a gas range. Stainless steel window screening can be substituted; do not use galvanized or plastic window screening or plastic nylon net, which could melt or catch fire.) Start the oven at 120° F, then raise it to 140° F. Leave the oven door open a little all through the drying process. You'll know the drying is complete when the food has no moisture left in it: fruits feel leathery, vegetables are brittle.

If food has been dried outside, in a solar drier or in any location where insect contamination is possible, it should be pasteurized after drying. Do the job either by spreading the food on baking sheets and heating it for 15 minutes in a 175° F oven, or by freezing it for a week in a plastic bag.

Conditioning is the next step. This is necessary to "even things out." Some of the pieces will have dried more thoroughly than others, so you'll want to let them absorb moisture from the damper pieces which might otherwise permit mold growth. Condition the food by putting it on a tray, loosely covered, for a few days; keep it in a warm, dry place, and stir occasionally. Alternately, place the dried fruit or vegetables in a sealed jar or plastic bucket. Leave it there for a week and check daily for moisture condensation on the edges. If you notice this, send the food back to the drier. Otherwise, you're ready to seal it up and put it on the shelf. Keep these tightly closed jars in a cool, dry, and dark place, or store them in the freezer.

Canning

Canning calls for care and special equipment, but the satisfaction derived from mastering this time-honored art is ample reward. For canning high-acid foods such as some fruits, you'll need a water-bath canner—a big, deep pot with a rack and a tight-fitting lid. For low-acid foods (most vegetables, soups, stews, certain fruits), invest in a pressure canner that has a rack and a tight lid equipped with a pressure gauge, a petcock, rubber seal, and safety valve. You also need canning jars specifically made for the purpose, self-sealing lids for them (to be used one time only), and accessories: jar tongs, ladles, a timer, paring knife, slotted spoon, jar funnel, saucepan, measuring cups and spoons, and for pickling, a household scale.

The reason for much of the equipment and procedures required in canning is to guard against botulism. Botulinus is a common spore that lives in and around many growing things. It does no damage at all until it's placed in an airless environment, at which point it produces the deadliest toxin known. Some experts believe that only 1 tablespoon of pure botulin toxin could kill the entire population of the earth! Since you need a vacuum in cans to keep food from spoiling, it is vital—a matter of life and death, in fact—to be sure that botulinus spores are prevented from growing. Unlike most organisms, this one isn't killed by boiling unless it is kept at the boiling point some 8 to 10 hours, a process that would leave the food a vitaminless mush. Therefore, food to be canned is cooked at 240° F, possible only in a pressure canner.

Home canning was on the decline for several years because of limited storage space in modern homes, the degree of care it demands, and the relative ease of home freezing. The wholefoods revolution and the renewed popularity of gardening, however, have sparked a resurgence in interest, and canning is undertaken by more families with every harvest season. If you're intrigued by the idea of putting up your own food, invest in first-rate equipment and follow the manufacturer's instructions for processing. Helpful books on the subject include *Farm Journal's Freezing and Canning Cookbook* and

Putting Food By, coordinated by Ruth Hertzberg. For additional information on all aspects of food preservation, contact the home adviser at your county offices or at the Agricultural Extension Department of a state college or university. Then clean out your pantry: it's about to be filled.

RECIPES

APPETIZERS

Appetizers should be light and satisfying without spoiling your appetite. In some cases, the appetizers we present here can be used as an interesting lunch—serve two or three to allow for a range of textures and flavors. Pâtés are served chilled, while dips and spreads should be given time to develop their full flavor at room temperature.

A range of breads or crackers (see Breads chapter) can be served with these appetizers.

Garnishes can be cut and served at the last moment, and be prepared to heat up hot appetizers quickly in a microwave or toaster oven. Serve the hot ones first, followed by the cold. Use fresh herbs as garnish.

Note: The symbol **(L)** is used next to those recipe titles that include some form of dairy product. All other recipes are vegan in nature; that is, they contain no meat, eggs, or milk products.

White Beans Vinaigrette

1 cup dried white beans, such as white kidney beans or pea beans
4 cups water
1 cup finely chopped onions
1 teaspoon finely minced garlic
2 tablespoons finely chopped parsley
2 tablespoons finely chopped basil
Freshly ground black pepper to taste
3 tablespoons red wine vinegar
½ cup olive oil

Unless the package specifies no soaking, place beans in a bowl and add water to cover about 2 inches above top of beans. Soak overnight.

Drain beans. Put in a pot or kettle and add 4 cups of water. Bring to a boil and simmer for 50 minutes to 1 hour or until beans are tender. Drain well.

Put beans in a mixing bowl and add remaining ingredients. Blend gently but well. Serve warm.

Serves 8

Hot-and-Sour Cucumbers

1 pound cucumbers
3 tablespoons peanut
    oil or corn oil
1 large clove garlic,
    lightly crushed and
    peeled
2–4 chili peppers, dried
2 tablespoons distilled
    white vinegar

Sauce:

1 tablespoon light soy
    sauce
2 tablespoons honey
½ teaspoon salt

Cut cucumbers in half lengthwise. Remove seeds and cut each half lengthwise into 4 strips. Cut these into 4 sections. Measure soy sauce and set aside. Mix honey and salt, and set aside.

Heat skillet over high heat until hot. Add oil, swirl, and turn heat to low. Add garlic and chili peppers (2 for a mild dish, 4 for a hot one). Press them against the pan, flipping until garlic is light brown and peppers have darkened.

Turn heat to high, add cucumbers, and stir immediately with fast, sweeping turns to tumble and roll them in the hot oil—about 25 seconds or until skin is bright green. Sprinkle with soy sauce and then honey-salt mixture. Stir rapidly for 5 seconds, then pour immediately into a dish. Let cucumbers cool, then cover and refrigerate until thoroughly chilled, stirring a few times for even marinating.

Transfer cucumbers to a serving dish without the marinade, garlic, or peppers. Add vinegar and toss to mix well.

Serves 4

Tofu Guacamole

1 ripe avocado
8–10 ounces tofu,
  drained
1 medium tomato,
  chopped
Canned jalapeño
  peppers to taste,
  diced
1 tablespoon chopped
  fresh cilantro or 1
  teaspoon dried
1 tablespoon freshly
  squeezed lemon juice
2 tablespoons
  mayonnaise
Pinch of garlic powder
  and/or cumin
2 tablespoons finely
  minced scallions or
  onions

Mash all ingredients together with a fork. Adjust seasonings to taste, adding a dash of salt, tamari, or tabasco if desired. Serve with corn chips.

Serves 4

Dill Wafers(L)

½ cup margarine or
  butter
3 ounces cream cheese,
  softened
1 cup all-purpose flour
1 teaspoon dill weed
¼ cup finely chopped
  nuts (optional)

Combine margarine and softened cream cheese, and mix until well blended. Gradually add flour and dill weed, and mix well. Chill. Roll dough on lightly floured surface to ¼ inch. Cut with assorted cutters. Put on ungreased cookie sheets. Bake at 425° F for 8–10 minutes or until lightly browned.

Yield: 2 dozen

Grape Leaves Stuffed with Rice

5 tablespoons chopped
  onions
1 cup oil
2 cups water
1 cup brown rice
1 teaspoon salt
2 teaspoons kelp
2 teaspoons dill weed
¼ teaspoon cinnamon
½ teaspoon peppermint
1 teaspoon paprika
½ teaspoon pepper
½ teaspoon allspice
Juice of 1 lemon
12 grape leaves

Sauté onions in oil until light brown. Add 1 cup of water, rice, salt, and kelp, and mix well. Cover and cook until all water is absorbed. Remove from heat, cool slightly, and add remaining spices. Place 1 generous teaspoon of filling onto each grape leaf. Make one fold up from the base of the leaf, tuck in the sides, and roll up tightly. Place in a heavy saucepan and fold down, packing the little rolls tightly. Add remaining cup of water and lemon juice. Cook slowly over low heat until almost all liquid is absorbed. Serve either hot or cold.

Variation: Add pine nuts or sunflower seeds to the filling if desired.

Serves 4

Taratoor Sauce

3 medium-size cloves
  garlic, finely chopped
1 cup tahini
¾–1 cup cold water
½ cup lemon juice
1 teaspoon salt

Mash garlic. Stir in tahini. Beat in water, lemon juice, and salt. While beating constantly, add up to ½ cup more water until sauce has the consistency of mayonnaise. Serve as a dip for raw or cooked vegetables.

Yield: about 2 cups

Hummus I

1⅓ cups dried chick-
    peas (garbanzo
    beans)
2 teaspoons salt
3 medium-size cloves
    garlic, finely chopped
¼ cup lemon juice
1 tablespoon kelp
1 cup taratoor sauce

Soak chick-peas for 12 hours. Drain. Add salt and enough water to completely cover peas. Bring to a boil and simmer for 2–3 hours or until peas are tender. Drain and reserve the liquid. In blender puree peas, garlic, and about ½ cup of cooking liquid, or mash peas in a mortar and pestle. (Unlike most peas or beans, chick-peas will not mash with a potato masher.) With a spoon, beat in lemon juice, a few tablespoons at a time. Add kelp. Beating constantly, pour in taratoor sauce very slowly and continue to beat until hummus is smooth—the consistency of mayonnaise. If it is too thick, add up to ½ cup more of cooking liquid, a tablespoon at a time.

Yield: about 2 cups

Hummus II

1 cup cooked chick-
    peas
6–7 tablespoons chick-
    pea liquid
Salt
3 tablespoons lemon
    juice
3 tablespoons tahini
1 clove garlic, minced
1 teaspoon sesame oil
Paprika

Combine in blender chick-peas, 6–7 tablespoons chick-pea liquid, pinch of salt, and lemon juice, and blend well. Stir in tahini and garlic. Refrigerate to blend flavors. Before serving, garnish lightly with sesame oil and paprika. Serve with sesame crisp crackers.

Serves 2

Eggplant Cream

**1 large eggplant
(about 2 pounds)
Lemon juice
Oil
Kelp
Garlic
Salt and pepper
1–2 tablespoons yogurt**

Bake eggplant in 450°F oven for about 30 minutes until evenly charred and soft all over. Peel off skin and mash pulp by hand or in blender. For each cup of pulp add 1 tablespoon of lemon juice, 2 teaspoons of oil, ½ teaspoon of kelp, ½ to 1 clove of garlic, finely chopped, and salt and pepper to taste. Stir in yogurt. Serve as a dip with pita or raw vegetables.

Serves 4

Yogurt Cheese (L)

**2 pints fresh yogurt
2 tablespoons olive oil
½ teaspoon dried mint**

Line a bowl with a triple or quadruple layer of cheesecloth. Scrape yogurt into the bowl and gather up ends of the cheesecloth. Tie ends with string. Lift up bag and let liquid from the yogurt drip into the bowl. It is best if you can hang the bag over the bowl in the refrigerator. Let it drip about 5 hours, no longer. Remove cheesecloth and put cheese on a plate. Refrigerate until ready to use.

Spread cheese on a round plate, rounding the edges. Make indentations all around the top and center of cheese. Sprinkle with oil and mint. Serve with unsalted bread.

Serves 6

Tofu-Garlic Dip

12 ounces tofu, drained
½ teaspoon crushed garlic
¼ cup crushed onion
2 tablespoons vegetable oil
Tamari, pepper, and honey to taste
Parsley

Blend tofu with garlic and onion. Whip in oil. Season with a few drops of tamari and pepper and a touch of honey. Garnish with parsley. Serve with raw vegetables.

Serves 8–10

Vegetable Pâté

1 quart chopped vegetables
Roux (your favorite recipe)
Herb salt
Parsley or olives (for garnish)

Cook chopped vegetables until firm-tender in enough water to cover. Add more water if necessary. In blender or processor, blend cooked vegetables with their cooking liquid. Thicken with roux to desired firmness. Season to taste. Garnish with chopped parsley or sliced olives.

Serves 4

Cold Stuffed Peppers(L)

4 medium-size green peppers
½ cup oil
¼ teaspoon mustard seeds
1 large onion, chopped
3 medium-size carrots, shredded
2 stalks celery, chopped
½ cup thick tomato sauce
½ teaspoon salt
Pepper
1 tablespoon sour cream
½ cup water

Cut off pepper tops and remove seeds and membranes.

Heat oil in a skillet and cook mustard seeds just until heated. Add and sauté onion, carrots, and celery, and cook until firm-tender. Add tomato sauce, salt, and pepper, and remove from heat. Stir in sour cream.

Stuff peppers with mixture and stand them in a saucepan. Pour water into the bottom of the pan, cover, and simmer about 20 minutes or until cooked. (A little more hot water might be needed after about 15 minutes.)

Allow to cool and serve at room temperature.

Serves 4

Lentil Pâté I(L)

1 small onion, minced
3 tablespoons olive oil
2 cloves garlic, minced
2 eggs, beaten
2 cups cooked lentils
½ teaspoon basil
½ teaspoon paprika
¼ teaspoon nutmeg
Turmeric and cumin to
  taste
1 teaspoon herb salt
1 tablespoon nutritional
  yeast
¼ cup chopped parsley
1 cup grated Swiss
  cheese
1 cup whole wheat
  bread crumbs

Sauté onion in oil until limp. Add garlic and sauté for 3 minutes. Combine eggs with lentils. Add garlic-onion mixture, seasonings, yeast, parsley, and cheese. Add bread crumbs gradually, using only enough to make mixture firm enough to form a ball. Press pâté into an oiled loaf pan. Bake at 350° F for 30–40 minutes until firm. Serve hot or cold.

Serves 4

Lentil Pâté II^(L)

1½ cups lentils
1 bay leaf
Vegetable broth or
  water
2 eggs, slightly beaten
1 cup chopped onions
3 tablespoons butter or
  margarine
1 clove garlic, minced
2 medium-size
  tomatoes (drain if
  canned), peeled and
  coarsely chopped
1 cup grated hard
  cheese
4 tablespoons chopped
  parsley
¼ teaspoon dried basil
¼ teaspoon paprika
¼ teaspoon pepper
Pinch of nutmeg
Pinch of turmeric
Pinch of powdered
  cumin
1 teaspoon salt
I cup bread crumbs +
  additional bread
  crumbs

Simmer lentils with bay leaf in just enough broth or water to cover. Stir frequently. Add hot broth or hot water as needed. After about 40 minutes, all liquid should be absorbed and lentils cooked. Taste for doneness. Remove bay leaf. Allow to cool, add eggs, and mix.

Preheat oven to 375° F. Sauté onions in butter and add garlic when onions are translucent. Add to lentils, together with all other ingredients including 1 cup of bread crumbs, and mix thoroughly.

Grease a 9-inch-square baking dish about 3 inches deep. Sprinkle with additional bread crumbs all around. Fill with lentil mixture and bake at 375° F about 1 hour or until an inserted knife comes out clean. Allow to cool for 10 minutes.

Serves 4

White Bean Pâté^(L)

1 cup navy beans or small white beans, washed and picked over
3 cups water
2 tablespoons olive oil, safflower oil, or butter
1 small or medium onion, chopped
5 large cloves garlic, minced or put through a press
1 large bay leaf
2 teaspoons salt or to taste
⅔ cup finely grated carrots
2 eggs
3 tablespoons beer
2 tablespoons + 1 teaspoon lemon juice
10 twists freshly ground pepper
½ cup whole-wheat bread crumbs
¼ cup chopped fresh parsley
¼ teaspoon ground coriander
¼ teaspoon dried basil
¼ teaspoon dried thyme

Soak beans in water for several hours or overnight, or bring to a boil, boil 2 minutes, cover, and let stand 2 hours.

Heat 1 tablespoon of oil in a heavy-bottomed saucepan, bean pot, or Dutch oven, and gently sauté half the onion and 2 cloves of garlic until onion is tender. Add beans and their liquid, raise heat, and bring to a boil. Add bay leaf, then cover, reduce heat, and simmer 2 hours or until beans are tender and aromatic. Remove bay leaf. Add up to 1 teaspoon of salt to taste. Drain beans and retain their cooking liquid.

Preheat oven to 400° F. Butter a 2-quart casserole or pâté tureen.

Heat remaining tablespoon of oil in a heavy-bottomed skillet and gently sauté remaining onion and garlic, along with carrots, until onion is tender. Remove from pan and place in a mixing bowl.

Put cooked beans in blender or food processor fitted with the steel blade. Add eggs, ⅓ cup stock from beans (freeze the rest for use in soups), beer, lemon juice, pepper, and up to 1 teaspoon of salt, to taste. Puree until smooth, adding more stock if the blades of your blender stick.

Pour bean puree into mixing bowl with onion, carrots, and garlic. Add bread crumbs, parsley, coriander, basil, and thyme, and mix well. Adjust salt and pepper.

Spoon pâté mixture into prepared casserole or tureen and cover tightly with a lid or foil. Bake in preheated oven for 50 minutes to 1 hour until top begins to brown. Remove from oven and cool. Serve warm or chilled. The flavors will mature overnight. This dish freezes well.

Yield: 4 cups

Ginger Root Pâté

2 medium eggplants
2 tomatoes
2 cloves garlic, crushed
½ cup fresh dill
⅓ cup chopped parsley
1 medium onion, chopped
¼ cup fresh ginger juice
Seasoned salt to taste

Bake unpeeled eggplants at 350° F for 1¼–1½ hours until soft. Plunge tomatoes in boiling water for a few seconds, peel off skin, and chop coarsely. Scoop out eggplant pulp and combine with other ingredients. Blend at low speed until spreadable but not liquified. Chill. Add salt and pepper.

Serves 12

Spiced Tofu Marinade

2 tablespoons olive oil
2 cloves garlic, minced
½ pound mushrooms, sliced
1 red onion, sliced
16 ounces tofu, cubed
16 ounces black olives, pitted
¾ cup tamari
¼ cup lemon juice
½ cup sherry

Heat olive oil. Add garlic and sauté until light brown. Add mushrooms and sauté until tender. Add all other ingredients and stir well. Let stand all day or overnight in the refrigerator. Stir occasionally.

Serves 4

Eggplant Caviar

1 **medium eggplant**
1 **large onion**
2–3 **cloves garlic**
   (optional)
2 **tablespoons**
   vegetable oil
Salt to taste
1–2 **tablespoons**
   homemade ketchup
   (see recipe p. 229)

Roast eggplant over a gas burner until the outside is charred and cracked and the inside soft. If smoked flavor is not desired, bake eggplant until soft (1–1½ hours) in a 300° F oven in a small pan of water. Eggplant is ready when it is soft but has not entirely collapsed.

Eggplant can be prepared by grinding it coarsely in food grinder or, if none is available, by chopping in blender at slow speed or chopping finely by hand. Finely chop onion and mince garlic; sauté in oil until golden. Mix in eggplant and continue to cook over a small flame until surface bubbles a little. Add salt and ketchup to taste. (If no "natural" ketchup is available, mix a little honey and vinegar with tomato paste.) Simmer, covered, for up to 2 hours. Serve cold as an appetizer with black bread or serve hot as an entree.

Variation: Use 3 tablespoons of mayonnaise and ⅓ cup of chopped walnuts in place of ketchup and onion. Remove dish from heat as soon as mayonnaise is added. Stir in 1 tablespoon of lemon juice if desired and serve chilled.

Serves 4

Zucchini Clafouti[(L)]

½ cup freshly grated
   Parmesan cheese
2 tablespoons dry
   whole-wheat bread
   crumbs
3 eggs
½ cup whole wheat
   pastry flour or
   unbleached flour
2 cups milk, half and
   half, or double-
   strength, reconstituted
   nonfat dry milk
1 teaspoon sea salt or 2
   teaspoons coarse salt
Ground red pepper
¾ pound zucchini
   (unpeeled), coarsely
   chopped
¼ cup coarsely
   chopped yellow
   onion
¼ cup coarsely
   chopped red bell
   pepper
1 teaspoon finely
   chopped garlic
2 tablespoons finely
   chopped fresh
   parsley (garnish)

Preheat oven to 375° F. Grease 10-inch pie plate or flan pan. Combine ¼ cup of cheese and bread crumbs in a small mixing bowl. Dust inside of pan with mixture, shaking out excess.

Beat eggs in processor or large bowl of electric mixer. Add flour and mix well. Add milk, salt, pepper, and remaining cheese, and beat thoroughly. Set aside.

Combine zucchini, onion, bell pepper, garlic, and egg mixture in medium bowl and mix thoroughly. Pour mixture into prepared pan. Bake until filling is firm, about 40 minutes. Garnish with parsley and serve in small squares.

Yield: 14–16 appetizer servings

Zucchini Fritters(L)

1½ pound zucchini, cut in ¼-inch slices
6 green onions, finely chopped
6 sprigs parsley, finely chopped
¼ cup grated Romano or Parmesan cheese
1 clove garlic, minced
Salt to taste
Freshly ground pepper to taste
2 slices bread, in crumbs
4 eggs
Olive oil

Boil zucchini for 10–15 minutes. Drain.

Mix zucchini, onions, parsley, cheese, garlic, salt, pepper, bread crumbs, and eggs.

Heat ½ inch of olive oil in skillet. Drop zucchini mixture by large spoonfuls into oil and cook until browned on both sides. Drain.

Yield: 6–8 fritters

Melon Bowl Ambrosia^(L)

2 medium-size
  cantaloupes
1 cup diced fresh
  pineapple
1 cup fresh raspberries
¼ cup toasted coconut
1 medium banana,
  frozen
1½ cups plain low-fat
  yogurt
¼ teaspoon nutmeg
1 tablespoon fresh
  lemon juice
Mint sprigs (optional)

Cut cantaloupes in half using zigzag cuts for attractive edge. Remove seeds and scoop out flesh, using melon-ball scoop. Trim a small slice from the underneath side of shell so it will balance on a plate. Scrap uneven ridges of cantaloupe flesh to measure 1 cup. Set aside.

Combine cantaloupe balls, pineapple, raspberries, and 2 tablespoons of toasted coconut. Spoon into cantaloupe halves.

Place 1 cup of cantaloupe trimmings into blender container and whirl until smooth and liquid. Slice frozen banana into chunks and add to cantaloupe. Blend until smooth and thick. Add ½ cup of yogurt, nutmeg, and lemon juice. Blend again until smooth. Spoon remaining 1 cup of yogurt onto top of fruit in shells (¼ cup each). Pour sauce over yogurt and fruit. Top with remaining toasted coconut and garnish with mint if desired.

Serves 4

Fresh Fruit Plate^(L)

4 circles cantaloupe, cut
  1 inch thick
Lettuce leaves
1⅓ cups low-fat cottage
  cheese
2 tablespoons raisins
1 tablespoon sunflower
  seeds
Dash of cinnamon
4 cups diced mixed
  fresh fruit
Mint sprigs
1 small banana
2 tablespoons plain
  low-fat yogurt
2 teaspoons finely
  chopped sunflower
  seeds or almonds

Place cantaloupe circles on lettuce-lined serving plates. Combine cottage cheese, raisins, 1 tablespoon of sunflower seeds, and cinnamon. Spoon into center of cantaloupe circles. Surround cottage cheese with mixed fresh fruit. Garnish with mint sprigs.

Peel banana and cut in half lengthwise. Spread cut surface with yogurt, then sprinkle with cinnamon and chopped sunflower seeds. Cut into bite-size pieces and place on serving dish. Serve as accompaniment to Fresh Fruit Plate.

Serves 4

BEVERAGES

Among the most creative components in the vegetarian diet are beverages. These beverages have it all: They are delicious, definitely nutritious, and are capable of serving as a meal.

Blenders pay for themselves rapidly if you make your own healthful drinks. And buying fruits and vegetables in season will allow you to make the most of your budget.

Top-of-the-stove juices, if you haven't tried them, are easy and fun to make, and give you the option of a good hot liquid form of refreshment and nourishment.

Tips to remember:

Vegetables have to be used in some quantity to get an appropriate amount of juice. It pays to use a juicer; a blender will also work, with a judicious amount of water added. Don't overwater. Use ripe fruit and vegetables to yield the most juice. If you are blending two or more juices of different colors, the colors will form a new one; for example, orange and cranberry combine to form an unwelcome brown.

Garnishes help all drinks, and you will find you have added a

Note: The symbol **(L)** is used next to those recipe titles that include some form of dairy product. All other recipes are vegan in nature; that is, they contain no meat, eggs, or milk products.

festive look with a slice of cucumber or an orange, a cherry, a carrot stick, or a piece of celery.

Add carbonated water (seltzer) at the last minute.

If you are making a punch, use a big block of ice—it will melt more slowly.

If you are heating citrus or other acid juices, use a steel or glass pan; aluminum will change the color and flavor of acidic juices.

Lemonade Delight with Fruit Kabobs

¾ cup raw wild honey
1 cup fresh water
2 cups lemon juice
1 cup orange juice
1½ tablespoons finely grated lemon peel
1½ tablespoons finely grated orange peel
Fresh fruit chunks

Pour honey and water into a saucepan with a tight-fitting lid. Stir over low heat until honey is blended with the water. Cover pan and boil for 3 minutes before setting aside to cool. Mix together citrus juices and grated peel; cool, then add water and honey syrup. Store in a screw-top glass jar until needed. Serve in tall glasses half-filled with the liquid and topped with ice and natural mineral water. Garnish with fruit kabobs made from pineapple squares, orange quarters, lime rounds, strawberries, or other seasonal fruit.

Serves 4

Gazpacho*

1 medium tomato,
  peeled and diced
¼ large cucumber,
  peeled and chopped
¼ large green pepper,
  seeded
2 onion slices
2 parsley sprigs
6 ice cubes

Combine and liquify in blender with
ice cubes.
Serves 1

* May also be served as a cold soup.

Pineapple-Cucumber Juice

3 ounces cucumber,
  peeled
1 ounce fresh pineapple
2 parsley sprigs
½ fresh apple, coarsely
  chopped
3 ice cubes

Combine and liquify in blender.
Serves 1

Carrot-Apple Juice

2 ounces fresh apple
  juice
2 ounces fresh carrot
  juice
1 small apple, coarsely
  chopped
3 ice cubes

Combine and liquify in blender.
Serves 1

Nut Milk

¼ cup nuts (almonds,*
    cashews, brazil nuts)
1 cup water
½ teaspoon honey or
    barley malt
¼ teaspoon vanilla
    (optional)

Grind nuts in blender until finely powdered. Add water to nut meal and blend for 2–3 minutes. Strain, then add sweetener and vanilla. Reserve nut meal for cereal or baking. Chill nut milk and shake before serving. Flavor with carob, molasses, or maple syrup for a delicious variation, hot or cold.

(Cashews are a softer nut and can be ground to a finer powder than the other nuts.)

Serves 1

* Blanch almonds by covering with boiling water, soaking for 1–2 minutes, then draining and rubbing nuts with fingers to remove skins.

Cranberry Delight (L)

1 cup cranberry juice
    cocktail, chilled
1 tablespoon lemon
    juice
1 egg white
½ cup crushed ice

Blend all ingredients until foamy. Serve immediately.

Serves 2

Orange Delight

1 cup orange juice
½ banana
1 cup apple juice
1 teaspoon honey
Shake of cinnamon
1 cup crushed ice

Blend at high speed until frothy.

Serves 2–3

Fruit Flip (L)

1 large peach or ½ cup
  cooked apricots or
  other fruit
1 cup milk or soymilk
½ cup cracked ice
1–2 drops almond
  extract
Mint sprigs (garnish)

Blend all ingredients in blender until smooth. Pour into small glasses and decorate with mint sprigs.

Variation: Mix fruits such as apples, pears, blueberries, or strawberries. Add a little honey for sweetener if desired.

Serves 2–3

Fruit Cooler (L)

1 cup cold milk
1 small or medium
  banana, sliced
½ cup orange juice
½ cup unsweetened
  pineapple juice

Whirl milk and banana in blender. Add remaining ingredients and whirl again.

Serves 2

Yogurt Whiz (L)

1 cup yogurt
1 cup ice
1 cup fresh fruit
  (strawberries or
  raspberries are good)
2 tablespoons sugar
Dash of salt

Combine ingredients in blender and serve immediately.

Serves 2–3

Snapple

4 cups fresh apple cider or juice
¼ cup whole cinnamon sticks
1 tablespoon whole cloves
⅛ teaspoon powdered cloves
⅛ teaspoon ginger
⅛ teaspoon allspice
1 whole vanilla bean or dash of vanilla extract

Place all but ¼ cup of cider in a saucepan. Wrap cinnamon sticks and whole cloves in a clean piece of cheesecloth and place in saucepan. Mix powdered spices in blender with remaining ¼ cup of cider and add to pan. Finally, add whole vanilla bean or dash of vanilla to mixture. Heat over low flame until warm. Remove cheesecloth mixture and vanilla bean, and serve snappy cider warm.

Variation: Add dash of orange or lemon extract in place of or in addition to vanilla.

Serves 4

Merry Nog (L)

2 cups plain yogurt
⅛–¼ cup honey or maple syrup
¼ teaspoon vanilla extract
½–1 cup unsweetened frozen strawberries
Dash of nutmeg

Blend everything but nutmeg in blender. Serve with a dash of nutmeg.

Variation: Use other fruits such as bananas, blueberries, or cherries, or mix bananas and berries. With bananas, add more yogurt if the mixture is too thick.

Serves 2

Banana Shake (L)

8 ounces plain yogurt
1 ripe banana, sliced
2 tablespoons honey
3 ice cubes

Combine ingredients in blender. Blend until smooth—about 30 seconds.

Serves 2

Fitness Nog^(L)

1 cup pineapple juice
1 banana
½ cup plain yogurt
½ cup milk or kefir
1 tablespoon honey
2 tablespoons ground
   pumpkin seeds
1 tablespoon honey
   bee pollen
Dash of nutmeg
6–8 ice cubes

Combine all ingredients in covered blender at high speed until well mixed. Pour into a thermos or glass bottle and store cold until ready to serve. Shake before serving.

Serves 2–3

Good Morning Drink

6 ounces unsweetened
   orange, pineapple,
   or apple juice
1 cup frozen
   unsweetened
   strawberries or other
   fruit, or substitute 1
   banana
1 tablespoon calcium-
   fortified brewer's
   yeast, mild-flavored
1 tablespoon wheat
   germ (optional)

Combine all ingredients in blender and serve in your favorite glass. (This drink is a lovely pink color when you use strawberries.) Fresh rather than frozen fruit may be used, but frozen fruit makes a thicker "smoothie."

Serves 1

Orange Nut Nog

½ cup unsulphured
  dried apricots
Spring water
½ cup raw cashew
  butter or peanut
  butter
½ cup orange juice
  concentrate
4 ice cubes
½ teaspoon freshly
  grated nutmeg

Soak apricots overnight in 1 cup of spring water. Add nut butter to blender with apricots and their "liquor." Blend, gradually adding remaining ingredients. You may want more or less liquid, and you may prefer more nutmeg. Adjust seasoning. Add another ice cube to thin and give additional frothiness to beverage.

Serves 2

Homemade Gingerale

4 lemons
2 quarts spring water,
  boiled
1 cup peeled and
  chopped fresh ginger
  root
Honey
1 quart sparkling water
Cinnamon sticks
  (garnish)

Peel lemons and cut peel into very thin strips. Pour boiling spring water over chopped ginger and lemon rind. (For a more pronounced ginger flavor, put chopped ginger through a garlic press and use both juices and pulp.) Steep for 10 minutes. Strain and add honey to taste. Juice the lemons and add this along with sparkling water. Pour into chilled glasses filled with ice cubes and a cinnamon stick "swizzler." For pink gingerale, add a little fresh pomegranate juice.

Serves 6–8

Clare's Hot Fruit-Tea Punch

8 cups boiling water
4 cinnamon sticks,
   broken
1 tablespoon whole
   cloves
A few dashes of nutmeg
4 teabags (herbal)
Juice of 2 lemons
¼ cup honey or to taste
1 large can
   unsweetened
   pineapple juice
1 6¼-ounce can frozen
   grapefruit juice or
   orange juice, or 1 48-
   ounce can apple juice

Bring water to a boil in a large stainless steel or enamel saucepan. Add spices and teabags. Remove teabags after 3 minutes of steeping; let remainder of spices simmer about 20 minutes. Add lemon juice, honey, pineapple juice, and one other juice. Bring just to a boil; leave on lowest heat to keep warm. For a larger crowd, add another can of pineapple juice.

Serves 40

Carrot Smoothie[L]

2 cups fresh, cold carrot
   juice
¼ cup light cream or
   milk or soymilk
Dash of cayenne
   pepper

Whirl in blender and serve while frothy.
Serves 2

White Lightning

3 cups white grape juice
1 cup grapefruit juice
1 40-ounce bottle
   cranberry juice
   cocktail
1 lemon, sliced

Combine juices and lemon in a large saucepan. Bring to a boil. Cover and simmer for 10 minutes. Remove lemon slices. Serve hot in mugs.
Serves 16

Harvest Punch

1 gallon apple cider
48 whole cloves
4 teaspoons whole
   allspice
6 cinnamon sticks
1 cup sugar, or to taste
1 cup orange juice
Juice of 1 medium
   lemon

Bring all ingredients to a slow boil and simmer about 10 minutes. Strain and serve hot.
Serves 20

Cider Cocktail

2 cups sweet cider
½ cup raw cranberries
1 medium-size banana
½ cup sunflower seeds
4 ice cubes

Whirl all ingredients in blender, adding ice cubes one at a time.
Serves 3–4

Hot Apple Toddy for One

1 cup apple juice or
  cider
1 teaspoon brown
  sugar, maple syrup,
  or honey (optional)
Slice of lemon
Sprinkle of cinnamon or
  cinnamon stick
¼ teaspoon butter
  (optional)

Heat apple juice or cider to boiling point. Pour into mug and add sweetener. Top with lemon slice. Add cinnamon or cinnamon stick for stirring. Top with butter if desired.

Serves 1

Cranberry Glog

1 40-ounce bottle
  cranberry-apple juice
½ cup raisins
¼ cup cranberries
  (optional)
4 orange slices, each
  studded with 2 whole
  cloves
½ teaspoon or 1 stick
  cinnamon
½ teaspoon cardamom
  (optional)

Combine all ingredients in medium saucepan. Let stand 1 hour or overnight. Bring to a boil, then simmer for 30 minutes. Serve hot in mugs.

Serves 6

Avocado Aperitif

1 medium-size avocado
1 large cucumber
Juice of 1 lemon
½ cup chopped parsley
1 tablespoon olive oil
2 cups crushed ice
Lemon slices or
  cucumber peel
  (garnish)

Peel avocado and cucumber, chop in chunks, and place in blender. Add lemon juice, parsley, and oil, and blend until smooth. Add crushed ice and blend together again. Strain into glasses. Garnish with lemon slices or cucumber peel.
Serves 4

Cranberry Tea Punch

5 tea bags or 5
  teaspoons loose tea
¼ teaspoon ground
  cinnamon
¼ teaspoon ground
  nutmeg
2½ cups boiling water
¾ cup sugar
2 cups cranberry juice
1½ cups water
½ cup orange juice
⅓ cup lemon juice

Steep tea and spices in hot water in covered teapot for 5 minutes. Remove tea bags or strain. Stir in sugar until dissolved. Cool mixture. When cool, add remaining ingredients. Chill. Pour over ice cubes in glasses to serve.
Serves 6–8

Spicy Mint and Apple Cooler

2 cups mint tea
1 tablespoon raw
honey
¼ teaspoon ground
ginger
Pinch of ground cloves
Pinch of ground
cinnamon
1 cup raw apple juice
1 bottle club soda or
sparkling water
Mint sprigs or apple
slices (garnish)

Prepare tea. Add honey, ginger, cloves, and cinnamon. Allow to cool. Mix apple juice and soda water together in a large pitcher. Add cooled tea and mix well. Store in a glass bottle. When ready to serve, shake bottle to agitate spices, which will have settled to the bottom. Garnish with fresh mint sprigs or slices of red apples.

Serves 4–6

SOUPS

Vegetable soup is a recycler's dream, and in the interest of saving vitamins that might go down the sink drain, every cook should conserve the juices and liquids from cooked fresh vegetables. Keep the liquid refrigerated in a covered jar. Odds and ends of leftover vegetables (potatoes, peas, string beans, corn removed from cobs, cabbage) may be added to canned or dried soups, but you can make the best soups with items that might ordinarily be thrown away: the ends of carrots, beet tops, the outside leaves of a head of lettuce that may be too unattractive to serve. When cooked with soup that is strained before serving, they serve up a hearty dish with a fresh, wonderful flavor. The tops of celery, run through a blender with cucumbers, make a delicious soup hot or cold.

As with stews, soups are traditionally meat-based. We hope that these fine selections from the world of soups will bear witness to the fact that they need not be. Each of these recipes yields a hearty and flavorful hot soup that will please the palate of the most discriminating taster.

Don't shy away from soups you know and love because you no longer eat meat. A hearty vegetable broth, such as the one we've

Note: The symbol **(L)** is used next to those recipe titles that include some form of dairy product. All other recipes are vegan in nature; that is, they contain no meat, eggs, or milk products.

provided here, can invariably substitute well for a meat stock. Experiment with herbs and spices for added fullness. Soups are a gradual affair—they require lots of tasting and building to reach their full potential—so work with a fearless hand and a loving heart when soup's on.

Vegetable Broth

6 cups water
2 medium onions, peeled and chopped
4 large carrots, peeled and chopped
6–8 celery stalks
1 bunch fresh dill or parsley
Salt to taste

Bring water to a boil. Add onions and carrots. Wash celery and add leaves and stalks to pot. Simmer 45 minutes. Strain. Pass ½ cup of cooked carrots through sieve and add to stock; discard remaining vegetables. Add dill or parsley. Reheat and serve steaming hot with matzo balls.

Serves 4

Corn Chowder(L)

4–6 ears corn on the cob
2 tablespoons butter or margarine
1 large onion, chopped
1 leek, sliced, or 1 green pepper, seeded and diced
2 potatoes, diced
3 cups vegetable broth
3 cups dairy or soy milk
Salt and pepper to taste
½ cup cream
Chopped parsley (garnish)

Remove the corn kernels from cobs by slicing downward on cobs with a small, sharp knife. Melt butter in a large, heavy saucepan. Add onion and sauté for 2–3 minutes. Add sliced leek and sauté a few minutes more. Add corn and potatoes, and toss together. Add broth and milk, and bring just to a boil. Salt and pepper to taste, then simmer for 20 minutes. Add cream and serve hot, sprinkled with chopped parsley.

Serves 6–8

Peanut Soup[(L)]

1 tablespoon butter or
  margarine
¼ cup peanut butter
1 teaspoon minced
  onion
¼ teaspoon ground
  cumin seed
¼ teaspoon ground
  coriander
2 tablespoons all-
  purpose flour
1½ cups vegetable
  broth
1½ cups heavy cream
Salt to taste
Cayenne pepper to
  taste

Combine butter, peanut butter, and onion in a heavy saucepan, and cook over a low heat for 5 minutes, stirring constantly. Add cumin seed, coriander, and flour, and blend. Slowly stir in vegetable broth. Cook over lowest heat for 10 minutes, stirring from time to time. Add cream and simmer for 10 minutes more. Do not boil. Season with salt and cayenne.

Serves 4–6

Black Bean Soup

1 cup black beans
4 cups water
3 bay leaves
4 cloves
2 onions, chopped
2 cloves garlic
¼ teaspoon dry
  mustard
1½ teaspoons chili
  powder
Salt to taste

Add all ingredients except salt to boiling water and simmer until tender. Puree. Salt to taste and serve.

Serves 4–6

Wax Bean Soup^(L)

1 small onion, finely
  chopped
2 tablespoons chopped
  parsley
3 tablespoons butter or
  margarine
1 pound fresh wax
  beans, washed and
  sliced
Salt and white pepper
  to taste (optional)
2 cups vegetable juices
4 cups water
2 cups milk
2 tablespoons wheat
  flour
Fresh chopped parsley
  (garnish)
1 cup sour cream
  (garnish)

In a heavy 3-quart saucepan, sauté onions and parsley in butter until onions become transparent. Add wax beans, salt, white pepper, vegetable juices, and water. Cover and cook until beans are tender, about 35–40 minutes. Thicken soup with mixture of milk and wheat flour. Serve garnished with parsley and sour cream.

Serves 8

Fresh Tomato Soup^(L)

3 quarts ripe tomatoes,
sliced
6 onions, finely sliced
Chopped parsley
30 whole cloves
4 teaspoons salt
1–2 teaspoons white
pepper
8 tablespoons butter or
margarine
6 tablespoons wheat
flour
½ cup water
1 cup sour cream

Boil tomatoes, onions, parsley, cloves, salt, and pepper until vegetables are thoroughly cooked. Strain through food mill and add butter. Add wheat flour dissolved with water. Boil until thickened. Serve hot with a heaping tablespoon of sour cream for each serving.

Variations: You can use carrot juice instead of water with this soup; carrots add sweetness which is natural and delicious. Also, if you have ½ cup or 1 cup of cooked rice left over from a meal, substitute the rice for the wheat flour.

Serves 8

Navy Bean Soup

1 pound navy beans
2 quarts water
2 quarts vegetable
juices
Parsley, celery, parsnips,
onions, or any
leftover vegetables
1 tablespoon salt
¼ teaspoon white
pepper
1 cup diced carrots
1 cup diced green or
red pepper

Wash beans and soak overnight in water. Cook beans in water in which they soaked, adding vegetable juices. Add other ingredients and cook until everything is tender, about 1 hour.

Serves 8

Portuguese Soup[(L)]

1 cup chopped onions
½ tablespoon olive oil
1 cup diced carrots
1 35-ounce can Italian
  tomatoes or 1 pound
  fresh tomatoes
1 cup water or
  vegetable juices
1 teaspoon salt
¼ teaspoon black
  pepper
½ teaspoon basil
½ teaspoon thyme
2 bay leaves
2 whole cloves
2 hard-cooked eggs,
  chopped (garnish)
¼ cup slivered almonds
  (garnish)

Brown chopped onions in olive oil. Add other ingredients and simmer, covered, for 20 minutes or until carrots are tender. Sprinkle surface with eggs and slivered almonds.

Serves 4–6

Split Pea Chowder

4 cups water
1 teaspoon salt
1 medium onion, diced
1 potato, diced
1 cup dry split peas
1 medium carrot,
  grated
½ teaspoon sweet basil
1 cup brown rice or
  whole wheat or
  whole-grain toast

Bring water to a boil and add salt. Add diced onion, potato, and split peas. Cook until tender. Add grated carrot and basil. Serve over whole-grain toast, cooked whole wheat, or rice.

Serves 6

Squash Soup with Tofu

1½ tablespoons oil

1 pound pumpkin or squash, seeded and cut into ½-inch squares

2 onions, thinly sliced

2 cups water or stock

¼ teaspoon nutmeg or cinnamon

1 clove garlic, minced

4 tablespoons miso

12 ounces tofu, cut into ½-inch cubes

3 tablespoons minced parsley (garnish)

½ cup croutons (garnish)

2 tablespoons ground roasted sesame seeds (garnish)

Heat oil in a casserole or large pot. Add pumpkin, onions, and stock. Cover and bring to a boil. Reduce heat and simmer for 25 minutes. Stir in nutmeg, garlic, and miso thinned in a little of the hot soup. Add tofu, return just to a boil, and remove from heat. For best flavor, allow to cool to room temperature. Serve cold or reheated, topped with parsley, croutons, and sesame seeds.

Serves 6

Vegetable Bean Soup

2 cups kidney beans
3 quarts stewed
tomatoes
6 quarts water
4 cups celery
3 large onions
½ cup tamari
2 tablespoons salt
Optional ingredients
(choose 1 or more):
12 cups cooked
noodles
2 large carrots, diced
4 small zucchini,
diced
4 cups fresh corn

Soak beans overnight; drain off water. Add fresh water, bring to a boil, and simmer for 1½ hours. Add remaining ingredients, simmer for 1 hour more, and adjust seasonings to taste.

Serves 25–30

Cold Sweet-and-Sour Tofu Soup

3 ounces olive oil
7 ounces onion,
chopped
10½ ounces cabbage,
chopped
10½ ounces tomatoes,
peeled and chopped
1 pint water
3¼ ounces lemon juice
4 tablespoons honey
3¼ ounces orange juice
1 ounce tofu balls
(Parisienne scoop)
Cabbage, julienne
(garnish)
Chervil leaves (garnish)

Heat oil and sauté onions until transparent. Add cabbage and sauté 5 minutes more. Add tomatoes, water, lemon juice, and honey, and simmer for 15–20 minutes. Season soup with salt and pepper, and remove from heat.

Pour soup into food processor and puree to a smooth, creamy consistency. Refrigerate soup for 6–8 hours.

Before serving, blend soup with orange juice. Place tofu balls into soup dish and pour soup over. Garnish with cabbage julienne and chervil leaves.

Serves 6–8

Garlic Soup

1½ quarts water
4 potatoes
1 carrot
2 stalks celery
1 onion
2 large bulbs garlic
½ teaspoon thyme
Dash of cayenne
Sea salt to taste

Bring water to a boil. Cut potatoes, carrot, celery, and onion into ½-inch pieces and place in boiling water. Break garlic bulbs and peel individual cloves. Place in soup together with spices. Cook soup over medium heat for 20–30 minutes. When soup is ready, it can be served in either of two ways: (1) strain and serve as a clear broth with 1 raw egg dropped into each serving, (2) eliminate eggs, puree in blender, and serve as a "cream of garlic" soup.

Serves 6–8

Cream of Carrot Soup(L)

3 cups grated carrots
1½ cups finely chopped
   celery
2 ounces onions
⅓ pound butter or
   margarine
1 quart hot water
2½ quarts milk or
   soyamilk
½ cups sifted
   unbleached flour
1½ tablespoons salt
1 teaspoon paprika
Chives or parsley,
   chopped (garnish)

Sauté carrots, celery, and onions in ⅓ of butter until tender but not brown. Add hot water; simmer until celery is thoroughly tender. Heat milk. Melt remainder of butter; add flour and blend until smooth. Add milk, stirring constantly with wire whisk. Cook until sauce has slightly thickened and starch flavor has disappeared. Add salt and paprika. Combine vegetable mixture with cream sauce. Garnish with chopped chives or parsley.

Serves 8–10

Northern Italian Spinach and Cornmeal Soup

4 tablespoons butter or margarine
1 clove garlic, minced
2 tablespoons all-purpose flour
1 pound fresh spinach, coarsely chopped
2 quarts heated vegetable broth
3 tablespoons yellow cornmeal
Salt and pepper
Grated Parmesan cheese

Heat butter in a large pot, add garlic, and sauté briefly. Add flour, blending it thoroughly. Add spinach and sauté about 5 minutes, stirring often. Add hot broth, slowly at first, stirring with a whisk. Cook about 20 minutes. Mix cornmeal with a little cold water and stir into soup. Season with salt and pepper, and cook, stirring often, about 20 minutes more. Serve with grated cheese.

Serves 4–6

Pimiento-Cheese Soup[L]

1 quart milk
4 ounces pimientos
¼ cup butter or margarine
⅓ cup whole wheat flour
1 teaspoon salt
Dash of cayenne pepper
1 cup sharp cheddar cheese, cubed

Put milk and pimientos in blender and whirl until pimientos are finely chopped. Melt butter in a 2-quart saucepan. Using a fork, stir in flour. Cook over medium heat, stirring frequently, until flour is browned. Gradually add milk mixture, still stirring with the fork to keep mixture smooth. Stir in salt and cayenne pepper. When mixture is bubbly and thickened, add cheese. Continue cooking until cheese is melted.

Serves 4

Chunky Potato Soup^(L)

2½ cups vegetable
   cooking water or
   water
½ cup sliced celery
¾ cup onions, cut in half
   lengthwise, then
   sliced across
½ cup sliced carrots
5 cups sliced unpeeled
   potatoes
2 teaspoons salt
½ teaspoon dry
   mustard
2 cups milk
1 teaspoon dried
   parsley flakes

Place first 5 ingredients in a 2½-quart saucepan and bring to a boil. Reduce heat and simmer, covered, until celery and carrots are tender. Mash mixture slightly in the saucepan with a potato masher. Add remaining ingredients and bring soup to a boil again. Reduce heat to simmer and continue to cook, stirring, about 2 minutes more.

Serves 4–6

Lima Cheese Soup^(L)

1 cup large dried lima
   beans
1 medium onion, diced
3 cups vegetable
   cooking water or
   water
1 cup milk
1 cup cubed cheddar
   cheese
1 cup cubed Monterey
   Jack cheese
Salt to taste

Cook dried limas and onion in vegetable cooking water in a 2-quart saucepan, covered, until limas are very tender. Put milk in blender container; add lima-onion mixture and cheeses. Blend until mixture is smooth. Return mixture to saucepan and season to taste with salt. Heat until soup is bubbly hot.

Serves 4

Hot Zucchini Soup^(L)

1 pound zucchini (3 to
  4 small), washed and
  sliced
1 cup chopped onion
1 cup vegetable broth
Sea salt to taste
⅛ teaspoon basil
⅛ teaspoon thyme
⅛ teaspoon marjoram
2 cups milk
Whipped cottage
  cheese or yogurt
Minced scallions

Place zucchini, onion, broth, and salt in a saucepan and bring to a boil. Cover and simmer gently until tender. Cool. Add basil, thyme, and marjoram, and puree in blender or food mill. Stir in milk, and heat but do not boil. Top with cottage cheese and minced scallions.

Serves 4

Carrot-Yogurt Soup^(L)

¼ cup soy butter
8 medium carrots,
  scraped and sliced
3 medium onions,
  chopped
4 cups stock, boiling
1 cup plain yogurt
½ cup soymilk
¼ cup chopped fresh
  chives or 2
  tablespoons freeze-
  dried chives

Melt butter in a large frying pan. Sauté carrots and onions until onions are tender. Add stock, cover, and simmer for 1 hour.

Puree carrots and onions with liquid in blender. Transfer mixture to a 2-quart saucepan. Add yogurt and milk, stirring until smooth. Keep on low heat until ready to serve, but do not allow to boil. Sprinkle with chives. Good hot or cold.

Serves 7

Bean Chowder

2 cups dry pinto beans
3 cups water
1½ teaspoons salt
2 medium potatoes,
  diced
1 medium onion, diced
2 tablespoons enriched
  flour
3 (or 1 can) tomatoes
1 green pepper,
  chopped
¼ cup vegetable
  margarine
1½ cups water or
  powdered milk or
  milk

Soak beans overnight in water. Add salt and cook until almost done. Add potatoes and onion. Cook for 30 minutes more, adding more water if needed. Mix flour with a few tomatoes and add to beans with rest of tomatoes, green pepper, and margarine. Cook for 10 minutes, stirring. Stir in water.

Serves 10

Pureed Cream of Field Pea Soup with Cheese^(L)

1 tablespoon butter or
  margarine
½ cup chopped onion
Water
½ cup dry milk powder
1 cup vegetable
  cooking water or
  water
2 cups dried field peas,
  cooked
Small amount of field
  pea cooking liquid
1 cup cubed Monterey
  Jack cheese
¼ teaspoon garlic
  powder

Melt butter in a 2-quart saucepan; add onions and sauté until limp. Add enough water to milk powder to make 2 cups. Put milk mixture, sautéed onions, and remaining ingredients except garlic powder in blender container, and blend until smooth. Pour mixture into the saucepan, add garlic powder, and bring to a boil. Reduce heat and simmer, covered, about 10 minutes.

Serves 4

Creamy Black Bean Soup

1 cup dried black beans
4 cups vegetable
  cooking water or 4
  cups water and 4
  teaspoons vegetable
  broth powder
¼ teaspoon ground
  marjoram
¼ teaspoon ground
  thyme
¼ teaspoon ground
  coriander
½ teaspoon garlic
  powder
2 cups water
2 tablespoons butter or
  margarine
1 cup chopped onions
Salt to taste

Put black beans, vegetable cooking water, marjoram, thyme, coriander, and garlic powder in a 2-quart saucepan. Bring mixture to a boil, reduce heat, and simmer, covered, until beans are tender and liquid is absorbed.

Pour 2 cups of water into blender container; add cooked bean mixture and blend until mixture is just creamy. Return mixture to saucepan.

Meanwhile, melt butter in a small skillet; add onions and sauté until tender. Add butter and onions to black bean mixture and cook together for 5 minutes or until mixture is bubbly hot. Season to taste with salt.

Serves 3–4

Cold Zucchini Soup^(L)

**5–6 small to medium
size zucchini
1 large onion, peeled
and thinly sliced
1½ teaspoons curry
powder
3 cups vegetable broth
1 cup heavy cream
½ cup milk
Salt and freshly ground
pepper
Chives, finely chopped**

Rinse zucchini and pat dry. Trim off ends. Cut one zucchini in two and thinly slice one half. Stack slices and cut into very thin, matchlike strips (there should be about 1 cup). Place in a saucepan and add cold water to cover. Boil for 3–4 minutes, then drain. Set aside.

Cut the other zucchini half and remaining zucchini into 1-inch lengths. Cut each length into quarters. Place pieces of zucchini in a kettle or saucepan and add onion slices. Sprinkle with curry powder and stir to coat pieces. Add vegetable broth and bring to a boil. Cover and simmer about 45 minutes.

Spoon and scrape mixture into blender or food processor container and blend to a fine puree. There should be about 4 cups. Add cream, milk, salt, and pepper to taste. Add reserved zucchini strips. Chill thoroughly. Serve sprinkled with chopped chives.

Serves 6–8

Cold Cucumber Soup^(L)

1½ cups diced
  cucumber
1¼ cups plain low-fat
  yogurt
1 cup water
1 clove garlic, pressed
1 teaspoon finely
  chopped fresh mint
  (optional)
½ teaspoon dillweed
2 tablespoons chopped
  chives (garnish)

Combine all ingredients except chopped chives. Mix well and chill for 2–4 hours. Serve garnished with chopped chives.

Serves 4

Fruit Soup

¼ cup dried apricots
¾ cup dried prunes
¼ cup dried peaches,
  cut in halves
¼ cup dried pears, cut
  in halves
6 cups cold water
1 cinnamon stick
2 lemon slices, thickly
  cut
2 tablespoons quick-
  cooking tapioca
3 tablespoons sugar or
  honey
2 tablespoons raisins
1 tablespoon dried
  currants
1 green apple, pared
  and cut into ½-inch
  slices

Wash and soak apricots, prunes, peaches, and pears in water for 30 minutes. Pour fruit and water into a pressure cooker. Cover and set control at 15. Cook over high heat until pressure is reached. Reduce heat; cook for 6 minutes more. Cool cooker naturally for 5 minutes; complete pressure reduction by placing cooker under cold, running water.

Add cinnamon stick, lemon slices, and tapioca; heat to boiling, stirring occasionally. Stir in remaining ingredients. Simmer, uncovered, until fruit is tender but not mushy, about 10 minutes. Remove lemon and cinnamon stick. Refrigerate until chilled. Serve soup in chilled bowls or in compote dishes if used as a dessert.

Serves 4–6

SALADS

Early Salads

An English recipe book of 1390 gives King Richard II's favorite salad: "Borage, cress, fennel, garlic, leeks, mint, onions, parsley, purslain, rosemary, rue, and sage. Wash, tear the leaves apart with the hands, mix well with oil, add salt and vinegar, and serve forth."

A royal gardener in the Elizabethan court stated that even plain salads should have a minimum of 35 ingredients, and he mentioned several that we would never consider: daisy, fennel, and rampion roots, served boiled, sliced cold, or candied; whole or candied flowers, including alder, broom buds, elder buds, and ash keys.

Crowned salads were far more grand and were served at great banquets. A large pastry castle was made, with carrot and turnip towers, and trees made of herbs in the courtyard. There were pastry steps all over the castle, with a different salad spread out on each one. At each corner was a carved vegetable statue holding a cruet.

A smaller version for regular dinners had a simple pastry tower in the center of a dish, surrounded with herbs, capers, sliced dates, raisins, almonds, figs, preserved oranges, and sugar. Lemon halves,

Note: The symbol (L) is used next to those recipe titles that include some form of dairy product. All other recipes are vegan in nature; that is, they contain no meat, eggs, or milk products.

their flat side down, sported branches of rosemary, with cherries dangling over them.

Rosemary snow was a popular table decoration; A rosemary branch was frosted with whipped cream and egg whites, beaten with sugar, and set in a loaf of bread in the middle of the table. This was said to promote the appetite.

Boiled Salads

By the seventh century, boiled salads were popular. Old peas and beans were boiled, mashed into a paste, and mixed with cinnamon, lemon rind, nutmeg, and butter. Finely shaped greens were added, and the whole spread on toast. Another variation had fresh spinach cooked and mixed with cinnamon, ginger, raisins, and butter, also served on toast. Boiled celery with French beans and dressing, and young asparagus boiled with a little vinegar and butter, were also relished. Cooked celery was chilled and served with thin lemon slices, julienne strips of beets, and a light dressing.

By the last century, salads were an accompaniment to vast, stodgy dinners and had little variation. Summer salad was lettuce, cress, radishes, cucumber, small green onions, and nasturtiums for garnish. Winter salads were endive, cress, beets, celery, and dressing. We know that salad is health-giving, natural, low in calories, good for the complexion, full of essential elements, and can be infinitely varied. We can experiment with new combinations as well as old ones.

The Ideal Meal for Spring and Summer

On a hot summer day nothing is more refreshing to the eye than alternating slices of cucumber and segments of grapefruit arranged on a crisp lettuce leaf. The traditional Brazilian salad of lettuce and orange segments with a sharp tarragon vinegar and oil dressing is a delicious combination, and for cooler days a dish of shredded young cabbage with a thick horseradish sauce makes a lively change. The combinations seem limitless, and a wise rule to remember is that the salad should be simple, elegant, and a symphony of a few delicate flavors. Anyone can throw 20 ingredients together and imagine that a masterpiece has been created, but the true salad lover appreciates restraint.

There is nothing quite like a crisp salad that was growing in the garden half an hour ago. The crunchy greens, the teasing hint of the herbs, the brightness of tomatoes or carrots—truly, the salad is a splendid invention.

Middle Eastern Pasta Salad[(L)]

½ pound small pasta
  shapes
1 teaspoon oil
1 large clove garlic
2 teaspoons salt
2 tablespoons finely
  chopped fresh mint or
  1 teaspoon dried
  mint
1–1½ cups yogurt
2 ounces pine nuts
1 tablespoon butter or
  margarine, melted

Cook pasta al dente for 8–10 minutes in salted water. Drain and add oil to prevent sticking. With a mortar and pestle, crush garlic, salt, and mint to a rough paste. Add to yogurt and blend well. Pour mixture over cooked pasta. Sauté pine nuts in hot melted butter until golden brown; drain and add to salad. Serve at once.

Serves 4–6

Sook Choo Na Mool (Korean Bean Sprout Salad)

4 tablespoons vegetable oil
2 tablespoons white wine vinegar
2 tablespoons soy sauce
1 clove garlic, minced
Freshly ground pepper and salt
8–10 ounces mung bean sprouts
1 small red pepper, cored, seeded, and finely chopped
4 scallions, trimmed and chopped
2 tablespoons toasted sesame seeds

For the dressing: mix oil, vinegar, soy sauce, garlic, and ground pepper. Add salt sparingly, since soy sauce is quite salty. Place bean sprouts, red pepper, and scallions in a large salad bowl. Add dressing and toss gently. Chill for at least 1 hour. Just before serving, add toasted sesame seeds and toss again.

Serves 6

Oriental Salad Dressing

1 tablespoon toasted sesame seeds
4 tablespoons light soy sauce
2 tablespoons Oriental sesame oil
2 tablespoons rice wine vinegar
1 teaspoon Chinese mustard dissolved in 1 teaspoon water

Toast sesame seeds in a roasting pan at 400° for 15–20 minutes or until golden brown. Shake occasionally and remove from heat when seeds begin to pop. Place all ingredients in a small jar with a tight-fitting lid. Shake well and chill. Just before serving, add sesame seeds to mixture, shake again, and pour over salad.

Yield: ½ cup

French Mushroom Salad

12 mushrooms
1 cup olive oil
12 small pearl onions
2 small heads Boston
    lettuce
2 large tomatoes
2 stalks celery, diced
Juice of 1 small lemon
2 teaspoons tomato
    paste
1 sprig fresh thyme,
    chopped, or ½
    teaspoon dried
    thyme
1 bay leaf
1 teaspoon coriander
    seeds
4 ounces dry white wine
Salt and freshly ground
    pepper

Clean mushrooms by gently wiping with a damp dish towel or paper towel. Leave caps whole but chop stems coarsely. Fry both caps and stems in ½ cup of oil until soft. Remove mushrooms and set aside to drain. Discard used oil.

Peel onions, cut lettuce into quarters, and slice tomatoes. Add onions, lettuce, and tomatoes to a frying pan with celery, lemon juice, tomato paste, thyme, bay leaf, coriander seeds, wine, and remaining oil. Season with salt and pepper, and simmer for 20–25 minutes or until onions are tender.

Remove mushrooms to a shallow serving dish and bring remaining ingredients to a rapid boil for 4–5 minutes. Pour over mushrooms and chill until ready to serve. Remove bay leaf.

Serves 4

Chef's Spinach Salad[(L)]

1 pound raw spinach
**⅔ cup chick-peas,
 cooked**
**½ cup sliced
 mushrooms**
½ cup sliced beets
**8 ounces farmer or
 ricotta cheese made
 from partially
 skimmed milk**
**⅓ cup shelled pumpkin
 or sunflower seeds**
2 tablespoons oil
Juice of 1 lemon

Wash spinach and tear into bite-size pieces. Toss chick-peas, mushrooms, beets, and crumbled farmer cheese with spinach. Just before serving, sprinkle in seeds and add lemon juice and oil as dressing.

Serves 10

Vinaigrette Sauce

⅔ cup oil
⅓ cup wine vinegar
2 teaspoons oregano
**½ teaspoon dry
 mustard**
2 cloves garlic, crushed
**Freshly ground black
 pepper**

Combine all ingredients in a jar, cover tightly, and shake to blend.

Yield: about 1 cup

Macaroni Salad Ricotta[L]

¼ pound whole wheat
  macaroni
2 teaspoons mustard
1 tablespoon or more
  low-fat yogurt
1 cup ricotta cheese
¼ cup sliced or
  chopped ripe olives
1 green pepper,
  coarsely chopped
2 scallions with tops,
  chopped
1 tablespoon chopped
  parsley
½ teaspoon dill
½ teaspoon basil
Red pimiento to taste
Freshly ground black
  pepper

Cook whole wheat macaroni until tender, about 8–10 minutes. Drain and chill. Make a dressing with consistency of mayonnaise by thinning mustard with 1 tablespoon or more of yogurt and then mixing with ricotta. Stir in all other ingredients. Serve on a bed of salad greens.

Serves 4

Yogurt and Radish Salad[L]

2 cups thinly sliced
  radishes
1 cup yogurt
1 clove garlic, pressed
2 tablespoons minced
  fresh parsley
½ teaspoon tamari
¼ teaspoon pepper

Mix all ingredients together and chill for 1–3 hours. Serve in small bowls.

Serves 4

Lemony Radish Salad

½ cup lemon juice
½ cup salad oil
2 tablespoons minced
  fresh chives
2 tablespoons minced
  fresh parsley
1 teaspoon tamari
¼ teaspoon pepper
4 cups thinly sliced
  radishes

Mix all ingredients together well and refrigerate until ready to serve.

Serves 6

Scalloped Radishes (L)

3 cups thinly sliced
  radishes
¼ cup minced green
  pepper
2 tablespoons
  unbleached white
  flour
4 tablespoons butter or
  margarine
1 teaspoon tamari
¼ teaspoon paprika
¼ teaspoon dry
  mustard
1¼ cups scalded milk

Preheat oven to 350° F.

Layer radishes and green pepper in a greased 2-quart casserole dish. Sprinkle each layer with flour and dot each with butter.

Stir tamari, paprika, and mustard into milk and pour mixture over radishes.

Bake, covered, for 30 minutes. Remove cover and bake for 45 minutes more.

Serves 6

Whole Meal Salad

1 head romaine lettuce, torn
1 cup alfalfa sprouts
1 ounce dulse, washed
2 carrots, sliced or grated
3 stalks celery, sliced
1 small head cabbage or cauliflower, chopped
¾ cup soya granules
3 tablespoons bacon-flavored chips (optional)
2 tablespoons sunflower or sesame seeds
Salad herbs to taste
Vegetable seasoning to taste

Toss all ingredients together. Serve with favorite dressing. Tomatoes may be added, but do not add tomatoes, salt, or dressing to salad that will be stored overnight.

Serves 4

Dressing for Whole Meal Salad

2 parts lemon juice
1 part peanut oil
Salt or salt substitute
Garlic powder
Onion powder
¼–½ teaspoon dried herbs of your choice

Mix first five ingredients. Rub herbs between palms to crumble into dressing. Toss and serve with salad. If more than 2 tablespoons of dressing are desired per serving, use more lemon juice.

Yield: 2 tablespoons

Rice Salad

2 cups brown rice,
  cooked
1/3 cup toasted sesame
  seeds
2 tablespoons minced
  fresh coriander
  (Chinese parsley) or
  regular parsley
1/2 cup sauerkraut
1/4 cup minced celery
  (use tender, inside
  stalks)
1/4 cup minced green
  onion
Olive oil

Combine ingredients, adding just enough olive oil to lightly coat vegetables. Additional salt is not needed—the sauerkraut will provide enough.

Serves 6

Macaroni-Vegetable Salad[L]

1 1/2 pounds whole
  wheat elbows
4 regular or 1 1/2 large
  packages frozen
  mixed vegetables
1 pint sour cream or
  yogurt
1 cup mayonnaise
3/4 cup cider vinegar
1 tablespoon salt
1 teaspoon celery seed
1/4 teaspoon bottled hot
  pepper sauce
2 large onions,
  chopped

Cook macaroni 8 minutes or until tender; drain, rinse with cold water, then drain again. Chill. Cook frozen mixed vegetables; drain and chill. In a large bowl, combine sour cream with mayonnaise, vinegar, salt, celery seed, and hot pepper sauce. Add macaroni, mixed vegetables, and onions. Toss to mix thoroughly. Serve on lettuce in 1-cup servings or in a large bowl.

Serves 24

California Vegetable and Tofu Salad

2 tablespoons olive oil
7 ounces zucchini,
    diced, unskinned
7 ounces tomatoes,
    peeled and
    quartered
5½ ounces tofu, cubed
6 mushrooms,
    quartered
3½ ounces snow peas,
    sliced
1¾ ounces broccoli
    florets
1¾ ounces onions,
    diced
1 teaspoon chopped
    garlic
Pinch of rosemary
Pinch of thyme
Salt and pepper
3 Belgian endive leaves

Heat oil in a pan and sauté zucchini briefly. Add remaining ingredients except endive. Cook briefly, just to warm through. Season to taste and remove from stove. Serve on a plate garnished with Belgian endive leaves.

Serves 2

Bean Sprout/Bean Curd Salad

3 cups mung bean or
    soybean sprouts
4 ribs celery, finely
    chopped
½ cup chopped walnuts
1 teaspoon caraway
    seeds
½ cup bean curd (tofu),
    cubed

Combine all ingredients. Toss lightly with vinaigrette sauce and serve on salad greens.

Serves 6

Tossed Green Salad

1 cup torn romaine
   lettuce
1 cup torn red leaf
   lettuce
1 cup torn spinach
   leaves
1 cup chopped
   watercress
¼ cup chopped parsley
1 tablespoon grated
   Parmesan cheese
1 teaspoon toasted
   sesame seeds
⅓ cup low-calorie herb
   dressing
4 red bell pepper rings
½ cup alfalfa sprouts
⅓ cup grated raw beets

Toss together first 8 ingredients. Divide into 4 salad bowls or plates, and top with red pepper rings. Fill rings with alfalfa sprouts and top with beets.

Serves 4

Sweet Corn Salad(L)

2 cups (about 6 ears)
   fresh corn kernels
½ cup homemade
   mayonnaise
½ cup sour cream
½ teaspoon Dijon-style
   mustard
Salt and freshly ground
   black pepper
Lemon juice
Roasted soybeans,
   sliced ripe olives, and
   strips of pimiento
   peppers for garnish

Remove corn from cobs by slicing downward on a cutting board with a very sharp knife, close to the cob. Steam corn until it is tender, about 4 minutes. Drain and cool. Mix mayonnaise, sour cream, and mustard and add corn when it is cool. Add salt, pepper, and lemon juice to taste. Serve on individual salad plates lined with lettuce or fresh spinach leaves, and garnish with roasted soybeans that have been cracked in the blender, sliced ripe olives, and strips of pimiento peppers.

Serves 4

Golden Nuggets Salad[(L)]

2 cups corn kernels,
    steamed and cooled
2 cups cottage cheese
4 scallions, minced
1 tablespoon minced
    fresh parsley
2 large ripe tomatoes,
    chopped
Salt and freshly ground
    black pepper

Toss all ingredients together lightly and season to taste. Chill salad and serve in lettuce-lined bowls.

Serves 4

Garden Salad with Italian or No-Oil Dressing

2 heads leaf lettuce
½ head cabbage,
    shredded
6 Swiss chard leaves,
    chopped
3 Chinese cabbage
    leaves, shredded
1 head cauliflower,
    broken into florets
3 stalks broccoli,
    chopped
1 zucchini, diced
5 large spinach leaves,
    chopped
3 carrots, diced
1 red pepper, diced
4 scallion tops, diced
1 beet, diced or grated
2 kohlrabi, diced

Tear lettuce into bite-size pieces and cut greens. Combine all ingredients in a large bowl. Add dressing, toss, chill, and serve.

Variation: Add sunflower seeds or cooked chick-peas to finished salad.

Serves 10

Italian Dressing

3 parts olive or other oil
1 part fresh lemon juice,
unstrained
⅛ part sea salt or onion
powder
⅛ part garlic, freshly
sliced

Add directly to salad.

No-Oil Italian Dressing

¼ cup lemon juice
¼ cup cider vinegar
¼ cup apple juice
½ teaspoon oregano
½ teaspoon dry
mustard
½ teaspoon onion
powder
½ teaspoon garlic
powder
½ teaspoon paprika
⅛ teaspoon thyme
⅛ teaspoon rosemary

Combine all ingredients in blender and blend well. Chill well and refrigerate overnight or longer to allow flavors to mix.

Yield: ¾ cup

Marinated Soybean Salad

3 cups hot, cooked soybeans or other small white beans, drained
¾ cup oil
⅓ cup vinegar
Sea salt and freshly ground black pepper to taste
1 clove garlic, finely chopped
1 teaspoon Dijon-style mustard
½ cup chopped scallions
½ cup chopped green pepper
⅓ cup chopped celery
2 tablespoons chopped parsley
2 tablespoons snipped fresh dill weed or 2 teaspoons dried dill
½ cup freshly grated Parmesan cheese (optional)

Place hot beans in a bowl. Combine oil, vinegar, salt, pepper, garlic, and mustard, and pour over hot beans. Cover and marinate in refrigerator for several hours. Stir in remaining ingredients. Chill again.

Serves 4

Creamy Tofu Dressing

6 ounces tofu, drained
2 tablespoons lemon
 juice
2 tablespoons cold-
 pressed oil
½ teaspoon salt
⅛ teaspoon ground
 pepper
1 tablespoon finely
 chopped parsley

Combine all ingredients in blender until smooth.

Yield: 1 cup

Tabouli Salad I

4 cups water
2 cups bulgur wheat
Pinch of salt (optional)
1 head lettuce,
 shredded
1 cucumber, finely diced
2 tomatoes, finely diced
2 radishes, finely diced
3 scallions, finely diced
¼ head cabbage,
 shredded
¼ cup finely chopped
 fresh parsley
3 tablespoons tamari
 soy sauce
2 tablespoons oil
¼ teaspoon garlic
 powder
¼ teaspoon paprika
¼ teaspoon basil

Boil water in a large saucepan over medium-high heat. Add bulgur and pinch of salt if desired. Reduce heat to low, cover, and simmer for 15–20 minutes or until bulgur is soft and all water is absorbed. Allow to cool. Combine all vegetables in a large bowl. Add bulgur, seasonings, and dressing if desired.

Variation: Soak bulgur in water for 1 hour or more until soft; drain and follow recipe as above. Add other salad vegetables such as beets, celery, or peppers, or add 2 tablespoons lemon or cider vinegar.

Serves 4

Tabouli Salad II

¾ cup boiling water
½ cup cracked wheat or
  bulgur
½ cup minced parsley
¼ cup minced mint
  leaves
½ cup finely chopped
  green onion
1 tomato, diced
3 tablespoons oil
1–2 tablespoons lemon
  juice or to taste
1 teaspoon sea salt
Pepper and allspice to
  taste

Pour boiling water over cracked wheat, cover, and let stand about 20 minutes until wheat is tender and most of water is absorbed. Add parsley, mint, onion, and diced tomato. Toss to mix. Combine oil, lemon juice, salt, pepper, and allspice. Add to wheat mixture. Chill. Serve on lettuce cups or in large bowl garnished with romaine or butter lettuce.

Serves 4

Tomato-Onion Vinaigrette

1 purple onion, peeled
  and thinly sliced
2 large ripe tomatoes,
  sliced
1 tablespoon chopped
  parsley
1 clove garlic, minced
1 teaspoon dried sweet
  basil
5 tablespoons salad oil
2 tablespoons red wine
  vinegar
Dash of salt and pepper
2 small heads Bibb
  lettuce

Separate onion slices into rings and arrange on top of tomato slices. Blend remaining ingredients in blender. Pour over onions and tomatoes, and chill until serving time. To serve, arrange atop lettuce leaves on individual plates and drizzle dressing over all.

Serves 4

Marinated Zucchini

½ cup oil
2 medium-size zucchini, thinly sliced
½ cup vinegar
1 clove garlic, finely chopped
1 tablespoon grated onion
1 tablespoon chopped fresh mint leaves

Heat oil in a skillet and sauté zucchini until tender and lightly browned, turning often. Place zucchini in a bowl and allow to cool. Stir in remaining ingredients and chill well before serving.

Serves 4

Zucchini Salad^(L)

3 small (about 1 pound) young zucchini, diced
3 scallions, finely chopped
2 tablespoons snipped fresh dill weed
1 tablespoon chopped parsley
¼ teaspoon oregano
1 cup yogurt
1 tablespoon lemon juice
1 teaspoon honey

Combine zucchini, scallions, dill, parsley, and oregano in a salad bowl. Mix yogurt, lemon juice, and honey, and pour over zucchini. Toss well. Refrigerate for 30 minutes or longer before serving.

Serves 4–6

Cold Bean Salad

1 cup cooked pinto
  beans
1 cup cooked navy
  beans
1 cup cooked kidney
  beans
1 stalk celery, diced
1 green pepper, diced
2 cloves garlic, diced
2 onions, diced
½ cup oil
3 tablespoons tamari
2 tablespoons apple
  cider vinegar
1 tablespoon sorghum
  or light molasses
3 tablespoons
  nutritional yeast
½ teaspoon sea salt
½ teaspoon garlic
  powder
¼ teaspoon paprika
¼ teaspoon oregano
¼ teaspoon basil
⅛ teaspoon red pepper

Combine beans and diced vegetables in a large bowl. Place remaining ingredients in blender and blend on high for 1 minute. Add to bean-vegetable mixture and stir well. Blend more seasoned liquid and add if desired. Chill for 2 hours to marinate. Season to taste.

Serves 4

Stuffed Avocados

2 avocados
2 scallions or chives, diced
1 cucumber, cut into chunks
2 radishes, diced
2 tablespoons tamari
¼ teaspoon sea salt
⅛ teaspoon garlic powder
2 tablespoons nutritional yeast
½ cup any kind of sprouts
½ teaspoon sesame meal*

Cut avocados in half; remove pits and gently scoop out insides, leaving shell intact. Mash avocados; add scallions, cucumber, radishes, tamari, and other seasonings, and mix well. Fill avocado shells with mixture. Top with yeast, sprouts, and sesame meal.

Serves 4

* *Sesame Meal:* Mix 1 cup of sesame seeds and ½ teaspoon of salt; grind in nut mill or blender in 2-tablespoon increments.

Salsa Fresca

3 medium-ripe tomatoes (1 pound), minced
½ small onion, minced
6 sprigs cilantro, minced
2 serrano or jalapeño peppers, minced
¼ cup red wine vinegar
⅓ cup water
Salt to taste

Mix all ingredients and serve. Or chill and serve. This is best when served very fresh, but it will keep for 2 days in the refrigerator.

Yield: 1½ cups

Eggplant à la Provençale

3 large eggplants
  (approximately 3
  pounds)
Coarse salt
Olive oil
2 pounds ripe tomatoes
3 cloves garlic, finely
  chopped
2 tablespoons finely
  chopped fresh
  parsley
1 tablespoon lemon
  juice
⅛ teaspoon sugar
Salt and freshly ground
  pepper to taste
Parsley

Cut unpeeled eggplants into ½-inch diagonal slices. Spread slices on a cutting board, sprinkle lightly with coarse salt, and top with a plate to press out excess liquid. Allow to drain about 30 minutes, then wipe with a damp paper towel.

Heat enough olive oil to cover bottom of a large enamel frying pan. Add eggplant and fry gently over medium heat, turning often until tender. Remove from pan and drain.

Plunge tomatoes into boiling water for a few seconds, then peel and deseed. Sauté remaining pulp in a little olive oil until just soft. Add garlic and chopped parsley. Cover and reduce heat to medium for 30–40 minutes. Remove from heat, cool, and add lemon juice, sugar, salt, and pepper.

Place eggplant in a shallow serving dish or glass bowl. Pour tomato mixture on top and chill until ready to serve. Garnish with a sprig of parsley.

Serves 4–5

Vegetables à la Grecque

½ cup olive oil
½ cup wine vinegar, or
  2 tablespoons lemon
  juice and 1 or 2
  lemon slices
1 teaspoon crushed
  coriander seed
1 teaspoon thyme
1 bay leaf
1 clove garlic, crushed
Freshly ground black
  pepper
2 cups water
4 cups assorted fresh or
  frozen vegetables
  (asparagus, artichoke
  hearts, Brussels
  sprouts, cauliflower,
  broccoli, green
  beans, carrots,
  mushrooms, zucchini,
  eggplant), prepared
  for cooking

Combine oil, vinegar, seasonings, and water. Bring to a boil and add vegetables. Reduce heat and simmer uncovered until tender-crisp. Do not overcook. Let vegetables cool in the sauce. Serve cold or at room temperature.

Serves 8

Tofu-Sesame Dressing

2 cakes soft tofu (about
  24 ounces)
1 cup sesame tahini
2 cups safflower oil
1 cup lemon juice
2 cloves garlic

Blend all ingredients until creamy or use electric mixer, first pressing the garlic.

Yield: approximately 4 cups

Dandy Salad

1 pound small spring
   dandelion leaves,
   shredded
3 tablespoons lemon
   juice
3 tablespoons maple
   syrup or other
   sweetener
1 teaspoon salt
½ teaspoon cayenne
   pepper
3 tablespoons peanut
   oil

Set dandelion leaves aside in a large bowl or pan. Combine all other ingredients in a small saucepan. Bring to a boil and boil for 1 minute. Remove from heat and immediately pour over dandelion leaves. Toss to coat thoroughly, then refrigerate to marinate for at least 1 hour before serving.

Serves 4

Plantain Pot

1 pound plantain
   leaves, washed and
   dried
2 cups rice, cooked
2–3 onions, sliced
1 teaspoon salt
1 cup stewed tomatoes
   and juice, well broken
   up

Heat oven to 350° F. Grease a 3-quart cooking dish, line with plantain leaves, a layer of rice, leaves, and onions, and repeat until all ingredients are used. Add salt to tomatoes and pour over other vegetables. Cover and bake for 2 hours.

Serves 4

Vinaigrette Dressing

2 cups safflower oil
1 cup apple cider
    vinegar
1 clove garlic
1 cup water
½ teaspoon salt
¼ teaspoon freshly
    ground pepper
2 tablespoons honey
1 tablespoon dry
    mustard

Blend all ingredients. If desired, add fresh or dried herbs: parsley, basil, oregano, ginger (fresh only), or green onion.
Yield: approximately 4 cups

East Indian Salad(L)

1 medium onion,
    minced
1 large cucumber,
    minced
3 medium tomatoes,
    diced small
1 green chili, minced
    (optional)
2 tablespoons chopped
    coriander leaf
½ teaspoon coriander
    powder
½ teaspoon powdered
    ginger
1 teaspoon salt
1 teaspoon garam
    masala
1 teaspoon lemon juice
1 cup plain yogurt

Dice all vegetables and place in a medium-size bowl. Combine spices and lemon juice with yogurt and blend into vegetables. Chill at least 30 minutes before serving.
Serves 2–3

Festive Melon and Grape Salad

1 medium-size
   honeydew melon or
   other green melon
½ pound seedless
   grapes
2 tablespoons crème de
   menthe or kirsch
Juice of 1 lime
Juice of 1 lemon
Juice of 1 orange
Lettuce leaves
6 mint sprigs

Halve melon, remove seeds, and scoop out as much flesh as possible with a melon cutter. Using a sharp knife, trim any remaining flesh from the shell so that neat hollows remain.

Cut grapes in half. In a large bowl, mix melon balls, grapes, liqueur, and fruit juices. Toss and chill for several hours, turning occasionally to macerate all the fruit.

Line a large serving dish with lettuce leaves and add melon shells. Fill shells with fruit salad, garnish with mint sprigs, and drizzle with fruit juice.

Serves 4

Bean Salad(L)

2 cups lima beans,
   cooked
2 cups green beans, cut
   (steam slightly if using
   fresh or frozen)
1 cup hard-cooked
   eggs, quartered
½ cup chopped dill
   pickle
2 cups kidney beans,
   cooked
1 cup chopped
   tomatoes
1 cup sliced celery

Mix all ingredients and toss with favorite French dressing. Marinate for several hours before serving.

Serves 10

MAIN DISHES:

FAST FOODS AND STEWS

Somewhere between a raw fruit-vegetable-nut meal and a fancy feast with twice-raised bread and beans that were soaked for 4 hours and simmered for 2, there is vegetarian fast-food. In this cuisine, there is limited, judicious use of certain processed foods. The resulting dishes are still delicious, nutritious, and far superior to conventional fast foods. This Indy 500 method for getting dinner is not meant to be an every-evening affair, but it is a real blessing for class nights, concert nights, or any time you are hungry now.

These are easy as well as time-saving entrees. Ingredients are interchangeable. Some options are given; others can be improvised. (A junket to the grocery store is not what fast food is for.) Any of these recipes can serve as a main dish. With a green salad and whole-grain bread, protein complimentary is provided.

Note: The symbol **(L)** is used next to those recipe titles that include some form of dairy product. All other recipes are vegan in nature; that is, they contain no meat, eggs, or milk products.

Eager Eggplant

1 medium eggplant
Oil and onion salt as needed
1 8-ounce can tomato sauce or puree
Sesame seeds, peanuts, wheat germ, or sprouts as topping

Slice eggplant in rounds about ⅜ inch thick. Dip each piece in vegetable oil on both sides and lightly sprinkle with onion salt. Place in large skillet with tomato sauce, garlic, and oregano. Heat until tender, turning at least once. (Oil, tamari, or more tomato sauce may be added to prevent sticking or burning.) Add 1 or more of suggested toppings (peanuts and wheat germ would be good for amino-acid balance).

Serves 2

Speedy Supper Sandwich

2 slices whole wheat bread
2 tablespoons peanut butter
1 banana
1 tablespoon shredded coconut
1 tablespoon sunflower or sesame seeds

Lightly toast bread. Add peanut butter and sliced banana. Put under broiler or in toaster oven for 3–4 minutes (don't let crusts burn). Top with coconut and seeds.

Serves 2

Timely Tofu

2 tablespoons onion
  flakes
2 ounces water
1 cup corn, frozen or cut
  from cob
1 tablespoon oil
1 pound tofu (solid
  block)
⅓ cup canned
  mushrooms, pieces
  and stems
Tamari to taste

Put onion flakes in water to soften. Add corn to oil in small skillet, then add onion flakes. Cut tofu in small squares and add to skillet, followed by mushrooms and liberal amount of tamari sauce. Sauté.

Serves 2

Simple Soup

1 cup frozen mixed
  vegetables
2 cups water or
  vegetable stock or
  whey left from
  making tofu
1 tablespoon brewer's
  yeast, calcium-
  fortified
3 tablespoons soy flour
Tamari to taste

Bring vegetables and water just to a boil. Put in blender with yeast, soy flour, and tamari. Blend to cream-soup consistency, adding more flour or water to make thicker or thinner. (Wheat germ, wheat flour, or bran may be used instead of more soy flour.) Garnish with sunflower or sesame seeds, alfalfa sprouts, or parsley.

Serves 2

Zucchini Stuffed with Cream Cheese[L]

5 medium zucchini
Water
3 tablespoons minced onions
1 cup chopped mushrooms
2 tablespoons oil
½ teaspoon salt
Dash of cayenne
¼ teaspoon cumin
6–8 ounces cream cheese
1 cup sour cream
2–3 egg yolks
Parsley, chili powder, and cherry tomatoes (garnish)

Preheat oven to 325° F.

Select fresh, firm, medium-size zucchini (6–8 inches). Put in a pan with enough boiling water to cover. Cook about 10 minutes or until barely tender. Lift carefully from pan and let cool in cold water. Drain, slice in half lengthwise, and scoop out seed cavities into a bowl. Sauté minced onions with chopped mushrooms in oil. Drain mushrooms, saving the juice for a soup, and mix with seasonings, scraped zucchini, and cream cheese. Stuff zucchini halves with seasoned cream cheese and mushrooms, and put in an oven-proof serving dish that has been lightly oiled. Combine sour cream with egg yolks. Spread sour cream mixture on each half and bake for 15–20 minutes. Garnish with parsley and a little chili powder. You may also garnish with a sliced cherry tomato either before or after baking.

Variation: Instead of cumin and chili powder, try seasoning with a little dill or ground caraway.

Serves 5–8

Curry of Zucchini and Tomatoes

8 cups (about 1¼ pounds) thinly sliced zucchini

½ pound tomatoes, cored and cut into ½-inch cubes

3 tablespoons sesame oil

2 teaspoons whole cumin seeds

¼ teaspoon hing* (optional)

1½ teaspoons ground coriander

1½ teaspoons ground cumin

¼ teaspoon turmeric

1 tablespoon paprika

1 teaspoon garam masala*

1 teaspoon salt

2 tablespoons water

4 teaspoons fresh coriander leaves, chopped

* Available in Indian food shops

Prepare zucchini and tomatoes, and set aside. Heat oil in a kettle and, when it starts to smoke, add cumin seeds. Stir briefly and add hing, coriander, cumin, turmeric, paprika, garam masala, and salt. Add zucchini and tomatoes, and stir gently to blend without breaking the slices. Add water and cover. Cook over gentle heat for 10 minutes. Sprinkle with chopped fresh coriander and serve.

Serves 8

Brown Rice Pizza[L]

Crust:

3 cups brown rice, cooked

1 cup grated mozzarrella cheese

½ cup sesame seeds

2 eggs, beaten

Sauce:

3 tablespoons butter or margarine

3 tablespoons whole wheat flour

1½ cups milk

½ teaspoon paprika

Topping:

1 cup broccoli, steamed

1 cup mushrooms, sliced and sautéed

1 cup zucchini, sautéed

2 tomatoes, sliced

½ pound Muenster cheese, sliced

½ teaspoon oregano

Allow rice to cool, then combine with remaining crust ingredients. Pat into a greased 12-inch pizza pan and bake at 400° F for 20 minutes.

To make the sauce, melt butter, add flour, and stir over medium heat for 1 minute. Whisk in milk and paprika, then continue stirring over medium heat until sauce thickens. Spread sauce over baked crust.

Prepare topping vegetables as indicated. Arrange, along with Muenster cheese and oregano, on top of pizza. Broil for 5 minutes until cheese melts.

Serves 4–6

Tofu Stroganoff[(L)]

1½ pounds tofu
2 tablespoons butter or margarine
1 medium onion, chopped
10 mushrooms
¼ teaspoon salt
¼ teaspoon pepper
2 tablespoons chives
½–1 teaspoon garlic powder
1 cup sour cream
¼ cup tamari soy sauce
1–2 tablespoons cooking sherry

Drain tofu on paper towel to remove excess water. In the meantime, melt 1 tablespoon of butter in a large saucepan. Sauté chopped onion. Wash mushrooms and slice each 2 or 3 times. Add to onions and sauté until tender. Add spices and let them blend together. Remove mixture from pan.

Slice drained tofu into long strips, about 3 inches by ¾ inch and ½ inch in height. Fry tofu on both sides in remaining tablespoon of butter until golden brown. Add mushroom-onion mixture to tofu. Before serving, add sour cream, tamari, and cooking sherry. Let cook for a few minutes to blend together. If sauce is too thick, add more sour cream. Adjust cooking sherry to taste.

Serve over noodles with a salad or vegetable.

Serves 4

Tofu-Stuffed Mushrooms^(L)

1 10-ounce package
  frozen spinach or 10
  ounces fresh spinach
1 pound tofu
15 large fresh
  mushrooms
1 tablespoon butter or
  margarine
1 teaspoon garlic
  powder
Salt and pepper to taste
Mozzarella cheese
2 tablespoons tamari
  soy sauce

Steam spinach until tender. As spinach is cooking, drain tofu on paper towel and then chop into very fine pieces. (It is important to chop it with a knife rather than mashing it with a fork because it comes out looking like tiny cubes.)

Wash fresh mushrooms. (They must be fresh because the first part of a mushroom to wilt is the stem, and it is used as part of the stuffing mixture.) Remove stems, being careful not to harm mushrooms. Set mushrooms aside; chop stems very finely.

When spinach is tender, cool and chop finely. Save excess liquid.

Melt butter in a medium saucepan. Add tofu, mushroom stems, spinach, garlic powder, salt, and pepper, and cook for 10 minutes. As it is cooking, grate enough mozzarella cheese to go over the top of the mushrooms.

Preheat oven to 350° F. Prepare a deep baking dish by putting tamari and enough leftover spinach juice to cover the bottom. Stuff each mushroom fully with the stuffing and place side by side in the dish. Top with grated mozzarella cheese, then bake for 20 minutes or until cheese is melted and golden brown. You may need to put it beneath the broiler to brown the cheese more.

Serve with bulgur or another grain and a fresh salad or vegetable, or by itself as an appetizer with a sprig of fresh parsley or watercress.

Serves 3

Shepherd's Pie (L)

6 medium potatoes
1 cup milk
2 tablespoons butter or
  margarine
Salt and pepper
2 pounds tofu
2 tablespoons oil
1 large onion, sliced
10 mushrooms, sliced
Garlic powder
Tamari
1 10-ounce can
  concentrated tomato
  soup

Dice potatoes (with skins) and cook until tender. Mash with milk, butter, salt, and pepper. Beat until potatoes are nice and fluffy. Depending on potatoes, you may want to add more milk or butter.

Drain tofu well on a paper towel to absorb any excess water. Mash tofu while heating 1 tablespoon of oil. Add tofu to pan, cooking and stirring until lightly browned. Remove tofu from pan, add 1 tablespoon of oil, and brown sliced onion and mushrooms. Return tofu to pan and continue browning while adding salt, pepper, garlic powder, and tamari to taste.

Preheat oven to 375° F.

You are now ready to begin layering. It is important to layer carefully to maintain each layer separately. The flavors will mingle, but you will achieve a nice effect.

Oil a 10-inch-square pan. In the bottom place browned tofu-mushroom-onion mixture. Spread evenly. Next, spoon tomato soup over mixture. Cover with mashed potatoes, taking care to spread them evenly. Bake about 35 minutes until lightly browned.

Serve with a salad or vegetable of your choice.

Serves 8

Italiano Zucchini

½ cup onions
¼ cup green peppers
2 celery stalks
1 garlic, minced
1 tablespoon soy oil
5 tomatoes, cored and
  chopped
1 large zucchini, sliced
  into spears
1 teaspoon Italian
  seasoning
Sea salt and pepper to
  taste
Parsley sprigs

Chop onions, peppers, and celery. Place in a pan with garlic and sauté in oil. Add remaining ingredients and cook, covered, until zucchini is done. Remove cover and evaporate tomato water. Serve with sprigs of parsley on top.

Serves 4

Eggplant and Cheese(L)

4 tablespoons olive oil
1 large eggplant, sliced
  ½ inch thick
1 cup chopped onion
1 clove garlic, crushed
1 pound tomatoes, cut
  up (or 1 16-ounce
  can)
2 tablespoons parsley
¾ teaspoon salt
⅛ teaspoon pepper
⅛ teaspoon cinnamon
1½ cups cottage cheese
1 egg
½ cup grated Parmesan
  cheese

Put 1 teaspoon of oil in a large skillet and lightly brown eggplant, adding oil as needed. Remove and drain on paper towels. Add 1 teaspoon of oil and sauté onion and garlic until just tender. Add tomatoes, parsley, salt, pepper, and cinnamon. Simmer, uncovered, for 5 minutes. Spread half of tomato mixture in a pan 12 inches by 8 inches by 2 inches. Mix cottage cheese with egg and spread over tomato mixture. Arrange eggplant on top, sprinkle Parmesan cheese, and spread tomatoes on top of that. Bake at 375° F for 35 minutes.

Serves 4

Tiropite (L)

1 pound filo dough
  sheets
Butter or margarine,
  melted
1 pound feta cheese
¼ cup Parmesan cheese
2 eggs
Oregano to taste
1 teaspoon olive oil
Pepper to taste

Preheat oven to 350° F.

Brush each filo sheet with melted butter, then cut into 9 squares.

Crumble feta and mix with Parmesan, eggs, oregano, oil, and pepper. Place 1 spoonful of mixture in the center of each square. Moisten edges, fold over into a triangle, press edges together, and brush with butter. Bake for 30 minutes. Serve hot.

Serves 4

Millet Cheese Soufflé (L)

½ cup millet
1½ cups water
½ teaspoon salt
½ teaspoon dillweed
3 ounces Swiss cheese,
  grated
2 egg yolks
3 egg whites
1 tablespoon chopped
  parsley

Combine millet, water, salt, and dillweed in a saucepan. Cover and bring to a boil. Lower heat and simmer very gently about 20 minutes until all liquid is absorbed. Remove from heat and let stand 10 minutes. Add grated cheese and egg yolks, and blend in thoroughly.

Preheat oven to 350° F.

Beat egg whites until stiff but not dry. Fold half the egg whites into millet mixture until thoroughly blended. Fold in remaining egg whites until just blended, being careful not to overmix. Turn into a greased 9-inch pie plate or 1½-quart casserole. Bake in preheated oven for 30 minutes or until puffed and browned. Sprinkle with chopped parsley and serve immediately.

Serves 4

Stir-Fry Vegetables

1 teaspoon oil
¼ onion, minced
1 clove garlic, minced
1 teaspoon finely
  minced fresh ginger
  root
1 cup diagonally sliced
  carrots
1 cup diagonally sliced
  celery
1 cup broccoli florets,
  sliced ¼ inch thick
¼ cup sliced water
  chestnuts
2 green onions, split
  and cut in 2-inch
  lengths
1 cup bean sprouts
1–2 tablespoons soy
  sauce

Heat oil in a heavy skillet. Sauté onion, garlic, and ginger root until onion is transparent. Add carrots, celery, and broccoli. Mix well. Add 3 tablespoons of water, cover, and cook for 2–3 minutes. Add water chestnuts and green onions. Cook 1 minute more, then add bean sprouts and soy sauce. Stir until well mixed and sprouts are heated through. Vegetables should be tender yet crisp. Serve immediately.

Serves 4

Stuffed Bell Peppers[L]

2 large bell peppers
1½ cups tomato sauce
2 cups brown rice, cooked
3½ ounces Monterey Jack cheese, grated
2 tablespoons chopped parsley
½ teaspoon herb seasoning salt

Cut bell peppers in half lengthwise; remove seeds and membranes. Steam pepper halves until cooked crisp-tender. Set aside.

Combine ½ cup of tomato sauce with cooked brown rice, half the grated cheese, 1 tablespoon of chopped parsley, and ½ teaspoon of seasoning salt. Heat over moderate heat, stirring gently, until well blended and cheese is melted. (Add a little water, if necessary, to prevent sticking.)

Spoon remaining tomato sauce into bottom of 9-inch pie pan. Place pepper halves on top of sauce, then fill with rice mixture. Top with remaining grated cheese. Bake at 350° F until hot and cheese is melted. Sprinkle with chopped parsley and serve.

Serves 4

Vegetarian Spaghetti[(L)]

Sauce:

4 ounces tofu

2 cups tomato sauce

¼ pound mushrooms, thinly sliced

½ cup thinly sliced celery

1 clove garlic, pressed

½ teaspoon basil

¼ cup Parmesan cheese

2 tablespoons chopped parsley

1 tablespoon chopped chives

Spaghetti:

6 ounces dry whole wheat spaghetti noodles

2 tablespoons half and half

½ teaspoon basil

1 tablespoon grated Parmesan cheese

Parsley sprigs (garnish)

Place tofu in a medium-size saucepan. Using a fork, mash tofu into small chunks resembling cottage cheese. Add tomato sauce, mushrooms, celery, garlic, and basil. Heat and stir until sauce is hot and mushrooms are cooked, about 5–10 minutes. Remove from heat and stir in Parmesan cheese, parsley, and chives. Keep warm.

Cook spaghetti in boiling water about 8 minutes until cooked al dente—tender yet firm. Drain thoroughly and return to saucepan. Blend in half and half, and season with basil and Parmesan cheese.

Pour tomato sauce over all and mix gently to coat spaghetti. Garnish with parsley sprigs.

Serves 4

Eggplant Parmesan(L)

⅔ cup (1 slice) whole
   wheat bread crumbs
¼ cup + 1 tablespoon
   grated Parmesan
   cheese
½ clove garlic, pressed
½ teaspoon thyme
½ teaspoon oregano
1 medium (1½ pounds)
   eggplant
2½ cups basic tomato
   sauce
½ teaspoon basil
4 ounces mozzarella or
   Monterey Jack
   cheese, grated
Parsley

Combine bread crumbs with 1 tablespoon of Parmesan cheese, garlic, thyme, and oregano. Set aside.

Peel eggplant and cut into 8 slices about ½ inch thick. Place in a greased baking pan 9 inches by 13 inches and sprinkle with seasoned bread crumbs. Bake in a 400 ° F oven about 20–25 minutes until crumbs are toasted and eggplant is tender. Remove from oven.

Combine tomato sauce with ¼ cup of Parmesan cheese and basil. Pour sauce over eggplant, covering all edges. Sprinkle with grated mozzarella cheese. Bake in a 400° F oven about 15 minutes or until cheese is melted and browned and sauce is hot. Sprinkle with parsley and serve.

Serves 4

Posole

2 cups posole (dried
   corn kernels)
Water to cover kernels
   in pot
2 cloves garlic, crushed
2 tablespoons red chili
   powder
½ teaspoon oregano
   (optional)
½ teaspoon cumin

Put all ingredients in a pot and bring to a boil. Simmer, covered, until kernels have softened and burst, approximately 2–3 hours. Drain and serve, topped with grated cheese.

Serves 4

Calabacitas

2 tablespoons oil for
  frying
2 small onions, thinly
  sliced
2 zucchini, sliced
1 summer squash,
  sliced
1 cup fresh or 2
  4-ounce cans green
  chilies, diced, peeled,
  and roasted
1½ cups corn kernels
Salt to taste
½ cup grated cheese
  (optional)

Heat oil in a large heavy skillet. Sauté onion lightly, then add zucchini and squash. When lightly cooked, add chilies and corn. Simmer, covered, stirring constantly until cooked to desired consistency. Add salt; sprinkle with cheese and stir through if desired.

Serves 4

Soybean Patties(L)

4 cups soybeans,
  cooked and well
  mashed
2 eggs
2 onions
4 cloves garlic, minced
2 cups bread crumbs
1 cup evaporated milk
2 teaspoons vegetable
  seasoning

Combine all ingredients and mix well. Shape into patties and brown. Serve on buns. Can also be made into loaves.

Serves 12–16

Cottage Cheese Luncheon Pie[L]

2 eggs
2 cups cream-style
    cottage cheese
2 cups hot mashed
    potatoes
¾ cup thick sour cream
    or yogurt
¼ cup finely chopped
    onion
2 tablespoons chopped
    red pepper or carrot
1 teaspoon salt
⅛ teaspoon white
    pepper
2 tablespoons butter or
    margarine

Preheat oven to 350° F.

Beat eggs until thick. Blend eggs, cottage cheese, potatoes, sour cream, onion, red pepper, salt, and pepper. Turn mix into a 9-inch unbaked pastry pie shell, spreading evenly. Dot surface with butter. Bake at 350° F for 1½ hours or until lightly browned. Serve hot or cold.

Serves 8

Whole Wheat Macaroni Casserole[(L)]

2 cups uncooked whole wheat macaroni
3 quarts boiling water
3 tablespoons butter or margarine
3 tablespoons whole wheat flour
2 cups milk
½ teaspoon sea salt
2 cups shredded cheddar cheese
¼ pound raw mushrooms, sliced
½ cup chopped onion
¼ cup chopped celery
1 tablespoon minced parsley
½ teaspoon marjoram

Cook macaroni in boiling water 8–10 minutes until tender. Drain and set aside. Melt butter in a saucepan. Stir in flour and mix well. Pour in milk and bring to a boil, stirring constantly. Remove from heat. Add sea salt and shredded cheese. Stir until cheese is melted. Pour sauce over cooked macaroni. Add remaining ingredients and mix well. Bake, covered, in a casserole dish at 350° F for 30 minutes. Top with a little more shredded cheese if desired and bake a few more minutes to melt the cheese.

Serves 6

Brown Rice and Carrot Casserole[(L)]

½ cup chopped onions
2 medium carrots, chopped
¼ cup chopped celery
2 tablespoons olive oil
1 tablespoon finely chopped parsley
½ teaspoon sea salt
3 cups brown rice, cooked
1 cup shredded cheese

Preheat oven to 350° F. Sauté onions, carrots, and celery in ¼ cup of water until almost tender, about 5 minutes. Add more water if necessary. Stir in olive oil, parsley, and sea salt. Add cooked rice. Bake, covered, in a casserole dish for 20 minutes. Sprinkle shredded cheese on top and bake, uncovered, a few minutes or until cheese melts.

Serves 4–6

Bean Burgers(L)

2 cups cooked pinto
  beans
1 cup fresh bread
  crumbs
2 tablespoons chopped
  onion
½ cup shredded mild
  cheese

Preheat oven to 400° F. Mash beans and combine with remaining ingredients. Place in a well-buttered baking pan and bake for 10 minutes at 400° F. Turn over and bake for 10 minutes more.

Serves 8

Lentil Casserole(L)

1 cup lentils
2 cups water
1 cup chopped
  tomatoes
1 green onion,
  chopped
1 clove garlic, minced
1 teaspoon chili powder
Dash of cayenne
  pepper
1 cup shredded cheese

Bring lentils and water to a boil in a saucepan. Reduce heat and simmer for 1–1½ hours until tender. Add tomatoes, onion, garlic, chili powder, and cayenne. Place in a baking dish and bake, covered, for 20 minutes at 350° F. Sprinkle cheese on top and bake, uncovered, 5 minutes more or until cheese melts.

Serves 4–6

Spicy Eggplant-Miso Sauté with Bulgur

1½ cups bulgur
3 cups boiling water
¼ cup miso
3 tablespoons water
1 tablespoon mild honey
2 teaspoons sesame oil
2 tablespoons safflower oil
1 medium (about 1½ pounds) eggplant, peeled and finely diced
1 clove garlic
1 teaspoon minced or grated fresh ginger
¼–½ pound pressed tofu to taste, diced
1 bunch green onions (both green and white parts), sliced
¼–½ teaspoon hot red pepper flakes or 1 small dried red pepper, seeds removed and crumbled

Place bulgur in a heat-proof serving dish and pour on boiling water. Let stand while you prepare rest of ingredients.

In a small bowl, mix together miso, water, honey, and sesame oil. Set aside.

Heat oil in a wok or a large heavy-bottomed skillet and sauté eggplant for 5 minutes, stirring. Add garlic and ginger, and sauté for 2 minutes. Add tofu and sauté for 5 minutes. Add miso mixture and stir-fry for 3–4 minutes. Add green onions and pepper flakes, and cook, stirring, until onions are tender.

Pour off any water that has not been absorbed by the bulgur. Fluff with a fork and top with eggplant mixture. Serve at once.

Serves 4

Enchilada Bake[(L)]

1 onion, chopped
1 clove garlic, minced
5–6 mushrooms, sliced
1 green pepper,
    chopped
½ cup dry beans,
    cooked, or 2 cups
    canned beans
1½ cups stewed
    tomatoes
1 tablespoon chili
    powder
1 teaspoon ground
    cumin seed
½ cup dry red wine
8 tortillas
¼ cup grated
    mozzarella cheese
    made from partially
    skimmed milk
½ cup ricotta cheese
    made from partially
    skimmed milk mixed
    with ¼ cup low-fat
    yogurt
6 black olives, sliced

Sauté onion, garlic, mushrooms, and pepper. Add beans, tomatoes, spices, and wine. Simmer gently about 30 minutes. In an oiled 1½-quart casserole, put a layer of tortillas, a layer of sauce, 1½ tablespoons of grated mozzarella, and 4 tablespoons of yogurt-ricotta mixture. Repeat until all ingredients are used, ending with yogurt-ricotta mixture. Top with black olives.

Serves 6

Sweet-and-Sour Lentils with Brown Rice

½ cup dry lentils
3 cups water
2 tablespoons vinegar
2 tablespoons honey
1 tablespoon tamari or soy sauce
½ teaspoon grated fresh ginger or 1 teaspoon ground ginger
½ cup water
1 teaspoon arrowroot powder or cornstarch
1 small onion, sliced
2 tablespoons oil
4–5 stalks diagonally sliced celery

To cook lentils, bring water to a boil, then reduce heat and cook about 25 minutes or until tender. Do not overcook. Drain and set aside.

To make sweet-and-sour sauce, combine vinegar, honey, tamari sauce, ginger, and ½ cup of water in a small saucepan. Bring to a boil. Put arrowroot powder or cornstarch in a small glass and add a little water. Mix thoroughly and add to boiling sauce to thicken it.

Sauté onion in oil in a large frying pan. When onion is soft, add pieces of celery and cook for 5 minutes more over medium heat. Drain cooked lentils and add to frying pan; mix well. Pour sweet-and-sour sauce into frying pan and simmer for 5 minutes more.

Serve over a bed of freshly steamed brown rice.

Serves 3–4

Spaghetti and Lentils

2 tablespoons oil
1 small onion, chopped
1 clove garlic, minced
½ cup dry lentils
1 large can (17 ounces)
    tomatoes, peeled
6 ounces tomato paste
1 cup water
½ teaspoon basil
½ teaspoon oregano
¼ teaspoon thyme
¼ teaspoon sea salt
¼ cup red wine
8 ounces spaghetti,
    cooked
Parmesan cheese

Put oil in a large skillet or Dutch oven, and sauté onions and garlic until soft. Add remaining ingredients except spaghetti. (Tomatoes can be chopped in blender for a smoother sauce.) Bring to a boil, then reduce heat to simmer, stirring occasionally. Cook for 1 hour. Serve over (or mixed with) cooked and drained spaghetti. Top with grated Parmesan cheese.

Serves 4

Ratatouille

3 cups cubed eggplant
2 cups sliced zucchini
1 green pepper,
    chopped
1 onion, chopped
1 clove garlic, minced
¼ cup water
½ teaspoon sea salt
2 tablespoons chopped
    fresh parsley
2 tomatoes, chopped
¼ cup olive oil

Combine all ingredients except parsley, tomatoes, and oil in a skillet and cook, covered, over medium heat for 10–15 minutes until vegetables are tender. Add parsley and tomatoes. Cook for 5 minutes more. Remove from heat, add oil, and stir well. Serve hot or cold.

Serves 6

The Devil's Chili

1 cup grated onions
1 clove garlic, minced
1 bulb shallot, minced
3 large scallions,
  minced
1 large bell pepper,
  chopped
1 ounce olive or other
  salad oil
2 quarts water
1 pound kidney, pink,
  or pinto beans,
  washed, sorted, and
  soaked
1 large bay leaf,
  crushed
1 teaspoon miso paste
1 teaspoon mild or hot
  curry
1 teaspoon basil
1 tablespoon paprika
Chili powder to taste
Salt and pepper to taste
3 large tomatoes,
  chopped, or 1
  15-ounce can
  peeled tomatoes
1 15-ounce can tomato
  sauce

In a large saucepan, sauté onions, garlic, shallot, scallions, and green pepper in oil. Add water, beans, and seasonings. Simmer for 1–1½ hours. Add tomatoes and tomato sauce. Simmer for 1 hour more or until fork-tender. For spicier chili, use 2 or more cloves of garlic. Serve piping hot with tacos, tofu, a scoop of cottage cheese, a cold glass of milk, or topped with melted cheese.

Serves 6

Potato Soufflé (L)

1 egg yolk
1 tablespoon butter or
  margarine
½ teaspoon dried dill or
  1 tablespoon fresh
  dill
2 cups mashed
  potatoes
1 egg white

Preheat oven to 350° F. Combine egg yolk, butter, and dill with mashed potatoes. Beat egg white until stiff and fold into potato mixture. Place in a buttered 1-quart dish and bake at 350° F for 25–30 minutes.

Serves 4

Okara-Millet Burgers (L)

1 cup okara
1 cup cooked millet
⅓ cup whole wheat
  flour
1 egg, lightly beaten
¼ cup chopped onion
1 small carrot, grated
1 clove garlic, minced
1 tablespoon shoyu soy
  sauce
½ teaspoon ground
  cumin

Combine all ingredients in a bowl and mix well. Form into patties and fry in an oiled skillet or broil until golden brown. These patties freeze well.

Serves 4

Zucchini Squash and Mushrooms[L]

4 green onions
(including stems),
sliced
5 6-inch zucchini
squash, washed
2 tablespoons butter or
margarine
Natural seasoning to
taste
¼ pound fresh
mushrooms

Steam onions and squash with butter and seasoning in a 2-quart saucepan until fork tender (about 15 minutes at medium heat). Do not allow squash to become mushy. Spread mushrooms on top of squash and steam for 5 minutes just before serving. Serve hot.

Serves 6

Brown Rice and Mushrooms

1 cup chopped green
onions
1 tablespoon vegetable
oil
1 cup mushrooms
2 cups brown rice,
cooked
1 teaspoon natural
seasoning salt

In a skillet, sauté green onions in vegetable oil until tender. Add mushrooms and sauté for 5 minutes more. Add rice and seasoning salt, and cook for 5 minutes more.

Serves 4

Spicy Brussels Sprouts

1 pound Brussels
    sprouts, fresh or
    frozen
¾ cup natural Italian
    salad dressing
¼ teaspoon seasoning
    salt
¼ teaspoon honey
1 teaspoon dry minced
    onion
Dash of Tabasco sauce
Dash of pepper

Boil or steam Brussels sprouts until tender. Drain for 5 minutes in a colander. Combine salad dressing, seasoning salt, honey, onion, Tabasco sauce and pepper. Marinate and toss Brussels sprouts in salad dressing until saturated. Marinated Brussels sprouts may be served hot or chilled.

Serves 6–8

Marinated Cauliflower

2 tablespoons chopped
    onion
2 tablespoons chopped
    green bell pepper
½ cup natural Italian
    salad dressing
1 medium cauliflower
    head, broken into
    small florets
1 teaspoon garlic
    powder
¼ teaspoon celery seed
½ teaspoon seasoning
    salt
1 tablespoon honey
2 tablespoons vinegar
1 cup halved cherry
    tomatoes

In a skillet, cook onions and green peppers in salad dressing until tender. Add cauliflower florets, seasonings, honey, and vinegar. Cook, covered, over low heat for 15 minutes until cauliflower is tender. Remove cauliflower from heat and add tomatoes. Toss tomatoes in salad dressing mixture until saturated. Return cauliflower to mixture. This dish may be served hot or cold.

Serves 6–8

Puerto Rican-Style Cabbage[(L)]

2 cups thinly shredded cabbage
2 cups cubed white potatoes or sweet potatoes
½ cup chopped onion
¼ teaspoon seasoning salt
4 tablespoons butter or margarine, softened
Parsley (optional)

Place cabbage in cold water for 30 minutes (optional), then drain. Steam cabbage, potatoes, and onions until tender. Thoroughly mash cabbage and potatoes together with a fork. Add onion, seasoning salt, and butter, and mix well. Place mixture in a greased casserole or baking dish. Bake at 350° F for 20 minutes. Dish may be topped with parsley before baking if desired.

Serves 4

Vegetable Fried Rice[(L)]

1 tablespoon butter or margarine
2 eggs, lightly beaten (optional)
2 tablespoons vegetable oil
1 medium onion, diced
1 cup bean sprouts
1 medium green pepper, diced
½ cup bamboo shoots
1 cup fresh mushrooms, washed and sliced
2 cups brown rice, cooked and cooled
1 teaspoon natural seasoning salt
3 tablespoons soy sauce

In a skillet, melt butter and scramble eggs until firm. Remove eggs and break them up in small pieces. Set aside. In vegetable oil, sauté onion, bean sprouts, green pepper, and bamboo shoots until tender but not brown (about 10 minutes); add mushrooms and cook for 10 minutes more. Add rice, seasoning salt, and soy sauce, and stir-fry for 10 minutes. Add eggs and stir-fry several minutes until dish is hot.

Serves 5–8

Cheese-Nut Main Dish Loaf (L)

2 tablespoons butter or
  margarine
1 large onion, chopped
1 cup rolled oats
½ cup whole wheat
  bread crumbs
1 cup finely chopped
  cashews
½ cup finely chopped
  pecans
½ cup milk
3 eggs, slightly beaten
1½ cups shredded
  sharp cheddar cheese
½ teaspoon sea salt
Dash of pepper

Preheat oven to 400° F. Melt butter in a
10-inch skillet. Add onion and sauté
until limp. Stir in remaining ingredients
until mixture is thoroughly blended.
Pack mixture into a well-buttered shallow 1-quart casserole. Bake at 400° F
about 50 minutes or until well browned.
  Serves 4

Lasagne (L)

1½ pints spaghetti
  sauce
¾–1 pound dry
  lasagne noodles,
  cooked and drained
2 cups ricotta or cottage
  cheese or shredded
  tofu
½ pound mozzarella
  cheese, grated

Preheat oven to 350° F. Layer ingredients in casserole, starting with spaghetti sauce, then noodles, ricotta,
mozzarella, etcetera, ending with a layer
of sauce and a sprinkling of grated
cheese. Bake for 35–40 minutes or until
cheese bubbles.
  Serves 4

Bean Burgers^(L)

**2 cups ground or
pureed cooked beans
(preferably red or
pink variety)**
**⅔ cup ground sunflower
seeds**
¼ cup chopped onion
**½ teaspoon chili
powder**
1 teaspoon salt
**2 tablespoons safflower
oil**
**3–4 tablespoons
ketchup**
½ cup wheat germ
**8 thin slices of cheddar
cheese**

Preheat oven to 350° F.

Combine all ingredients except cheese, adding enough wheat germ so that mixture will hold its shape. Form into 8 small patties. Cover each with cheese slice. Place on a lightly oiled baking sheet and bake for 25 minutes, basting occasionally.

Serves 6–8

Zucchini Parmesan^(L)

Oil
3 medium zucchini
**1 tablespoon butter or
margarine, sliced
paper-thin**
**3 ounces Parmesan
cheese**

Preheat oven to 350° F. Oil a 9-inch glass baking dish. Grate zucchini. Pile zucchini ½ inch deep in dish, cover with butter slices, and generously sprinkle with cheese. Bake for 20 minutes or until cheese lightly browns.

Serves 4

Stewed Garbanzos

2 tablespoons oil
2 medium onions, chopped
1 teaspoon ground coriander
1 teaspoon ground roasted cumin seed
½ teaspoon turmeric
4 cups dried garbanzo beans, cooked
2 large tomatoes, chopped
1 6-ounce can tomato paste
1 cup vegetable broth
2 tablespoons chopped parsley

Heat oil and sauté onions until transparent. Add spices and stir for 1–2 minutes. Add garbanzo beans, tomatoes, tomato paste, and vegetable broth. Simmer together about 30 minutes, then add chopped parsley. Serve hot over cooked brown rice or millet.

Serves 6

Curried Yellow Squash[(L)]

4 medium-size yellow crookneck squash
4 tablespoons butter or margarine
½ teaspoon curry powder
½ teaspoon natural seasoning salt

Wash and cut squash crosswise (about ¼ inch thick), and steam until slightly tender. In a large saucepan, combine butter, curry powder, and seasoning salt. Add squash to curry butter. Sauté until tender and thoroughly coated.

Serves 6

Green Bean Almondine[(L)]

1 pound green beans, fresh or frozen
¼ cup slivered almonds
2 tablespoons butter or margarine
1 teaspoon lemon juice
¼ teaspoon natural seasoning salt

Cook green beans. Cook almonds in butter over low heat until golden brown, stirring occasionally so that almonds do not burn. Remove almonds from heat and add lemon juice and seasoning salt. Pour almond mixture over green beans (which should be hot) and serve.

Serves 4

Twenty Carrots[(L)]

2 large baking potatoes
20 small (finger) carrots
3 eggs, separated
1 teaspoon sea salt or vegesalt
¼ teaspoon paprika

Wash, peel, and grate potatoes. Grate carrots finely. Beat egg yolks until thick and mix in potatoes, carrots, salt, and paprika. Preheat oven to 350° F. Beat whites until they hold stiff peaks, then fold gently into vegetable mixture. Turn into a well-oiled casserole and bake for 30–40 minutes.

Serves 4

Vegetarian Stew

2 cups millet or coarse-ground cornmeal or cracked wheat
6 cups water
⅓ cup oil
¼ cup tamari sauce
1 teaspoon kelp
½ teaspoon cayenne pepper
2 cups chopped vegetables (such as potatoes, green peppers, onions, celery, carrots, etcetera)
¼ cup smoked yeast (optional)

Dry-roast millet in a large skillet or pot. (Dry-roast means cooking over medium heat with no oil or water until brown.) Add water, oil, and seasonings. Bring to a boil, then reduce heat. Cook over low heat, covered, for 10 minutes. Add vegetables. Continue to cook until vegetables reach desired tenderness and millet is soft (like rice). Add yeast, if desired, and stir lightly with a fork before serving.

Serves 6–8

Vegetable Stew

2 medium onions, sliced
3 cloves garlic, crushed
2 medium potatoes, cut
  in small chunks
1 eggplant, diced
Butter or margarine for
  sauté
Salt and pepper to taste
2 stalks celery, sliced
1 stalk fresh broccoli,
  sliced
3 carrots, sliced
½ cup Burgundy
2 medium-small
  zucchini, cut in chunks
¼ pound fresh
  mushrooms, sliced
3 tablespoons tomato
  paste
3 fresh tomatoes, diced
1 teaspoon dill weed
3 tablespoons molasses
Sour cream and parsley
  for topping

In a stew pot, begin sautéing onions, garlic, potatoes, and eggplant in butter. Salt and pepper lightly. When potatoes begin to get tender, add celery, broccoli, and carrots, along with Burgundy. Steam until all vegetables begin to get tender, then add zucchini, mushrooms, tomato paste, tomatoes, dill, and molasses. Cover and simmer over low heat about 20 minutes. Correct seasoning. Serve piping hot, topped with sour cream and freshly chopped parsley.

Serves 6

Mushroom Stew^(L)

5 tablespoons butter or
  margarine
1 tablespoon olive oil
2 bay leaves
2 cloves garlic, minced
1 large yellow onion,
  chopped
2 tablespoons flour
1 cup vegetable broth
1 cup tomato juice
2 cups peeled and
  quartered tomatoes
1 teaspoon thyme
1½ pounds fresh
  mushrooms, washed
1 pound boiling onions
Red wine to taste
Chopped fresh parsley
  to taste
Salt and pepper to taste
1 cup ripe green olives,
  pitted

In a medium-size saucepan, melt 2 tablespoons of butter with 1 tablespoon of olive oil and add bay leaves, garlic, and yellow onion. Sauté until the onion is golden, then stir in flour and lower heat.

Cook this roux for several minutes, stirring constantly, then add vegetable broth and tomato juice. Stir with a whisk to remove all lumps, then add peeled tomatoes.

In larger pot, melt remaining tablespoons of butter and add thyme and washed mushrooms. Sauté mushrooms over high heat for several minutes, turning them over often, then add boiling onions and tomato sauce. Turn down heat and simmer stew about 20 minutes. Add a little red wine, some chopped parsley, and salt and pepper to taste. Last but not least, add green olives. Cook only a few more minutes, remove bay leaf, and serve hot with a good bread and some red wine.

Serves 6

MAIN DISHES: RICE

No mystery, hocus-pocus, or razzle-dazzle surrounds the preparation of rice. It is simple. Rice is hydrogenous; it absorbs moisture. (This is why rice grains are placed in salt shakers to keep the salt flowing and why you have "more" rice after it is cooked than when you started.) Therefore, successful preparation depends on the ratio of rice to water. Here is a rough guideline: 2½ cups of liquid for every 1 cup of brown rice; 2 cups of liquid for every 1 cup of white rice. One cup of uncooked brown rice yields between 3 and 4 cups of cooked rice; 1 cup of uncooked white rice yields 3 cups of cooked rice.

Always start with boiling liquid—it insures the shortest possible cooking time. In terms of nutrition, this means less vitamin and mineral loss. Add salt, seasonings, and/or butter after the rice has been placed in the boiling liquid. Stir occasionally.

To cover or not to cover the pot is a lively issue among some rice connoisseurs. You can do it either way. Simmer brown rice for 45 to 50 minutes covered or uncovered; allow 20 to 25 minutes for white rice.

Well-cooked rice is tender and firm, not hard or mushy. All the

Note: All recipes can be made with either white or brown rice.

The symbol **(L)** is used next to those recipe titles that include some form of dairy product. All other recipes are vegan in nature; that is, they contain no meat, eggs, or milk products.

liquid should be absorbed. You will be throwing away precious vitamins and minerals if you start with too much liquid and have to drain it when the rice becomes tender.

If the rice is not the right tenderness at the end of the suggested time guideline, simmer an additional 2 to 6 minutes, being careful that all the fluid does not evaporate and you are left with a pot of scorched rice. Pudding or dessert dishes usually call for very tender rice, and for these treats you may want to start with 2 additional ounces of water and an additional simmering time of 4 to 6 minutes. Conversely, if you plan to bake the rice after boiling it, you may wish to undercook it slightly.

Rice can be baked without prior simmering. For this method, place rice and suggested amount of liquid in a moderate oven (350° F), cover, and use the following times as guidelines only: brown rice, 65 minutes; white rice, 45 minutes. Stir the rice occasionally. Again, the fluid should be absorbed when the rice is tender and firm.

Leftover cooked or baked rice can be stored in the refrigerator if it is well covered. Otherwise, it will dry out and absorb the flavors of the other foods in the refrigerator. To reuse the rice, serve cold, if you prefer, or heat in a warm (350° F) oven for between 10 and 20 minutes. You may want to add several tablespoons of water for each cup of rice reheated. This will help you recapture some of the moisture that may have been lost in refrigerator storage. Some people, however, prefer the less moist, leftover rice.

Cooked rice has a good freezer life if it is stored in airtight containers or casserole dishes. Again, you might want to add several tablespoons of liquid for each cup of frozen rice to recapture some of the lost moisture.

The rice dishes given here show the delectability and versatility of the vitamin-rich grain. If it is flavor, good nutrition, and sensible calories that you seek in your diet—in other words, snap, crunch, and punch—add rice . . . and some spice in your life.

BROWN RICE AND WHITE RICE

Some facts to be considered:

Brown rice has more calories—220 per cup compared with 195 for white rice.

There are other differences too. Expect double the cooking time for brown rice than for white rice. Responsible for this increase in cooking time is the high fiber and oil content of the bran layer. This also means more liquid is needed for cooking brown rice.

Like white rice, however, brown rice expands during cooking, but because the bran coating "explodes" in brown rice, the bran adheres to the rice grain. Although white rice has less nutritional value than brown rice, it may be preferred by those who savor a blander accompaniment to their main dish. Because of its lower fiber content, white rice may be the choice of those on low-residue diets and those allergic to gluten. Rice may have shortcomings as a nutritious meal in itself, but when combined with other proteins, fruits, or vegetables, it becomes an integral part of a well-balanced meal.

Rice Pancakes (L)

2 cups brown rice, cooked
4 ounces carrots, shredded
1 onion, grated
2 eggs, well beaten
1 teaspoon salt
1 teaspoon ground black pepper
½ teaspoon mild curry*

Blend rice, carrots, onion, eggs, salt, pepper, and curry in blender or mixer. Form into 10 medium-size patties. Place patties on well-greased skillet. Brown each side. Serve with plain yogurt, sour cream, apple sauce, butter honey, or molasses.

Serves 4

* See recipe for Madras-Style Curry Powder, p. 237

Rice Soup (L)

1 clove garlic, minced
1 clove shallot, minced
3 tablespoons olive oil
4 large tomatoes,
   peeled
2 large onions, finely
   chopped
1 cup shredded carrots
6 stalks celery, chopped
8 sprigs parsley,
   chopped
1 tablespoon crushed
   basil leaves
1 bay leaf, crushed
1 teaspoon ground
   white pepper
1 teaspoon salt
1 quart water
1½ cups uncooked rice
1 cup vegetable stock
1 cup light cream

In a large kettle, sauté garlic and shallot cloves in olive oil. Discard cloves. Simmer tomatoes, onions, carrots, celery, parsley, and spices in water for 30 minutes. Add rice and vegetable stock and simmer for 45 minutes more. Remove from heat. Put soup mixture in blender with light cream until smooth and creamy. Simmer for 20 minutes. Remove bay leaf. Serve piping hot.

Serves 6

Rice Jarlsberg (L)

2 cups uncooked brown rice

12 ounces Jarlsberg, Icelandic, or Swiss cheese

6 ounces milk

6 tablespoons sweet butter or margarine

4 ounces almonds, chopped

1 cup shredded carrots

1 large tomato, peeled and chopped

1 tablespoon wheat germ

1 teaspoon paprika

1 teaspoon nutmeg

1 teaspoon mild curry

½ teaspoon crushed cumin seeds

1 teaspoon salt

1 teaspoon ground white pepper

1 tablespoon chopped chives

1 large egg, slightly beaten

¾ cup cooked mushrooms

4 parsley sprigs

4 ounces hard cheese (such as Parmesan), grated

In a large saucepan, simmer rice, cheese, milk, butter, almonds, and carrots until cheese is melted. Stir constantly. Add tomato, wheat germ, and spices, and blend thoroughly. Remove from heat. Add beaten egg, cooked mushrooms, and parsley sprigs. Spoon mixture into a casserole dish. Top with grated cheese. Bake at 350° F for 45 minutes or until crust is a golden brown. Serve hot or cold.

Serves 4

Fried Rice, Chinese-Style[(L)]

2 ounces peanut oil
2 large green peppers,
  chopped
1 onion, finely chopped
2 cups rice, cooked
6 tablespoons soy
  sauce
3 tablespoons sugar
1 egg, slightly beaten
1 teaspoon pepper

Heat peanut oil in a hot wok. When oil begins to sizzle, add green peppers and onion. Stir-fry for 5 minutes. Add rice, soy sauce, sugar, egg, and black pepper. Stir-fry for 5–7 minutes. Serve piping hot.

Serves 4

Stir-Fried Rice

3 cups rice, cooked
  (long- or medium-
  grain)
½ cup peanuts
1 package (about 10
  ounces) tofu
2 tablespoons sesame
  oil
2 onions, chopped
2 carrots, diced
½ bunch minced
  watercress
2 tablespoons minced
  fresh parsley
½ teaspoon turmeric
½ teaspoon ginger
  powder
Soy sauce to taste

Break up rice with a wooden spoon and set aside. Dry-roast peanuts in the oven if they are raw. Rinse tofu in cold water, cut into small cubes, and place on paper towels to drain. Heat oil in a large skillet or wok and sauté onions; when they become transparent, add carrots and sauté for a few minutes before adding the greens. Add spices and mix thoroughly before adding rice, peanuts, and tofu. Stir-fry for a few minutes. Season with soy sauce and serve.

Serves 6

Herbed Rice[L]

1 clove garlic
1 clove shallot
2 tablespoons olive oil
2 cups vegetable broth
1 large onion, chopped
2 teaspoons chives
½ teaspoon crushed
  tarragon leaves
½ teaspoon crushed
  savory leaves
1 teaspoon crushed
  basil leaves
1 teaspoon crushed
  cumin seeds
½ teaspoon marjoram
  leaves
1 teaspoon ground
  black pepper
¼ teaspoon ginger
¼ teaspoon dry
  mustard
¼ teaspoon nutmeg
¼ teaspoon crushed
  celery seeds
3 cups rice, cooked
½ cup shredded carrots
8 ounces cheddar,
  Muenster, or other
  cheese
1 egg, well beaten
1 cup plain yogurt
  (optional)
5 tablespoons hard
  cheese (such as
  Parmesan), grated

In a large saucepan, sauté garlic and shallot cloves in olive oil. Remove cloves. Add vegetable broth, onion, and all seasonings. Simmer for 1 hour. Remove from heat. Add cooked rice, carrots, cheese, egg, and yogurt. Mix thoroughly and place in a large casserole dish. Top with grated cheese. Bake at 350° F for 35 minutes or until top is brown. Serve piping hot.

Serves 6

Baked Rice^(L)

1 large onion, chopped
1 large tomato, peeled
   and chopped
1 large bell pepper,
   chopped
1 clove garlic
1 clove shallot
Olive oil
3 8-ounce cans tomato
   sauce
16 ounces water
1 tablespoon crushed
   basil leaves
1 teaspoon crushed
   oregano
1 bay leaf, crushed
1 vegetable bouillon
   cube (optional)
1 teaspoon salt
1 teaspoon ground
   black pepper
½ teaspoon paprika
½ teaspoon nutmeg
4 cups rice, cooked
1 egg, well beaten
4 slices mozzarella or
   Swiss cheese

In a large saucepan, sauté onion, tomato, green pepper, garlic, and shallot cloves in olive oil. Remove garlic and shallot cloves. Add tomato sauce, water, and seasonings. Simmer for 90 minutes. Remove from flame and set aside. In a large bowl, mix cooked rice with sauce mixture. Add well-beaten egg and mix thoroughly. Spoon mixture into a casserole dish. Top with cheese slices. Bake at 350° F for 35 minutes. Serve piping hot or cold.

Serves 6

Stuffed Bell Peppers with Herbed Rice (L)

1 clove garlic
1 clove shallot
1 medium tomato, sliced
Olive oil
1 15-ounce can tomato sauce
1 cup water
1 teaspoon salt
1 teaspoon ground black pepper
½ teaspoon crushed oregano
1 teaspoon crushed basil
1 bay leaf, crushed
½ teaspoon crushed celery seeds
½ teaspoon crushed savory
½ teaspoon curry
2 parsley sprigs, chopped
3 cups brown or white rice, cooked
1 egg, slightly beaten
6 tablespoons Parmesan cheese
6 large bell peppers, pared and seeded
6 slices mozzarella or Jarlsberg cheese (optional)

In a large skillet, sauté garlic and shallot cloves and tomato in olive oil. Remove cloves. Add tomato sauce, water, and spices. Simmer for 45 minutes. Add 3 cups of cooked rice, egg, and Parmesan cheese to sauce. Mix well. Spoon rice-sauce mixture into green peppers. Top each pepper with cheese slice. Bake at 350° F for 35 minutes or until cheese is melted and browned. Serve hot.

Serves 4–6

MAIN DISHES: TOFU AND SOY

Tofu is soybean cheese, also known as bean curd. You will find it in firm and soft forms, a custardlike product created from soymilk; the firm form (also known as the Chinese-style versus the soft Japanese) has had more of the water pressed out of it. If you want tofu to keep its shape in your recipe, use the firm; the soft form mixes easier in recipes.

Tofu recipes are limitless, and we have some excellent examples of its use in this section, along with uses for other forms of soybean products. The soybean itself in the dried state is also versatile and is cooked in the same manner as any dried bean.

A bland dish by itself, tofu lends itself to any type of cuisine you enjoy, for it mixes so well. You will note liquid on the tofu when purchased; this is natural but should be drained before use. In storing it, however, add a bit of insulating water to the top in order to keep it for about a week in a covered refrigerator container.

Tofu works well in hot and cold dishes, in salads, and on sandwiches. We believe you will enjoy every one of these choice recipes, from Soy Burgers to Tofu Terrine to Tofu Noodle Kugel.

Note: The symbol **(L)** is used next to those recipe titles that include some form of dairy product. All other recipes are vegan in nature; that is, they contain no meat, eggs, or milk products.

Soysage (L)

1½ cups okara
¾ cups whole wheat
   flour
2 tablespoons shoyu
1 teaspoon wet
   mustard
½ teaspoon salt
¼ teaspoon oregano
¼ clove garlic, crushed
Pepper to taste
1—5 tablespoons milk
   (soy or dairy) or
   water

Combine all ingredients but milk, mixing well. Then add just enough milk to make a medium-firm dough.

Oil the inside of several slender sausage-shaped tin cans or sturdy oven-proof cups or bowls. Pack mixture into containers and cover with aluminum foil. Stand containers upright in 1 inch of water in a pressure cooker, and bring cooker to full pressure (15 pounds). Simmer for 45 minutes. (Or stand containers in a tray of water and bake at 350° F for 30 minutes.)

Remove containers from cooker or oven and allow mixture to cool until firm. Then remove soysages by inverting containers and shaking.

Cut soysages into ¼-inch-thick rounds and fry on both sides in a well-oiled skillet. Serve as is or top with shoyu or ketchup and mustard. Also use as sandwiches.

If baking method is used and soysage is cooked in an oven-proof bowl, scoop out mixture and shape into patties.

Variation: Try adding a little fennel, cayenne, honey, or allspice to the dough.

Serves 3–4

Simple Tofu Vegetables

2 medium onions,
   cubed
1 medium green
   pepper, cubed
½ pound mushrooms,
   halved
1 pound dry tofu, cubed
½ cup sunflower seeds
1 cup water
1 teaspoon basil
1 teaspoon sage

In hot oil, sauté onions until limp. Add green pepper, mushrooms, tofu, sunflower seeds, water, and herbs. Simmer until vegetables are limp. Serve over cooked rice.

Serves 4–6

Tofu-Stuffed Peppers

3 ounces olive oil
2 ounces onions,
   chopped
1 clove garlic, chopped
14 ounces tofu,
   squeezed and
   mashed
2 ounces cooked wild
   rice
1 teaspoon oregano
½ teaspoon basil
Salt and pepper to taste
4 medium-size red
   peppers

Heat olive oil and sauté onions and garlic until transparent. Add crumbled tofu, wild rice, oregano, and basil. Cook ingredients for 5 minutes, stirring constantly to avoid burning onions. Add salt and pepper and set aside to cool slightly.

Cut off bottoms of peppers, remove seeds, and wash peppers. Fill peppers with tofu mixture and steam for 10–15 minutes or until stuffing is heated through.

Remove peppers from steam, cut out a wedge, and arrange nicely on a plate. Serve with a miso sauce.

Serves 4

Tofu Brochettes with Vegetables

3 ounces zucchini
2 ounces onions
1½ ounces carrots, blanched
3 ounces tofu
8 mushroom caps
Pinch of curry powder
1 tablespoon sesame oil
Salt and pepper
3¼ ounces curry sauce, hot

Cut vegetables and tofu in cubes (approximately 1 inch) and alternate on 2 skewers. Marinate skewers in curry powder, sesame oil, salt, and pepper for 1 hour. Pan-fry until golden brown on all sides. Vegetables should still remain crisp. Serve brochettes with curry sauce.
Serves 2

White Tofu Sauce(L)

3 tablespoons soy margarine
3½ ounces onions, chopped
10½ ounces tofu, crumbled
1 teaspoon crushed garlic
3¼ ounces white wine
6¾ ounces soymilk
Pinch of nutmeg
Salt and pepper to taste

Melt soy margarine and sauté onions until soft. Add crumbled tofu and garlic, and blend well. Add white wine and soy milk, and bring to a boil. Taste for seasoning and puree in a food processor. Bring sauce to a boil again, stirring constantly, then simmer for 5 minutes.
Serves 8–10

Tofu Terrine[(L)]

18 ounces tofu
3 eggs
3 tablespoons spinach
puree, very dry
3 tablespoons carrot
puree, very dry
Salt and pepper to taste
1 teaspoon sesame oil
2 tomatoes, sliced
Chervil

Crumble tofu and puree in food processor. Add eggs and divide puree into 3 equal parts. Add 1 of the vegetable purees to each portion of tofu, leaving the third plain. Season with salt, pepper, and sesame oil. Spread puree in a mold 9 inches by 3 inches lined with cheesecloth, starting with the white, followed by the spinach, and then the carrot. Close the cheesecloth and steam for 10–15 minutes. Let the terrine cool completely before slicing. Pour Asparagus Sauce (see recipe that follows) on a plate and place terrine in the center. Garnish with asparagus spear, tomato slices, and chervil.

Serves 4

Asparagus Sauce

4 ounces cold White
Tofu Sauce (see
recipe on p. 161)
1 tablespoon
asparagus puree, dry

Blend ingredients well; serve chilled.
Serves 8–10

Tofu Rainbow Sandwich

10½ ounces tofu
½ teaspoon paprika
1 ounce chopped
  radish
1 tablespoon chopped
  chives
1 teaspoon chopped
  parsley
Salt and pepper to taste
4 slices pumpernickel
  bread
4 endive leaves
2¾ ounces carrots,
  julienne
4 tablespoons alfalfa
  sprouts

Place tofu in a food processor and blend until creamy. Blend ⅓ of tofu with paprika and chopped radish, ⅓ with chives and parsley, and leave remaining ⅓ plain. Season with salt and pepper. Spread 3 slices of bread, each with a different mixture. Stack together and top with fourth slice. Press together firmly. Slice into 2 portions and garnish with endive, carrots, and alfalfa sprouts.
  Serves 2

Although America has only recently discovered tofu, some predict that it will revolutionize the American diet, duplicating the success stories of such other once-foreign foods as yogurt and pizza. There is a good reason to believe this will happen. Tofu, a natural food made from soybeans, is low in cost, in fats, and in calories; it contains no cholesterol and is high in protein. It is ideal for dieters: a 3½-ounce serving contains just 72 calories yet contains about as much protein as a hamburger.

Some food marketing experts predict that tofu will replace dairy products to about the same extent that margarine has replaced butter.

Tofu Cutlets^(L)

11 ounces tofu
1 tablespoon soy sauce
3 tablespoons
**   nutritional yeast flakes**
1½ teaspoons
**   margarine or oil**
Garlic powder to taste

Slice tofu into pieces 2½ inches square and ½ inch thick, and wrap in a triple layer of dish toweling for 30 minutes until firm. Dip tofu slices into soy sauce on a plate, then dust in yeast flakes. Melt margarine in a skillet and fry tofu for 3–4 minutes on each side or until nicely browned, then sprinkle with garlic powder. They are nice as is or as open-faced sandwiches with burger-type trimmings (tomato and alfalfa sprouts or lettuce, onion, mustard, and ketchup).

Serves 2

Stuffed Mushroom Caps^(L)

1½ ounces tofu,
**   crumbled**
1 teaspoon chopped
**   onions**
1 teaspoon chopped
**   scallions**
1 teaspoon tomato
**   concasse**
½ teaspoon crushed
**   garlic**
Pinch of chopped thyme
Salt and pepper to taste
6 medium-size
**   mushroom caps**
1 teaspoon grated
**   Parmesan cheese**
3¼ ounces fresh tomato
**   sauce**

Mix crumbled tofu with onions, scallions, tomato concasse, and garlic. Season with thyme, salt, and pepper. Fill mushroom caps with tofu mixture. Sprinkle with Parmesan cheese and bake at 350° F for 10 minutes until the cheese is golden brown. Pour tomato sauce on a plate and arrange mushroom caps nicely.

Serves 1–2

Tofu Burgers

30 ounces tofu
6 tablespoons grated carrots
4 tablespoons minced leeks, scallions, onions, or ginger root
2 tablespoons ground roasted sesame or sunflower seeds, peanuts, or chopped nut meats
¾ teaspoon salt
Oil for deep-frying
Shoyu

Cut tofu into thin slices and arrange between double layers of cotton toweling. Set aside for 15 minutes, then place pieces at the center of a dry dish towel. Gather the corners and twist to form a sack. Squeeze tofu in sack firmly to expel as much moisture as possible. Combine tofu with next 4 ingredients in a large shallow bowl. Mix well, then knead mixture about 3 minutes, as if kneading bread. When dough is smooth and holds together well, moisten your palms with a little oil or warm water and shape dough into 8 patties, each 3–3½ inches in diameter.

Fill a wok, heavy skillet, or deep fryer with oil to a depth of 1½–2 inches. Heat to 300° F. Slide in patties and deep-fry for 4–6 minutes or until they float high in the oil. Turn patties over and deep-fry for several minutes more or until crisp and golden brown. Drain briefly, then serve crisp and hot, and topped with a sprinkling of shoyu or between buns with burger trimmings. Leftovers may be frozen.

Yield: 8 patties

Teriyaki Tofu[(L)]

16 ounces tofu
2 tablespoons butter or margarine

Teriyaki Sauce:
½ cup soy sauce
¾ cup water
1½ tablespoon honey
1½ teaspoon powdered ginger, ground
¼ teaspoon garlic powder
1 teaspoon dark (toasted) sesame oil
½ teaspoon prepared mustard

Slice tofu into pieces 2 inches by 2¾ inches by ½ inch thick. Press tofu slices between a double layer of dish toweling topped with a 3-pound board for 3 minutes. Arrange slices in a shallow baking pan. Mix ingredients for teriyaki sauce. Pour sauce on tofu slices and marinate for 1½ hours on each side. Drain briefly on paper towels. Melt butter in a large skillet. Add tofu slices and fry for 2½–3 minutes on each side or until golden brown. (Nice as is or in sandwiches.)
Yield: 9–10 slices

Tofu Italian Meatballs[L]

12 ounces tofu, well
  pressed or squeezed
¼ cup chopped walnut
  meats
½ onion, minced
¼–⅓ cup bread crumbs
1 egg, lightly beaten
3 tablespoons minced
  parsley
Pepper to taste
  (optional)
4 teaspoons red miso
  or ½ teaspoon salt
Oil for deep-frying
¼ cup tomato juice or
  soup
¼ cup ketchup
Oregano to taste
3 tablespoons grated
  Parmesan cheese

Combine first 7 ingredients and 1 tablespoon of miso. Mix well and shape into 1½-inch-diameter balls. Heat oil to 350° F in a wok, skillet, or deep fryer. Drop in balls and deep-fry about 3 minutes or until golden brown. Drain balls, then arrange in a loaf pan. Preheat oven to 350° F. Combine remaining teaspoon of miso with tomato juice, ketchup, and oregano, mixing to form sauce, and pour over tofu balls. Top with a sprinkling of cheese and bake for 15 minutes or until nicely browned. For best flavor, set aside for 6–8 hours. Serve hot or cold as is or as a topping for spaghetti or in a spaghetti sauce.

Serves 2–3

Bean Curd with Ginger

3 pads fresh bean curd
8 tree ears (available in
  Chinese markets)
2 tablespoons peanut,
  vegetable, or corn oil
1 tablespoon finely
  chopped ginger
1½ tablespoons finely
  chopped garlic
¾ cup chopped
  scallions
1 teaspoon chopped
  fresh hot chilies or ½
  teaspoon crushed hot
  red pepper flakes
½ cup cooked fresh
  peas (optional)
1 teaspoon sugar
1 tablespoon red wine
  vinegar
1 teaspoon sesame oil
  (optional)

Cut bean curd into ½-inch cubes. Soak tree ears in warm water until softened. Drain and chop coarsely. Heat oil in a wok or skillet and, when very hot, add ginger, garlic, and scallions. Add bean curd, stirring quickly. Add tree ears, chopped chilies, and peas, and stir. Add sugar and vinegar, and toss. Spoon mixture onto a serving dish and sprinkle sesame oil over all if desired.

Serves 4

Foo Young (L)

6 ounces tofu
6 eggs
1 cup coarsely chopped
  bean sprouts
½ cup minced celery
3 tablespoons grated
  Parmesan cheese
2 tablespoons soy
  sauce
2 green onions, minced
¼ cup chopped parsley
1 teaspoon sesame oil

Place tofu in a small bowl and mash with fork until pieces resemble cottage cheese. In a larger bowl, beat eggs until fluffy. Add mashed tofu, bean sprouts, celery, Parmesan cheese, soy sauce, green onions, and 2 tablespoons of chopped parsley. Mix well.

Heat oil in a heavy skillet until quite hot. Drop egg batter by tablespoons. Turn when bottom is lightly browned, brown the second side, and serve immediately. Garnish with remaining chopped parsley.

Serves 4

Baked Potatoes with Tofu Stuffing (L)

4 baked potatoes
12 ounces tofu, pressed
2 ounces cheese,
  grated or diced
½ teaspoon salt
Pepper to taste
1½ tablespoons butter
  or margarine
1 onion, minced
1 tablespoon oil

Preheat oven to 350° F.

Cut potatoes lengthwise and scoop out shells. Spoon 1 cup of potato into a mixing bowl and reserve remainder. Mash tofu and cheese with potato in a bowl. Season with salt and pepper. Melt butter in a skillet and sauté onion until nicely browned. Mix onion into potato-tofu mixture, then divide mixture among potato shells. Coat a cookie sheet with oil and bake stuffed potatoes about 30 minutes or until nicely browned. Delicious served topped with butter (or sour cream) and minced chives (or parsley).

Serves 6–8

Tofu with Tacos(L)

12 ounces tofu
⅔ cup cooked brown
   rice or bulgur wheat
¼ cup peanuts
½ green pepper, diced
2 cloves garlic, crushed
¼ teaspoon chili
   powder
¼ cup ketchup
½ teaspoon salt or 1
   tablespoon red miso
2–3 tablespoons oil
6 tortillas
Tabasco or taco sauce

Garnishes of your choice,
   such as chopped
   tomato, minced
   onion, shredded
   lettuce, grated cheese

Combine first 8 ingredients in a large bowl, and mash thoroughly. Heat oil in a skillet and fry tortillas. Fill each tortilla with tofu mixture. Spoon your choice of garnish on tofu mixture and season with Tabasco sauce.

Serves 6

Scrambled Tofu

1 pound block tofu
1 teaspoon oil
¼ teaspoon turmeric
   (optional for
   coloring)
½ teaspoon onion
   powder
½ teaspoon kelp
½ teaspoon mixed
   herbs

Mash tofu. Stir in other ingredients. Heat in skillet.

Serves 4

Curried Rice and Tofu Salad

18 ounces tofu
2½ cups brown rice, cooked and chilled
3 tablespoons minced green onion or leek
2 tablespoons minced parsley
2 green peppers; one slivered and one cut into rings
4 lettuce leaves
1 tomato, cut into wedges

Dressing:
6 tablespoons oil
⅓ cup rice vinegar
1 tablespoon lemon juice
1 tablespoon curry powder
¼ teaspoon red pepper
1 clove garlic, crushed
¾ teaspoon salt
Pepper to taste

Press tofu and break into very small pieces. Combine first 4 ingredients with slivered green pepper. Add blended dressing, mix lightly, and for best flavor set aside for several hours. Serve mounded on lettuce leaves in a large bowl. Garnish with tomato wedges and green pepper rings.

Serves 6

Soy Nut Meat

1 cup lightly toasted
  peanuts or cashews
2 cups water or tomato
  juice (or
  combination)
2 teaspoons salt or 2
  teaspoons salt and 1
  tablespoon soy sauce
2½ tablespoons
  arrowroot or
  cornstarch
1⅓ cups soy flour
1 tablespoon bakon
  yeast
2 teaspoons onion
  powder or a few
  garlic drops

Mix all ingredients together well. Fill greased tin cans and cover. Steam for 3 hours in boiling water (water should not go over top of cans). Or fill greased cans and bake in the oven at 350° F for 2 hours (baking changes the texture).

Serves 4

Un-Salmon Loaf

1 cup tomato juice
1 cup water
1 cup soy flour
1½ teaspoons onion
   salt

Preheat oven to 400° F. Whirl ingredients in blender until smooth and pour into floured baking dish. Bake about 40 minutes until tan crust forms. Cool and turn onto a platter. Serve hot or cold as a main dish with a sauce. Use sliced for sandwiches. (It is expected that loaves made with soy flour will fall slightly. Do not be disappointed. The flavor is not altered, and the "falling" develops a cheeselike consistency. This particular dish keeps nicely refrigerated for reuse or reheating but is not best when frozen.)

Serves 4

Fried Tofu with Vegetables

½ pound tofu
1 tablespoon soy oil
½ cup shredded
   cabbage
1 stalk celery, sliced
½ cup thinly sliced
   carrots
1 onion, chopped
1 clove garlic, minced
1 tablespoon tamari
¼ cup sesame or
   sunflower seeds

Cut tofu into ½-inch cubes and fry for 5 minutes in oil. Add all vegetables and sprinkle with tamari and seeds. Fry on hot flame until vegetables wilt but still crunch.

Variations: Add 1 or more of the following: ½ cup mushrooms, ½ cup sprouts, ½ green pepper, 3–4 broccoli florets.

Serves 4–6

Soy Burgers^(L)

2 tablespoons chopped
   green onions
2 tablespoons oil
1 cup cooked soy pulp
   or coarsely chopped
   soybeans
1 cup brown rice,
   cooked
½ cup grated cheese
1 cup ground sesame
   and/or sunflower
   seeds, toasted
⅓ cup whole wheat
   flour
2 eggs, beaten
1 teaspoon salt
2 teaspoons soy sauce
½ teaspoon basil

Sauté onions in oil. Mix in remaining ingredients. Shape into patties and cook on a griddle or in a skillet, or bake in a 350° F oven for 20 minutes. To keep them from sticking, sprinkle griddle or baking dish with sesame seeds.

Serves 8

Pan-Fried Tofu^(L)

½ pound tofu
1 tablespoon
   margarine or soy oil
1 tablespoon tamari
1 clove garlic, minced
2 tablespoons
   nutritional yeast
¼ cup sunflower seeds

Slice tofu ¼ inch thick. Fry tofu in margarine until one side is lightly browned. Sprinkle on tamari, garlic, and yeast, and fry other side. Add seeds and cook until lightly browned.

Serves 4

Scotch Eggs (L)

2 cups cooked
soybeans
1 cup finely chopped
onions
½ teaspoon dried
thyme
1 teaspoon dried sage
Salt to taste
Freshly ground pepper
to taste
2 eggs, well beaten
4 eggs, hard-cooked
¼ cup whole wheat
flour
¼ cup dried whole
wheat fine bread
crumbs
Oil for deep-frying

Mince or blend soybeans with onions and herbs, and season well with salt and pepper. Add half of the beaten eggs and bind mixture together thoroughly. Divide into 4 portions. Pat 1 portion out into a round, put a hard-cooked egg in the center, and wrap soy mixture evenly around it.

Roll each Scotch egg in flour, dip it in remaining beaten egg, then coat thickly with bread crumbs.

Heat oil to 350° F in a deep-fat fryer. Lower Scotch eggs carefully into oil and deep-fry for 2–3 minutes or until golden brown. Remove with a slotted spoon and drain well on paper towels. Leave to cool, then serve cold with a salad.

Serves 4

Scheherezade Casserole^(L)

¾ cup raw soybeans
1 cup raw bulgur
1½ cups chopped
  onions
2 cloves garlic, crushed
2 medium green
  peppers, chopped
4 medium-size fresh
  tomatoes, chopped
¼ cup freshly chopped
  parsley
3 tablespoons tomato
  paste
1 teaspoon ground
  cumin
1 teaspoon basil
Salt, pepper, and
  Tabasco to taste
1½ cups crumbled feta
  cheese

Soak soybeans in lots of water for at least 4 hours. Then puree in blender with 1½ cups of water. Soak bulgur for 15 minutes in 1 cup of boiling water. Combine pureed soybeans and soaked bulgur. Sauté onions and garlic in a little lightly salted oil. When soft, add peppers and sauté for 5 minutes. Combine all ingredients except feta cheese. Place in a large buttered casserole. Sprinkle feta cheese on top. Bake for 1 hour at 375° F (covered for first 45 minutes, uncovered for last 15 minutes).

Serves 4–6

Spicy Szechuan Tofu

24 ounces fresh soft tofu
2 tablespoons oil
1 teaspoon minced
   fresh ginger
1 clove garlic, minced
3 tablespoons chopped
   scallions
1 tablespoon Szechuan
   hot bean paste*
1 tablespoon tamari or
   soy sauce
½ teaspoon salt
½ teaspoon sugar
½ cup stock
½ tablespoon
   cornstarch dissolved
   in 2 tablespoons
   water
1 teaspoon sesame oil
A few drops hot chili oil
   (optional)
¼ teaspoon Szechuan
   peppercorn powder
   (or more, to taste)

* Available in Oriental markets.

Drain and rinse tofu, and drain again. Cut into 1-inch-square pieces.

Set wok over a high flame and add oil. When oil is hot, stir in ginger, garlic, and 2 tablespoons scallions, and cook about 30 seconds. Add hot bean paste and tofu. With a spatula, stir tofu very gently. Add soy sauce, salt, sugar, and stock, and bring to a full boil. Thicken sauce with dissolved cornstarch, then add sesame oil, hot chili oil, and peppercorn powder.

Transfer to a hot serving dish and sprinkle with the remaining chopped scallions. Serve hot with brown rice.

Serves 4–6

Mushroom Stroganoff with Tofu[L]

Sauce: (make first)
8 ounces tofu
⅓ cup water
2 tablespoons soy sauce
2 tablespoons lemon juice or apple cider vinegar
1 clove garlic
1 teaspoon chopped lemon rind
1 teaspoon chopped ginger root

Stroganoff:
½ onion, minced
1 clove garlic, minced (optional)
1 teaspoon oil
¾ pound fresh mushrooms, sliced
4 ounces tofu
2 tablespoons sour cream
½ teaspoon oregano
1 tablespoon toasted slivered almonds
1 tablespoon chopped parsley
2 cups brown rice, cooked

To make the sauce: combine all ingredients in blender container. Blend until very smooth. Be sure garlic, lemon rind, and ginger root are finely chopped and not left in big chunks. Set aside or refrigerate to use later; this improves flavor. Sauce will keep up to 1 week.

To make the Stroganoff: sauté onion and garlic in oil until onion is transparent. Add mushrooms and sauté until slightly limp and moisture has evaporated. Set aside. Cut tofu into 1-inch cubes and brown slightly.

Pour sauce over all. Mix well and heat through, stirring. Blend in sour cream and oregano. Serve over cooked brown rice (½ cup per person) and sprinkle with toasted almonds and parsley.

Serves 4

MAIN DISHES: NUTS

Not long ago, nuts were considered just a snack—something you served in a dish as an accompaniment to a drink. This, of course, is still true, and in their natural form they make an excellent, fast, and healthful food. They are a fine energy food, supplying protein, fiber, minerals, and vitamins E and B. However, they also have a high fat content.

Because of the high and tasty quality of nuts, they also lend themselves to creative gourmet vegetarian cooking. They blend well with vegetables, rice, honey, potatoes, and more, as the recipes that follow prove. Their texture adds to softer dishes. Seeds of a grand variety can also be used in your recipes in much the same manner, by the way.

In addition to being blended with other ingredients in recipes, nuts serve as a fine garnish to virtually any hearty dish or dessert.

Use them in abundance in season. You can buy them shelled and raw, blanched (no skins), roasted, and in the shell. When you buy, be sure you are getting fresh nuts, and use them within a three- to five-month period. And keep them refrigerated—nuts kept stored in covered jars will keep at room temperature about half the refrig-

Note: The symbol **(L)** is used next to those recipe titles that include some form of dairy product. All other recipes are vegan in nature; that is, they contain no meat, eggs, or milk products.

erated time. Your unshelled nuts should keep about a year in a dry, cool spot. We suggest buying unsalted nuts for any cooking use.

Macadamia-Stuffed Mushrooms[L]

1 pound medium-size mushrooms
4 tablespoons butter or margarine
½ cup chopped onions
½ cup chopped macadamia nuts
½ cup soft bread crumbs
1 tablespoon dry white wine, apple juice, or water
½ teaspoon salt
⅛ teaspoon ground black pepper

Preheat broiler. Remove stems from mushrooms, reserving caps and stems. Chop enough stems to yield 1 cup. In a large skillet, melt 2 tablespoons of butter. Add stems and onions; sauté until tender, about 3 minutes. Add nuts, bread crumbs, wine, salt, and black pepper. Continue to cook until hot, about 1 minute, then set aside. On a baking sheet, place mushroom caps hollow-side down. Melt remaining 2 tablespoons of butter. Brush each cap with butter. Broil 4 inches from heat source until tender, about 2 minutes. Turn caps hollow-side up. Spoon an equal amount of reserved bread-crumb mixture into each cap. Broil until lightly browned, about 1 minute.

Yield: 20–39 mushrooms

Cheese and Walnut Stuffed Peppers[(L)]

6 large green peppers
4 medium onions, chopped
Butter or margarine
2 cups brown rice, cooked
1 cup walnuts, finely chopped or run through a meat or nut grinder
½ pound cheddar cheese, grated
4 eggs, beaten
2 teaspoons caraway seeds
Sea salt

Preheat oven to 350° F.

Remove stem caps, pulp, and seeds from peppers. Stir-fry onions in butter. Place in a large bowl and mix in remaining ingredients. Stuff each pepper as full as possible. Arrange peppers open-end up in a baking dish and pour a little water into the dish. Bake for 30–40 minutes or until peppers are tender. (If you have any extra filling, bake it separately in a small oiled casserole for a side dish or save it for a main dish for another day.)

Serves 6

Chestnuts with Rice

1 medium-size onion,
  finely sliced
¼ pound mushrooms
Butter or margarine as
  required
1 teaspoon all-purpose
  flour
½ cup vegetable water
1 pound chestnuts,
  boiled
Salt and black pepper
  to taste
½ cup white wine
2 cups rice, cooked

Sauté onion and mushrooms in butter until brown. Add flour and blend, then gradually add heated vegetable water, stirring until smooth. Add peeled and chopped chestnuts, and mix well. Flavor with salt and black pepper. Add white wine, heat to boiling point, and serve on plain boiled rice.

Serves 4

Filbert-Stuffed Artichokes[L]

4 medium artichokes
½ cup chopped toasted filberts
½ cup seasoned dry bread crumbs
¼ cup chopped pimiento-stuffed green olives
1 clove garlic, pressed
2 tablespoons butter or margarine, melted
1 teaspoon salt
Boiling water

Wash artichokes. Cut off stems at base and remove small bottom leaves. Trim tips of leaves with scissors and cut off about 1 inch from top of artichokes.

Combine nuts, bread crumbs, olives, garlic, and butter. Stir with a tossing motion to coat mixture with butter. Spoon butter sauce between artichoke leaves.

Stand artichokes upright in a deep saucepan large enough to hold them snugly. Add 1 inch of boiling water and salt, pouring water around, not over, artichokes. Cover and boil gently for 35–40 minutes until base of artichoke can be easily pierced with a fork. Add more boiling water if needed.

Drain artichokes and serve with additional melted butter if desired.

Serves 4

Peanut Cutlets[L]

2 eggs
½ cup water
1 onion
2 tablespoons margarine or vegetable oil
4 ounces peanuts, chopped
1 teaspoon lemon juice
1 cup bread crumbs
Parsley sprigs (garnish)

Beat eggs with 1 tablespoon of water and set aside half of liquid for dipping the cutlets. Cook onion in oil for 5 minutes, then add water and rest of ingredients except bread crumbs and parsley. Shape the paste into cutlets, dip into bread crumbs, then into egg reserved for the purpose, and again into bread crumbs. Fry in oil to a golden brown. Serve with tomato or any other sauce and garnish with parsley.

Serves 4

Vegetable Stew with Nut Dumplings

½ pound potatoes
1 parsley sprig
¼ pound carrots
1 celery leaf
¼ pound parsnips
2 ounces onions
¼ pound turnips
2 tablespoons
  vegetable oil
½ tablespoon all-
  purpose flour

Dumplings:
2 tablespoons cooking
  oil
4 tablespoons whole
  wheat flour
¼ cup whole wheat
  bread crumbs
¼ cup finely chopped
  walnuts or other nuts

Cut peeled and washed vegetables into small cubes. Combine oil and about 1½ cups of vegetables. (Any combination of vegetables may be used.) Cook until light brown. Add flour and mix well. Add pint of water and rest of vegetables. Cook slowly about 90 minutes. Season to taste and serve with dumplings made as follows: Work oil into flour, crumbs, and chopped nuts. Add water to make stiff dough. Roll and cut into walnut-size pieces. Cook for 25 minutes in rapidly boiling water. (Also good in soups.)

Serves 4

Peanut Roast I⁽ᴸ⁾

½ pound potatoes,
  mashed
2 ounces onions,
  chopped
½ cup milk
2 cups whole wheat
  bread crumbs
½ cup peanut butter
1 egg, well beaten

Boil and mash potatoes and finely chop onions. Mix with milk, bread crumbs, and peanut butter, and add well-beaten egg. Season to taste. Bake in a 350° F oven for 30 minutes.

Serves 4

Peanut Roast II [L]

½ pound onions,
  chopped
Butter or margarine
½ cup ground peanuts
½ teaspoon salt
2 eggs, beaten
Pinch of nutmeg
2 cups bread crumbs
Pinch of pepper
½ cup vegetable stock
½ teaspoon mixed
  dried herbs

Preheat oven to 375° F. Fry onions in a small amount of butter. Mix with remaining ingredients. Turn into a well-greased baking dish. Bake for 45 minutes at 375° F.

Serves 4

Vegetable Nut Loaf [L]

2½ cups cooked green
  beans
2½ cups cooked corn,
  creamed in blender
2½ cups cooked yellow
  hominy
2½ cups cooked carrots
2½ cups cooked peas
1 tablespoon meatless
  soup base
2 cups bread crumbs
1 medium onion,
  ground
1½ cups chopped
  pecans or other nuts
4 eggs or equivalent
  egg substitute
Salt and pepper or
  substitutes to taste

Grind all vegetables in food grinder. Add remaining ingredients and mix well. Fill well-greased loaf pans. Set in pan of hot water and bake at 300° F until set on top (about 2 hours). Remove from pan of hot water and bake 1½ hours more. Serve with a favorite sauce. (Leftover vegetables may be used.)

Yield: 2 loaves

Peanut and Potato Loaf (L)

**2 cups mashed
  potatoes**
Milk to taste
**1½ cups chopped
  peanuts**
**1 cup whole wheat
  bread crumbs**
2 eggs
**1 teaspoon chopped
  onions**
**1 teaspoon chopped
  parsley**

Preheat oven to 350° F. Beat mashed potatoes with a little milk until they are light. Put peanuts in blender, then mix with potatoes. Add bread crumbs; if too stiff, add a little more milk. Whip eggs and fold in. Season and place in a greased baking pan. Bake in 350° F oven for 30 minutes.

Serves 4

Hot Nut Loaf Delight (L)

1 cup ground walnuts
1 cup ground almonds
**½ cup soybean grits
  soaked in 1 cup
  vegetable broth**
**3 eggs (or arrowroot
  powder or other
  suitable thickener)**
¼ cup wheat germ
¼ cup parsley
1 teaspoon salt
1 teaspoon pepper
**¼ cup brown rice,
  cooked**

Preheat oven to 350° F. Mix all ingredients together. Mixture should be slightly moist. If necessary, add more liquid or dry ingredients, whatever the case may be. Bake in oiled loaf pan for 30 minutes at 350° F. Serve hot with tomato sauce or your own sauce.

Serves 4–6

Squash with Peanuts [L]

4 cups thinly sliced summer squash
6 tablespoons whole wheat flour
6 tablespoons butter or oil
2 cups half and half
Salt and pepper to taste
⅓ cup grated Gruyère cheese
1½ cups salted peanuts

Cover squash with lightly salted boiling water and cook for 5 minutes. Drain. Combine flour and butter in top part of double boiler over hot water and blend. Add half and half, and cook, stirring constantly, until smooth and thickened. Add salt and pepper to taste. Stir in grated cheese and stir until cheese has melted. Crush peanuts with a rolling pin on a sheet of wax paper. Do not roll them to a paste, however; the texture should be uneven.

Preheat oven to 350° F. Arrange a layer of squash in a buttered baking dish. Spread with sauce and then sprinkle with peanuts. Repeat until all are used, ending with peanuts on top. Bake until sauce is bubbly and peanuts are lightly browned. Serve immediately.

Serves 6–8

Peanut Spaghetti [L]

3 tablespoons butter or
  margarine
3 tablespoons flour
1 teaspoon salt
1 teaspoon dry mustard
¼ teaspoon pepper
½ cup chopped onions
2 cups buttermilk or
  regular milk
1 pound spaghetti,
  cooked
½ cup sliced black
  olives
1 cup grated cheddar
  cheese
1 cup chopped peanuts
3 drops hot pepper
  sauce
⅓ cup bread crumbs

Melt butter and blend in flour, salt, mustard, pepper, and onions. Add milk and stir until thickened. Put half of cooked spaghetti in greased casserole with half of olives, cheese, and peanuts on top. Repeat layers. Pour sauce over top. Sprinkle with bread crumbs that have been moistened with butter. Bake at 350° F for 25 minutes.

Serves 4

Nut Loaf (L)

1 cup chopped cooked
  carrots
Salt to taste
1 cup chopped walnut
  meats
1 cup bread crumbs
1 small onion, chopped
2 eggs, well beaten
½ stalk celery, chopped
1 8-ounce can tomato
  sauce
1 tablespoon oil

Preheat oven to 350° F. Mix all ingredients except tomato sauce. Spoon into oiled pan. Bake for 30 minutes. Five minutes before removing from oven, cover with sauce.

Serves 4

Baked Nut Croquettes (L)

½ cup ground nuts
1 cup boiled brown rice
1 cup mashed potatoes
1 cup bread crumbs
1 onion, grated
2 eggs, beaten
Salt and pepper to taste
Grated cheese

Mix together nuts, rice, potatoes, bread crumbs, onion, eggs, salt, and pepper. Shape into croquettes, adding more crumbs if necessary. Sprinkle with cheese. Place on well-greased baking sheet. Bake at 375° F for 30 minutes. Serve with mushroom sauce (recipe follows).

Serves 4

Mushroom Sauce

4 tablespoons oil
4 tablespoons flour
2 cups vegetable stock
Salt and pepper to taste
1 cup chopped
   mushrooms

Make a brown sauce of oil, flour, and stock. Season, add mushrooms, and cook for 5 minutes or until thickened.

Serves 4

Meatless Meatballs(L)

½ cup grated cheese
½ clove garlic, minced
½ cup chopped pecans
½ teaspoon parsley
1 cup cracker crumbs
½ teaspoon sage
1 egg
½ teaspoon salt
1 onion, finely chopped

Mix all ingredients well and form into small balls. Fry until brown. Add meatballs to spaghetti sauce 30 minutes before serving.

Serves 4

BREADS

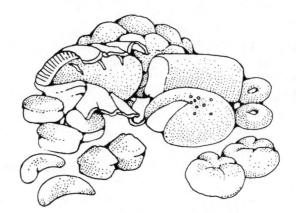

Ah, bread! Freshly baked, swollen with whole grain goodness, it stands proud on the counter as it cools. Let your bread be as hale and hearty as the fruits of the earth it is made from. Use whole grains—don't devitalize your bread by using white flour. Deprived of its heart (the germ) and its outer covering (the bran), the noble wheat berry is rendered just a shadow of its former self by the refining process.

Though the ingredients of bread are basic, numerous pages could be written about them. Many cookbooks go into detail about both the parts and the process of bread making at home. *Wings of Life, The Tassajara Bread Book,* and *Laurel's Kitchen* offer especially good overviews. Read a chapter on bread before you get started. A smattering of good bread recipes are offered here, some yeasted and some not, one steamed, one in pockets, one baked in a skillet. There are many fabulous breads that can be created in your kitchen, and some do not take a lot of time. Happy baking!

Note: The symbol **(L)** is used next to those recipe titles that include some form of dairy product. All other recipes are vegan in nature; that is, they contain no meat, eggs, or milk products.

Wheat Gluten

10 cups whole wheat
   flour
4 cups unbleached flour
5 cups cold water
2 teaspoons salt

Mix flours and add water in which the salt has been dissolved. Knead in a large bowl. The dough will not make good gluten unless it is well kneaded. That is the elastic part of the flour, and only strong kneading will bring it out. Knead for at least 20 minutes.

Set dough in a spot about 40 minutes to dry out a bit. Then place bowl in a sink and add 8–10 cups of cold water. Knead vigorously and wring out all cream-colored starch from dough. Change water, reserving starch water. This can be used for soup stocks and gravy. Place dough in colander, set that into a bowl, and add fresh water. This process must be repeated several times until the gluten becomes stringy and shiny and the starch is washed out.

Bring 12 cups of water to a boil in a large pot. Pull off sections of gluten with your fingers—they should be about the size of a walnut. Drop pieces into boiling water and remove with a slotted spoon as soon as they float to the top. Place gluten in a colander and wash with cold water.

At this stage the gluten is rather bland. You can fry it, use it in vegetable dishes (seasoned any way you like), or make seitan to use in gravy.

Yield: 5 cups.

Scrumptious Corn Bread[(L)]

1 cup yellow corn meal
1 cup whole wheat
 pastry flour
2 eggs
1 cup buttermilk or sour
 milk*
¼ cup honey
2 tablespoons molasses
3 tablespoons butter or
 margarine, melted
2 tablespoons dry milk
 powder
2 teaspoons baking
 powder
½ teaspoon baking
 soda
1 teaspoon salt

Preheat oven to 350° F. Mix dry ingredients in a bowl. Make a well in the center and crack in the eggs. Beat with a fork and then beat in buttermilk, honey, and molasses. Slowly stir all ingredients together, gently mixing wet with dry. Do not overmix or beat. Spread into a buttered 8-inch-square cake pan or a medium-size cast-iron skillet. Bake in a 350° F oven about 35–40 minutes or until top is lightly browned and center is firm.

Yield: 1 loaf

* To make sour milk, add 2 tablespoons of lemon juice or vinegar to regular sweet milk.

Banana-Oatmeal-Pecan Bread[(L)]

½ cup butter or margarine, at room temperature
¼ cup honey
2 eggs
3 bananas, mashed
¼ cup buttermilk
1 teaspoon vanilla
1 teaspoon baking powder
1 teaspoon baking soda
½ teaspoon sea salt
½ cup rolled oats
2 cups whole wheat flour
1 cup broken pecans

Preheat oven to 350° F.

In a medium-size bowl, cream together butter and honey until mixture is smooth. Beat in eggs, one at a time. Stir in bananas, buttermilk, and vanilla. When well-blended, mix in baking powder, soda, and salt, then blend in oats, flour, and pecans until all ingredients are well combined.

Turn mixture into a buttered loaf pan 9 inches by 5 inches by 3 inches. Bake at 350° F for 55 minutes or until a toothpick inserted in center comes out clean. Remove from pan and cool on wire rack. Serve warm or cooled. This bread is slightly sweet and is good served with fresh fruit for breakfast.

Yield: 1 loaf

Old-Fashioned Oatmeal Bread^(L)

**2 envelopes active dry
  yeast**
**½ cup warm water
  (105°–115°)**
½ cup molasses
⅓ cup oil
1¼ cups water
2 eggs, beaten
1 tablespoon sea salt
2 cups rolled oats
**5 cups whole wheat
  flour**

Stir yeast into warm water and set aside for 5 minutes. Stir again to dissolve.

In a large bowl, mix together molasses, oil, 1¼ cups of water, eggs, and salt. Stir in yeast and then oats. Add whole wheat flour, using just enough to form a soft dough. (You may need to use up to 5½ cups whole wheat flour.)

Knead dough in the bowl for several minutes to develop gluten. Cover and let rise in a warm, draft-free place about 1 hour and 15 minutes or until doubled in bulk. (An ideal place for the dough to rise is inside a cold oven.)

Punch dough down and knead again. Divide dough in half and place in 2 buttered loaf pans 9 inches by 5 inches by 3 inches. Cover and let rise again until doubled in bulk, about 45 minutes. Bake at 375° F about 45 minutes or until loaves sound hollow when tapped.

When done, remove from pans and cool on a wire rack.

Yield: 2 loaves

Oat Flour Biscuits[(L)]

1⅓ cups whole wheat flour
⅔ cup oat flour
1 tablespoon baking powder
1 teaspoon sea salt
⅓ cup oil
⅔ cup milk

Preheat oven to 450° F.

In a medium-size mixing bowl, mix together whole wheat flour, oat flour, baking powder, and salt. Add oil and milk all at once and stir until a soft dough forms.

Turn dough out onto a floured sheet of wax paper and knead a few times until dough is smooth. Cover with another sheet of wax paper and roll out ½ inch thick. Cut with a 2½-inch-diameter cutter

Place biscuits on an ungreased baking sheet and bake for 15–20 minutes or until biscuits are nicely browned. Serve hot with butter, honey, or molasses.

Yield: 12–14 biscuits

Whole Wheat Sesame Bread[(L)]

2 envelopes active dry yeast
3½ cups very warm water
½ cup honey
2 tablespoons oil
Dry milk powder to make 1 quart of milk
½ cup soy flour
1 tablespoon salt
1 cup sesame seeds
9 cups whole wheat flour (approximately)

In a large mixing bowl, soften yeast in warm water. Stir in honey and set aside for 5–10 minutes. Stir in oil, milk powder, soy flour, salt, and sesame seeds. Add enough whole wheat flour to make a stiff dough.

Knead dough in the bowl for 5–10 minutes or until smooth and elastic. Cover with a clean cloth and let rise until doubled in bulk, about 1 hour.

Punch dough down, then knead for 1–2 minutes. Divide dough in half and shape into loaves. Place each half in a greased loaf pan 9 inches by 5 inches by 3 inches, cover, and let rise again until doubled in bulk, about 35 minutes. Bake at 350° F for 30–35 minutes or until done. (Bread should sound hollow when tapped.) Cool on wire rack.

Yield: 2 loaves

Sunflower Ginger Bread[(L)]

1½ cups honey
1 cup butter or
  safflower oil
5 eggs
2 cups molasses
6 cups whole wheat
  pastry flour
5 teaspoons cinnamon
3 teaspoons ginger
2 cups buttermilk or 2
  cups fresh milk with
  the juice of 2 lemons
  added
2 cups toasted
  sunflower seeds or
  chopped walnuts

Preheat oven to 325° F. Beat honey well with butter. Add eggs and beat. Add molasses and beat. Sift dry ingredients and fold in alternately with milk. Add sunflower seeds. Bake in oiled, floured pan for 35–40 minutes. Cool in pan for 10 minutes before removing to cut.

Serves 24

Apple Bran Muffins[L]

2 cups whole wheat
   flour
1 ½ cups wheat bran
½ teaspoon salt
1 ¼ teaspoons baking
   soda
½ teaspoon nutmeg
1 teaspoon cinnamon
1 heaping tablespoon
   grated orange rind
1 cup chopped apple
½ cup raisins
½ cup chopped nuts
½ cup orange juice
1 ½ cups buttermilk
1 egg, lightly beaten
½ cup molasses
2 tablespoons oil

Preheat oven to 350° F. Mix together dry ingredients, then stir in fruits and nuts. Combine liquid ingredients, then stir into flour mixture with a few quick strokes. Pour into greased muffin pans, filling them ⅔ full, and bake for 25 minutes.

Yield: 24 muffins

French Bread

2 tablespoons yeast
(1 tablespoon if using
unbleached white
flour)
½ cup lukewarm water
or milk
1 teaspoon blackstrap
molasses
¾ cup lukewarm water,
milk, potato water, or
vegetable water
1½ teaspoons salt
1 tablespoon honey
3 cups whole wheat or
unbleached white
flour
1 tablespoon oil or
margarine

Glaze:
1 teaspoon cornstarch
1 teaspoon cold water
½ cup boiling water

Sprinkle yeast on top of ½ cup of water and molasses. Set aside for 10 minutes in a warm, draft-free place.

Beat ¾ cup of lukewarm water, salt, honey, flour, and oil. Add yeast to mix. Stir until well mixed.

Turn dough onto a lightly floured board. Knead. Place in an oiled bowl. Brush lightly with melted margarine and cover with a clean towel. Let rise in a warm place until doubled in bulk, about 40 minutes. Punch down and let rise again until almost double in bulk, about 30 minutes.

To make the glaze: combine cornstarch and cold water. Gradually add boiling water. Cook until smooth, then allow to cool slightly.

When bread has risen, divide into 2 equal portions. Press each piece of dough into an oblong about 15 inches by 10 inches. Beginning with the wide side, roll up lightly. Seal edges by pinching together. With hands on each end, roll gently back and forth to lengthen loaf and taper ends.

Place loaves on a greased baking sheet. Brush loaves with cornstarch glaze. Let rise, uncovered, about 1½ hours. Brush again with cornstarch glaze. Make ¼-inch slashes in dough at 2-inch intervals. Bake at 400° F for 10 minutes.

Remove from oven and brush again with cornstarch glaze. Return to oven and bake for 20 minutes or until golden brown.

For a crustier French loaf, place a pan of boiling water in the bottom of the oven during baking.

Because of its shape, this bread is best eaten right away (it tends to dry out quickly). Using all milk for the liquid may make it stay moist longer.

Yield: 2 loaves

Rye Bread(L)

3 cups scalded milk,
   buttermilk, yogurt,
   stock, or potato water
¾ cup cornmeal
1 tablespoon molasses
½ tablespoon salt
2 tablespoons butter or
   margarine
1 tablespoon yeast
¼ cup lukewarm water
1½ cups gluten
6 cups rye flour
2 cups whole wheat
   flour
2 cups mashed
   potatoes

In a heavy saucepan, pour scalded milk over cornmeal and stir until smooth. Cook, stirring occasionally, for 2 minutes until mushy. Add molasses, salt, and butter. Set aside until mush is lukewarm. Dissolve yeast in lukewarm water and let rise. Mix gluten with rye flour and whole wheat flour. Add to corn mush along with mashed potatoes and yeast. Mix until it forms a stiff dough.

Turn onto floured board and knead, using more whole wheat flour until it is no longer sticky. Set in oiled bowl, turning dough until well oiled. Cover and let rise in a warm place until dough doubles in size.

Shape into 3 or 4 loaves and place in buttered bread tins. Let rise until at top of tins. Cross-cut twice in each loaf. Bake for 1 hour or more at 350° F.

Yield: 3–4 loaves

Whole Wheat Bread with Egg (L)

¼ cup blackstrap molasses
¼ cup honey (optional)
4½ cups warm water or milk
3 tablespoons yeast
1–2 eggs
¼ cup cold-pressed oil
1–2 teaspoons salt
8–10 cups stone-ground whole wheat flour
½ cup powdered milk
2 cups soy flour

Dissolve molasses and honey in warm water. Add yeast, stir lightly, and set aside for 10 minutes. Add eggs, oil, and salt, and beat.

Add 4 cups of whole wheat flour and beat 100 times, with ½ cup of gluten if necessary. Mix milk powder with soy flour and add to dough. Keep adding flour until too stiff to beat.

Turn onto floured board and knead. When dough is rounded and full (you'll know it is full when you see it), place in a warm oiled bowl. Oil top of dough and cover with oiled aluminum foil. Keep in a warm place until doubled in bulk (about 2 hours).

Turn out and lightly knead, then let rest for 10 minutes. Divide into 3 rounded loaves, oil tops, cover with damp cloth or foil, and set in warm place for 20 minutes. Bake at 350° F for 40 minutes or until nicely browned. The loaf should come away from the side of the loaf pan. Turn on sides to release from pans; cool.

Yield: 3 loaves

Irish Potato Bread(L)

2 medium-size potatoes
½ cup lukewarm water
1 teaspoon molasses
1 tablespoon baker's
  yeast
2 eggs
Milk
½ cup oil
½ cup mixture honey
  and molasses
2 teaspoons salt
6 cups unbleached or
  whole wheat flour (or
  3 cups of each)

Scrub potatoes and boil, unpeeled, until tender; reserve liquid. In lukewarm water, thoroughly dissolve molasses. Dissolve yeast on top of water. Set aside for 10 minutes in a warm place, then stir well.

Break 2 eggs in a measuring cup. Beat lightly with a fork. Add enough milk to make 1 cup.

Measure ¾ cup of water in which potatoes were cooked; place in a bowl and let cool to tepid. Remove skin from potatoes and mash them in the tepid water (or blend chopped, unskinned potatoes with water in blender).

Add oil, honey-molasses mixture, and salt. Mix well and add yeast and egg mixtures. Blend thoroughly and add flour.

Turn onto a lightly floured table and knead for 10 minutes. Cover and let rise in a warm place for 2 hours or until doubled in bulk.

Punch down dough and knead again for at least 5 minutes. Divide dough into 3 loaves. Place in well-oiled loaf pans and let rise until double in bulk. Bake at 400° F for 20 minutes. Lower heat to 300° F and bake for 10 minutes more.

(This dough can be kept overnight. Place in refrigerator right after second kneading and first rising. When ready to bake, shape in loaves and allow to rise once. Bake as above.)

Yield: 3 loaves

Oatmeal Yeast Bread(L)

½ cup molasses
1½ tablespoons salt
3 tablespoons oil
1 cup scalded milk, or 2 cups of scalded milk and omit water
1 cup boiling water
3 cups rolled oats, uncooked
2–4 tablespoons dry yeast
½ cup lukewarm water
½ cup gluten
3½–4 cups whole wheat flour

Add molasses, salt, and oil to scalded milk. Pour milk and boiling water over rolled oats and combine well. Set aside until lukewarm.

Dissolve yeast in lukewarm water and let rise.

Mix gluten with whole wheat flour. Add to oat mix and beat well. Add yeast to mixture and mix thoroughly—do not beat.

Turn onto a floured board and knead for 5 minutes, using more flour if necessary. Dough should be smooth and easy to handle.

Place in an oiled bowl, oil top of dough, and cover. Let rise until nearly double in size, about 45 minutes.

Punch and divide in half. Cover and let dough rise for 10 minutes, then form into 2 loaves. Put into 2 well-greased pans and oil top of each loaf. Let rise until nearly double, about 30 minutes.

Bake at 400° F for 10 minutes, then reduce to 350° F and bake for 60–65 minutes more.

Remove from pans, brush with melted butter, and let cool.

Yield: 2 loaves

Basic Bread

⅓ cup + 1 teaspoon
  blackstrap molasses
2 tablespoons salt
½ cup oil
4 cups boiling water
6 cups whole wheat
  flour
¼–½ cup gluten
3 tablespoons yeast
2 cups warm water
2 cups soy flour

Mix ⅓ cup of molasses, salt, oil, and boiling water. Set aside until it is just warm.

In a big bowl, mix 4 cups of whole wheat flour with gluten. Meanwhile, dissolve yeast in warm water to which 1 teaspoon of molasses has been added. Set aside for 10 minutes.

Make a hole in the flour-gluten mixture and pour in molasses-oil mixture. Beat well until it becomes very elastic. Add yeast to this dough; mix but do not beat.

Mix soy flour with 2 cups of whole wheat flour separately. Then add to batter until a stiff dough forms.

Turn onto a floured board and knead. Oil a bowl and place dough inside. Let rise for 1 hour or until dough doubles in size.

Place raised dough on an oiled board. Roll into a long sausage. Cut into loaves. Place in pans and let rise for 1 hour.

Bake at 375° F about 1 hour.
Yield: 3 loaves

Spoonbread(L)

2 tablespoons butter or margarine
1 cup buttermilk and 1 cup milk, or 2 cups milk
¾ cup cornmeal
3 eggs, separated
½ teaspoon baking soda (omit if all milk is used)
¾ teaspoon salt
Pinch of cream of tartar

Preheat oven to 400° F.

Lightly butter a soufflé dish. In a saucepan, scald milk, then add cornmeal and remaining butter. Simmer and stir until mixture thickens. Remove from heat and cool to lukewarm.

Beat in egg yolks and baking soda if used. In a separate bowl, beat egg whites with salt and cream of tartar until stiff. With a spatula, carefully fold beaten egg whites into cornmeal mixture. Pile it into the soufflé dish and bake about 40 minutes until it is set and golden brown. Serve at once.

Serves 4

Delicious Cornbread(L)

½ cup soy flour
¾ cup whole wheat pastry flour
¾ cup stone-ground whole-grain yellow cornmeal
4 teaspoons baking powder
½ teaspoon salt
1 egg
1 cup buttermilk or milk
½ teaspoon baking soda (omit if milk is used)
2 tablespoons butter or margarine, melted
¼ cup honey

Preheat oven to 375° F. Sift all dry ingredients. Combine all other ingredients and mix well. Combine all ingredients and stir. Spread into a buttered 9-inch cast-iron frying pan or a 9-inch pie dish, and bake for 30–35 minutes or until light brown around the edges.

Serves 6

Okara Crackers

¾ cup okara
¾ cup whole wheat flour
¾ cup brown rice flour
1 teaspoon salt or 1 tablespoon nutritional yeast
1–2 teaspoons mixed herbs (optional)
2–4 tablespoons sesame or poppy seeds (optional)
3 tablespoons oil
4 tablespoons tofu or yogurt
1–2 tablespoons water, as needed

Mix dry ingredients together, breaking up okara with your hands. Add oil and mix well with a fork. Add tofu, mixing with your hands. Add water as needed to form a pie dough consistency. Let dough rest for 5 minutes. Roll out on a lightly floured board and cut into cracker shapes, ⅛ inch thick or less. Bake on a lightly greased cookie sheet at 375° F until crackers are golden, about 10 minutes.

Yield: 3 dozen small crackers

Okara Waffles^(L)

¾ cup brown rice flour
¾ cup whole wheat flour
¼ cup wheat germ
1½ teaspoons baking powder
¼ teaspoon baking soda
2 eggs, separated
3 tablespoons oil or melted butter
2 cups soy or dairy milk
½ cup okara
¼ teaspoon nutmeg

Combine first 5 ingredients in a mixing bowl. In another bowl, beat egg yolks, then add oil, milk, okara, and nutmeg. Mix well. Beat in flour mixture gradually. Beat egg whites until stiff and gently fold them into the batter. Bake on a preheated waffle iron.

Yield: 4 waffles

Blue Cornbread

3 cups blue cornmeal
½ cup whole wheat
flour
1½ cups unbleached
white flour
2 tablespoons baking
powder
4 tablespoons ground
arrowroot
2 teaspoons sea salt
2 ears fresh corn off the
cob
2 cups water
1 cup honey

Preheat oven to 350° F. Mix dry ingredients together. Heat water to warm and add honey. Let cool and add to batter. Pour this thin batter into a greased 9-inch-square glass dish. Bake for 30–40 minutes. Check often.

Serves 6

Walnut and Honey Scones(L)

4 cups whole wheat
pastry flour
4¼ teaspoons baking
powder
1 teaspoon salt
½ cup butter or
margarine
2½ tablespoons
granulated sugar
½ cup finely chopped
walnuts
2½ tablespoons clear
honey
¾ cup cold milk
Egg or milk for coating

Preheat oven to 425° F. Sift flour, baking powder, and salt into a bowl and rub in butter. Add sugar and walnuts, and mix to a soft but not sticky dough with honey and milk. Turn onto a lightly floured board, knead quickly, and roll out to ½ inch thickness. Cut into rounds and put on a greased baking sheet. Brush tops with beaten egg or milk and bake for 10 minutes.

Yield: 20 scones

Herb-Onion Bread

6 cakes yeast
3 tablespoons honey
7½ cups + 3
   tablespoons warm
   water
15 cups whole wheat
   flour
3 cups bran
2 tablespoons salt
12 tablespoons herbs,
   dried or fresh
   (rosemary, dill,
   caraway, fennel or
   anise, oregano,
   tarragon)
1 onion, chopped and
   sautéed in oil

Mix together thoroughly yeast, honey, and 3 tablespoons of warm water. Set in a warm place for 15–20 minutes until frothy. Mix dry ingredients in a warmed bowl. Make a well and add yeast mixture and 7½ cups of water. Mix until doughy. Knead for 10 minutes, adding enough flour to make it workable but not too much or the dough will become dry. Keep it soft but not very sticky. Put in a clean, oiled bowl in a warm place for 1–1½ hours until double in size. Knead for 3 minutes, then form 6 loaves. Let rise in greased pans for 35–40 minutes. Bake at 475° F for 15 minutes, then reduce heat to 375° F and bake for 25 minutes more. Remember, slightly underbake it.

Yield: 6 loaves

Steamed Date-Nut Loaf (L)

½ cup whole wheat flour
½ cup yellow cornmeal
¼ cup wheat germ
1 tablespoon brewer's yeast
2 tablespoons Familia or crunchy granola
2 tablespoons sesame seeds
½ teaspoon sea salt
½ teaspoon baking soda
½ teaspoon baking powder
½ teaspoon vanilla
½ cup buttermilk
1 egg, lightly beaten
¼ cup blackstrap molasses
¼ cup honey
¼ cup chopped almonds
½ cup chopped pitted dates
¼ cup raisins

Combine all ingredients in a large bowl and mix well. Pour mixture into a 1-pound coffee can or 1-quart pudding mold that has been lightly greased with safflower oil. Cover tin with aluminum foil and secure tightly. Place plastic cover over foil to keep it in place. Place tin on a rack in a large kettle of boiling water so that the water extends halfway up the tin. Cover the kettle. Keep the kettle simmering for 3½ hours, maintaining the level of boiling water by replacing it as needed. The bread is done when it is firm to the touch on the top surface. Remove from tin and serve warm or cool the bread on a rack. It will keep in the refrigerator for 2 weeks, and it can be mailed.

Yield: 1 loaf

Pita Bread

**2 teaspoons active dry
yeast**
1 cup lukewarm water
1 tablespoon honey
1½ teaspoons salt
**3 cups whole wheat or
all-purpose flour**

Dissolve yeast in water. Add honey. Set aside about 5 minutes until it froths. Add salt and flour. Mix well with a wooden spoon. Turn out onto a floured board and knead for 10 minutes. Add flour if sticky.

Return dough ball to its bowl, now oiled. Turn until it is coated with oil, cover with a damp towel, and set to rise in a warm place about 1½ hours.

Punch dough down, turn it out, and knead again for a couple of minutes. Divide into 6 equal parts. Form each part into a smooth round dough ball. Set to rise again about 15 minutes, covered with a clean towel.

Preheat oven to 475° F. Do it now— the oven must be fully heated for baking. The high temperature is the magic that makes the bread's pocket!

Roll each ball out to about ½ inch thickness. Put them on an ungreased cookie sheet and bake on lowest possible oven rack about 10 minutes or until they are puffed and golden brown.

To help maintain their pockets and keep them soft, place baked breads on a towel, wrap up, and keep in a brown paper bag until serving time.

Yield: 6 large rounds

CONDIMENTS AND DIPS

If you thought about it, you would probably agree that it does not make sense to top that wholesome homemade tofu burger with sugary store-bought ketchup or mayonnaise laden with potassium sorbate, BHT, and all manner of chemical wonders. What is more, you would be amazed at just how easy it is to make these and other condiments and dips (which we find attractive when used as condiments with most vegetables).

Mayonnaise falls just this side of magic for its uncanny ability to keep oil and vinegar mixed. The inside story is this: The egg yolks mix with the vinegar and spread out to coat tiny droplets of oil and keep them separated. Since the oil droplets cannot cluster to form larger droplets which would settle out, they remain suspended in the egg-vinegar liquid. Even if you are not impressed with the physics, you will be with the thick, creamy, lemon-yellow, rich tasting mixture that results.

For those who shun dairy products, we have included a good cashew mayo. And the calorie wise will take note of the recipe for tofu mayo, which is also delicious. Thinned with a little more yogurt, it makes a fine salad dressing as well.

Note: The symbol **(L)** is used next to those recipe titles that include some form of dairy product. All other recipes are vegan in nature; that is, they contain no meat, eggs, or milk products.

Condiments, relishes, and garnishes, incidental as they may seem, have the ability to turn a bland dish into an enticing one. Sandwiches especially stand to benefit from a little creativity in this department. Your daily bread with a slab of cheddar cheese will provide the sustenance you need, but sneak some apple rings sautéed in butter under the cheese and pop the whole thing into the broiler for a couple of minutes, and you have an adventure in good eating.

Pickles and chutneys are good harvest-time projects, but the amount of time and ambition to create them is not necessary for the quick recipes we have included in this section. You will find them truly tasty, often unusual, highly nutritious, and fun to serve.

DIPS

Creamy Tofu Dip or Dressing

10 ounces tofu
½ cup oil
**2 teaspoons lemon
juice**
1½ tablespoons honey
¼ cup minced parsley
**2 tablespoons minced
dill pickles**
**1 tablespoon minced
onion**
**½ teaspoon prepared
mustard**
½ teaspoon salt

Combine all ingredients in blender and puree for 30–60 seconds or until smooth. Great with chips or sticks of freshly sliced carrots, green peppers, jicama, cucumbers, cauliflower, cherry tomatoes, Jerusalem artichokes, and celery.

Yield: 2 cups

Frijoles con Queso Dip⁽ᴸ⁾

**⅔ cup kidney or pinto
beans**
**2 teaspoons cumin
seeds**
2 tablespoons oil
1 clove garlic, minced
1 cup sour cream
**¾ cup grated Monterey
Jack or cheddar
cheese**
**Salt and cayenne
pepper or hot pepper
sauce to taste**

Soak and cook beans until very tender. Drain and mash. Roast whole cumin seeds in a dry cast-iron pan for a few minutes, shaking often, until they are aromatic. Grind in a seed grinder or a mortar. Heat oil in a skillet. Add cumin and garlic, and sauté for 1 minute. Add mashed beans and mix well. Cook for a couple of minutes, then remove from heat and cool. Beat in sour cream, cheese, salt, and pepper to taste. Serve with corn tortilla chips.

Yield: about 2½ cups

Blender Vegetable Dip[(L)]

2 onions, chopped
2 tablespoons butter or unsaturated margarine
3 hard-cooked eggs, quartered
1 tablespoon milk
½ cup chopped walnuts
½ cup non-fat dry milk powder
½ cup very well cooked green beans, sliced
½ teaspoon salt

Sauté onions in butter until softened. Place in blender along with remaining ingredients. Blend until smooth. Turn into a serving dish and chill well.

Yield: about 2 cups

Curry Dip[(L)]

½ cup mayonnaise
1 cup plain yogurt
2 teaspoons curry powder
½ teaspoon turmeric
¼ teaspoon powdered ginger
¼ teaspoon paprika
¼ teaspoon chili powder

Mix well and chill.
Yield: about 1½ cups

Horseradish and Nut Dip^(L)

¾ cup salted peanuts
2 tablespoons grated
horseradish
⅔ cup heavy cream or
thick yogurt

Process peanuts in blender or food processor until finely chopped. Add horseradish and cream and process until you have a thick, smooth dip. Serve with celery sticks and chips.

Yield: about 1½ cups

Hot Dahl Dip^(L)

1 teaspoon ground
cumin
1 teaspoon turmeric
½ teaspoon mustard
seeds
½ teaspoon ground
ginger
¼ teaspoon chili
powder
2 tablespoons butter or
oil
1 cup finely chopped
onion
1 cup yellow lentils
2 cups water
Salt to taste

Heat spices in butter or oil until they are aromatic. Add onions and fry until golden brown and soft. Add lentils and water, and cook, stirring occasionally, until they have formed a soft, thick puree (about 30 minutes). Taste for seasoning. Serve hot with whole wheat crackers for dipping.

Serves 6–8

Tofu Dill Dip

¼ cup fresh dill or 1
   tablespoon dried
3 tablespoons finely
   minced fresh parsley
¼ cup olive oil
¼ cup water
3 tablespoons lemon
   juice
1 tablespoon
   Worcestershire sauce
1 teaspoon tamari
1 teaspoon vinegar
1 small clove garlic,
   minced
1 pound tofu, drained

Chop greens in food processor or blender. Add remaining ingredients except tofu and process until smooth. Break tofu into chunks and add, processing again until smooth. This is equally good served with fresh vegetables or crackers.

Yield: 2 cups

Spinach Dip with Sweet Red Peppers

10 ounces fresh spinach
12 ounces tofu
3 tablespoons lemon
   juice
2 teaspoons olive oil
2 small cloves garlic,
   minced, or 3 scallions,
   finely chopped
1½ teaspoons oregano
Salt and freshly ground
   pepper to taste
Sweet red peppers, cut
   in strips

Wash and stem spinach. Blend all ingredients except red pepper in food processor or blender. Correct seasoning. Place dip in a small bowl in the center of a platter and surround with red pepper strips.

Yield: 3 cups

Herbed Dip for Fresh Vegetables[L]

**2 medium cucumbers,
  peeled, seeded, and
  grated**
**2 3-ounce packages
  cream cheese,
  softened**
⅓ cup light cream
1 clove garlic, pressed
**1 tablespoon minced
  fresh chives**
**2 tablespoons minced
  fresh parsley**
**1 tablespoon minced
  green onion**
2 tablespoons brandy
2 teaspoons tamari
¼ teaspoon pepper

Dry cucumber very well. Mix with remaining ingredients. Chill until ready to serve.

Yield: about 2 cups

Curry Dip for Raw Vegetables[L]

**1 cup sour cream or
  yogurt**
**8 ounces cream cheese,
  softened**
**2 tablespoons freshly
  chopped green onion
  or chives**
**2 teaspoons fragrant
  curry powder**
½ teaspoon salt
**Fresh carrot strips,
  zucchini strips, celery
  sticks, and cauliflower**

Beat the sour cream little by little into cream cheese. Add remaining seasonings. Blanch vegetables in boiling salted water for 2 minutes and refresh under cold water.

Serves 6–8

Black Bean Dip

8 ounces dried black
  turtle beans (frijoles
  negros), cooked and
  drained
1 large onion, chopped
1 jalapeño pepper,
  seeded and sliced
  (optional)
1 small green pepper,
  chopped
2 large scallions,
  chopped
1 bulb shallot, chopped
1 clove garlic (optional)
1 teaspoon paprika
1 teaspoon dried
  mustard
3 parsley sprigs,
  chopped
Chili powder to taste
Salt and pepper to taste

Combine all ingredients in blender, making certain that they are evenly distributed. If mixture becomes too thick while blending, add water. If after adding water dip is too thin, add 1 tablespoon of matzo meal and mix well. Refrigerate in plastic or glass containers until ready to use. Serve with tortilla chips, tacos, or melba toast. Keep refrigerated until ready to use.

Serves 4

Tofu Sour Cream

1 pound tofu
1–2 tablespoons fresh
  lemon juice
½ teaspoon salt or 1
  tablespoon shoyu soy
  sauce
1 tablespoon mild oil
  (optional)

Steam tofu for 3–4 minutes (unless very fresh), then cool. Process all ingredients in blender until very smooth. Use as you would any sour cream, or more liberally because this topping has only one-third the calories of regular sour cream.

Yield: 2 cups

Lentil Dip

½ cup dry lentils
¼ cup minced onions
1 clove garlic, minced
3 cups water
1 teaspoon ground
  cumin
2 tablespoons lemon
  juice
1 teaspoon chili powder
½ teaspoon sea salt
4 teaspoons green taco
  sauce
¼ cup tomato sauce

Place lentils, onions, and garlic in water. Bring to a boil, then reduce heat to low. Cook until lentils are soft (about 30 minutes). Drain. Save liquid for stock. Put mixture into blender or food processor. Add cumin, lemon juice, chili powder, sea salt, green taco sauce, and tomato sauce. Puree until smooth. Chill.

Yield: 1½ cups

Cashew Nut Cream

½ cup cashews
1 cup water
1 tablespoon honey or
  3 dates
⅛ teaspoon vanilla
  (optional)
Salt to taste

Blend all ingredients until very smooth, about 2 minutes. Use on cereals and desserts like apple crisp. For an almond cream, used blanched almonds and dates, and substitute ⅛ teaspoon of grated orange rind for the vanilla.

Yield: 1 cup

SAUCES

Chestnut Horseradish Sauce[(L)]

2 tablespoons sweet
  butter or margarine
¾ cup roasted
  chestnuts, shelled*
½ cup half and half,
  light cream, or milk
½ cup plain yogurt
2 tablespoons dry
  sherry
1 tablespoon prepared
  horseradish

In a heavy saucepan, melt butter over low heat. Add chestnuts and half and half. Cook over low heat about 5 minutes until heated through. Allow to cool slightly, about 5 minutes.

Puree mixture in food processor or blender, slowly adding yogurt. Return to saucepan and cook over low heat for 3–5 minutes until again heated through. Blend in sherry and horseradish, and cook about 5 minutes more.

Yield: 1½ cups

* To roast chestnuts, slice a cross on the flat side of each nut. Spread on a cookie tin and roast at 425° F for 15–25 minutes until soft inside. Be sure to remove entire shell and any furry inner skin before grinding them.

Spicy Peanut-Tomato Sauce

2 cloves garlic, minced
2 tablespoons safflower
  or vegetable oil
½ cup finely ground
  unsalted peanuts
1 16-ounce can
  tomatoes or
  equivalent fresh
  tomatoes
½ teaspoon coriander
½ teaspoon turmeric
¼ teaspoon cumin
¼ teaspoon salt or to
  taste

In a heavy saucepan or skillet, sauté garlic in oil about 5 minutes until soft. Add ground peanuts and tomatoes, and blend well until smooth. Mash tomatoes slightly with spoon or fork, leaving slightly chunky. Blend in spices and salt. Allow to cook until heated through. Serve warm, or chill and serve as a cold condiment.

Yield: 2 cups

Oignon Noisette Sauce[L]

1 tablespoon sweet
  butter or margarine
½ cup chopped green
  onion
⅔ cup finely ground
  roasted hazelnuts
¾ cup concentrated
  unsalted vegetable
  stock
¼ cup cream
¼ cup white wine
¼ teaspoon salt or to
  taste
1 tablespoon chopped
  fresh chives

Melt butter in a heavy saucepan. Sauté onion for 7–10 minutes until fairly soft. Add ground nuts and mix. Blend in stock, then cream, stirring gently. Cook about 5 minutes until slightly thickened. Add wine and leave on heat about 3 minutes more. Add salt and chives, and serve immediately.

Yield: 1½ cups

Curried Sunflower Seed Sauce

½ cup sunflower seed
  butter
1¼ teaspoons garam
  masala
1 clove garlic, minced
¾ cup soymilk
1½ teaspoons lemon
  juice
1 teaspoon wine
  vinegar

In a heavy saucepan or skillet, toast sunflower seed butter, garam masala, and garlic together for a few minutes over moderate heat. Mash mixture around pan with a wooden spoon to toast evenly. Turn off heat and blend in soymilk until mixture is a smooth emulsion. Return to low heat and stir sauce until it is desired consistency. Stir in lemon juice and vinegar. Remove from heat and let stand 3 minutes before serving.

Yield: 1¼ cups

Sesame Mustard Sauce

1½ cups concentrated unsalted vegetable stock
1-inch-piece of fresh ginger, cut into 4 pieces
2 cloves garlic, cut in halves
⅓ cup tahini
2 teaspoons Dijon mustard
¼ teaspoon salt
1 teaspoon honey
1 tablespoon lemon juice

In a heavy saucepan, heat vegetable stock with ginger and garlic about 5 minutes. Blend in remaining ingredients and cook over low heat about 7 minutes. Remove ginger and garlic before serving.

Yield: 1½ cups

Cashew Sauce

¼ cup safflower or vegetable oil
½ small onion, finely minced
1 cup soft tofu, pureed
½ cup finely ground cashews
1 tablespoon dried tarragon or 2 tablespoons fresh
¼ teaspoon salt
1½ teaspoons lemon juice
Freshly ground black pepper

Heat oil in a heavy saucepan. Add onion and sauté over medium heat for 5 minutes until soft. Blend in pureed tofu, then ground cashews. Add tarragon, salt, lemon juice, and pepper, and stir well. Allow sauce to heat through about 5 minutes and serve. If mixture seems to thicken slowly, blend in soymilk or hot water until desired consistency is reached.

Yield: 1½ cups

Tomato-Nut Mélange Sauce[(L)]

1 cup canned tomatoes
  with juice
¼ cup each pecans,
  walnuts, and cashews
1 clove garlic, minced
2 tablespoons sour
  cream or yogurt
¼ teaspoon salt
⅛ teaspoon cayenne
  pepper
2 tablespoons fresh
  cilantro or 1
  tablespoon dried

Combine all ingredients except cilantro in blender and mix on high speed until smooth. Thin with tomato juice if needed. Pour sauce into a bowl and add cilantro. To serve hot, heat mixture slowly in a heavy saucepan.

Yield: 1½ cups

Brazilian Spice Cream

1 cup finely ground
  brazil nuts
1 cup soft tofu or ½ cup
  firm tofu blended with
  ½ cup hot water or
  soymilk
¼ cup maple syrup
½ teaspoon cinnamon
¼ teaspoon nutmeg
¼ teaspoon ground
  cloves

Place all ingredients in blender or food processor and blend until smooth. This rich-tasting dessert sauce is excellent for fresh fruit salads and as a topping or filling for cakes, crepes, and pancakes.

Variations: Add 2 or 3 tablespoons of your favorite liqueur, or add ¼ cup of grated coconut, raisins, or currants to the blended sauce.

Yield: 1¾ cups

Pecan Duxelles Sauce (L)

1 tablespoon butter or
   margarine
2 cloves garlic, minced
½ cup finely minced
   mushroom caps
¾ cup whole pecans
½ cup cream
¼ cup milk
1½ teaspoons shoyu
   soy sauce
1 teaspoon thyme
1 teaspoon parsley
1 bay leaf
Salt to taste

Melt butter in a heavy saucepan. Sauté garlic, mushrooms, and pecans about 7 minutes. Add cream and milk, and cook just until heated through. Cool mixture slightly, then puree in blender or food processor about 2 minutes. When smooth, return to saucepan. Over low heat blend in shoyu and herbs, and cook about 5 minutes, stirring frequently. When heated through, remove bay leaf. Serve immediately.

This sauce may turn out thick enough to be a dip. If you prefer a thinner sauce, blend in a little more milk until it is the desired consistency.

Yield: 1¼ cups

PESTO

Lemon-Walnut Pesto[L]

1½–2 cups fresh basil
    leaves
¾ cup walnuts
2 cloves garlic
¼ cup grated Parmesan
    cheese
¼ cup ricotta cheese or
    tofu
2 tablespoons fresh
    lemon juice
1 tablespoon olive oil

In a mortar (at least 1-quart capacity), mash basil, walnuts, and garlic to a very moist, even pulp. Blend in cheeses, lemon juice, and olive oil. Serve immediately or store in refrigerator.

If using blender or food processor, add all ingredients at once and blend until smooth.

Yield: 1¾ cups

Herbed Spinach Pesto Cream[L]

2 cloves garlic
2 cup fresh spinach,
    cleaned, dried, and
    tightly packed
½ cup pine nuts
⅓ cup grated Parmesan
    cheese
¼ cup dry bread
    crumbs
⅓ cup olive oil
¼ cup hot water

In a mortar (at least 1-quart capacity), pound garlic to a pulp. Blend in spinach leaves, pounding until quite pulpy. Blend in pine nuts, crushing well. Add cheese and bread crumbs, and mix well. Stir in olive oil. Slowly add hot water, making a smooth emulsion. (If using blender or food processor, add all ingredients at once and blend until smooth.) Serve or store in refrigerator.

Yield: 1¾ cups

GRAVIES

Cashew Milk Gravy

2 cups water
½ cup cashews
2 tablespoons
  arrowroot
2 teaspoons onion
  powder
2 tablespoons oil
½ teaspoon salt

Blend all ingredients together. Cook over medium heat, stirring constantly, until thickened, about 3 minutes. Dilute if necessary. Use as a white sauce.

Yield: 2 cups

Nutritional Yeast Gravy[L]

3 tablespoons oil or
  butter
¼ cup nutritional yeast
¼ cup whole wheat
  flour
1 tablespoon red miso
1½ cups hot water
1 clove garlic, crushed
  (optional)

Heat oil in a skillet. Add nutritional yeast and mix well for 30 seconds. Add flour and continue cooking, stirring, for 1 minute. Dissolve miso in hot water and add a little at a time, stirring constantly, to create a thick and creamy consistency. Add garlic if desired. Bring just to a boil, then remove from heat. Add more water if needed.

Yield: 1½ cups

CHUTNEY

Cranberry Chutney

3 cups clean cranberries
1 cup honey or more to taste
½ cup water
1 medium navel orange
1 teaspoon ground ginger
Ground cloves to taste
Ground cinnamon to taste
½ teaspoon ground cardamom (crushed seeds from 4 pods)

Combine cranberries, honey, and water in a saucepan. Simmer, covered, for 10 minutes, then for 10 more uncovered, stirring occasionally. Cut unpeeled orange into chunks and chop finely in food processor or grinder. Add orange, seasonings, and another ½ cup of water to cranberries. Simmer chutney for 20 minutes more, stirring often. Chill before serving.

Yield: 4–5 cups

OTHER CONDIMENTS

Cashew Mayonnaise

½ cup raw cashews
1 teaspoon kelp or
  dulse
½ teaspoon paprika
1 clove garlic, crushed
1 cup water
1 cup unrefined oil
⅓ cup lemon juice
¼ teaspoon chervil
¼ teaspoon summer
  savory

Put first 5 ingredients in blender and blend until smooth. While still blending, add oil in a slow, steady stream until mixture is thick. Add lemon juice and herbs. Refrigerate.

Yield: about 3 cups

Homemade Ketchup

1 12-ounce can tomato
  paste
½ cup cider vinegar
½ cup water
1 teaspoon sea salt
1 teaspoon oregano
¼ teaspoon ground
  cumin
⅛ teaspoon nutmeg
⅛ teaspoon black
  pepper
½ teaspoon mustard
  powder
Garlic powder to taste

Mix all ingredients together very well.

Yield: 2 cups

Tofu Mayonnaise(L)

Juice of ½ lemon
2 tablespoons wine or
  cider vinegar
1 clove garlic, minced
  (optional)
1 teaspoon Dijon-style
  mustard
½ cup mayonnaise
1 teaspoon miso
1–1½ cups cubed tofu
2 tablespoons olive oil
2–4 tablespoons plain
  yogurt
Salt and freshly ground
  pepper to taste

Combine all ingredients in blender until smooth. Add additional 2 tablespoons of yogurt if necessary to thin.

Yield: about 2 cups

Tartar Sauce(L)

1 cup mayonnaise
¼ cup pickled and
  chopped vegetable
  or relish
2 teaspoons mustard

Mix all ingredients together. Two teaspoons of a spice blend (see recipes on pages 235–239) may replace or be combined with mustard to change the sauce's flavor. In addition to cucumbers, other pickled vegetables work well, although they change the traditional tartar taste. Give it even more of a face-lift by using pickled or fresh herbs that have been finely chopped. Scallions and chives would be the most common choices, but most culinary herbs lend themselves as long as they are added with a light hand.

Yield: about 1¼ cups

Tomato Ketchup

2 cups tomato puree
½ cup oil
¼ cup honey
¼ cup vinegar
1 teaspoon salt
  (optional)
½ teaspoon cinnamon

Combine all ingredients, adding more honey if a sweet ketchup is desired. The spice may be replaced with 1 teaspoon of one of the combinations. For a stronger flavor, use up to 1 tablespoon of spice. The puree can be made from scratch by cooking down tomatoes. Adding a tablespoon of arrowroot per cup will thicken it to a paste and eliminate some cooking. Otherwise, use canned tomato paste. Ketchup does not have to be made from tomatoes, although that is by far the most common type. Use any fruit or sweet vegetable to make a sweet-and-sour sauce. For chili sauce, double the amount of cinnamon and add an equal amount of cayenne or other chili pepper, or combine with the Mexican chili spice blend. Keep refrigerated.

Yield: about 3 cups

Mustard

2 tablespoons
   powdered mustard
2 tablespoons finely
   ground all-purpose
   flour
½ teaspoon turmeric
½ teaspoon ground
   ginger
1 cup cider vinegar
½ cup water
1 tablespoon honey

Mix mustard, flour, and spices together. Mix vinegar, water, and honey together. Combine dry and liquid ingredients. Bring to a boil, lower heat, and simmer for a few minutes. Pack into sterilized jars (if you want it to keep for a while), being sure to push out any air spaces, and seal. Refrigeration is not necessary but do keep in a cool place away from light. The consistency may be thinned by adding more water, thickened with more flour, or made slightly gritty with whole mustard seeds. A dash of powdered cloves and/or dill is often added to mustard, or replace the spices called for with a teaspoon of one of the spice blends (see recipes on pages 235–239).

Yield: about 2 cups

PICKLES

Quick Sweet Pickle Slices

Cucumbers (can be
large or odd shaped
if seeds are small)
Boiling water
3¾ cups vinegar
3—6 cups sugar (to
taste)
3 tablespoons salt
4½ teaspoons celery
seed
4½ teaspoons turmeric
¾ teaspoon mustard
seed

Wash and cut cucumbers into sticks. Place in glass, enamel, or crockery container. Pour boiling water to cover cucumbers. Let stand for 4–5 hours. Drain water and pack cucumbers solidly into hot jars. Make pickling solution of vinegar, sugar, and spices. Boil for 5 minutes. Pour over cucumbers to ½ inch of jar neck. Seal.

Yield: 2 quarts

Oil Pickles

5 dozen small
cucumbers
Salt
20 small onions
5 cups vinegar
½ teaspoon white
mustard seed
1½ tablespoons celery
seed
1 cup salad oil

Wash cucumbers. Place in a large enamel, glass, or crockery container. Do not pare but slice in rounds. Sprinkle liberally with salt. Let stand for 24 hours. Drain. Slice onions and add to cucumbers. Pack into sterilized jars. In a saucepan, mix vinegar, mustard seed, celery seed, and salad oil, stirring until well blended. Bring mixture to a rolling boil. Pour over cucumbers to ½ inch of top. Seal.

Yield: 5–6 quarts

Pickled Okra

2½–3 pounds small
  okra, uncut
Celery leaves
Garlic
Dill
1 quart water
1 pint white vinegar
½ cup pickling salt

Wash okra well. Pack into sterilized pint jars with 3–4 celery leaves, 1 clove garlic, and 1 head dill per jar. In a saucepan, mix water, vinegar, and salt. Heat to a rolling boil. Pour over okra to ½ inch of top. Seal.

Yield: 4–6 pints

Pickled Prunes

1 pound prunes
½ cup vinegar
1½ cups sugar
1 tablespoon stick
  cinnamon, broken
  into small hunks
1 teaspoon whole
  cloves
½ teaspoon allspice

Wash prunes. Place in a saucepan, cover with cold water, and bring to a rolling boil. Cover and simmer until tender. Add vinegar, sugar, and spices. Simmer for 15 minutes. Pour into hot pint jars and seal. Process in boiling water that covers the jar tops by ½ inch for 10 minutes. (This one sounds weird but is surprisingly good.)

Yield: 4–6 pints

SPICE BLENDS

How to Make Your Own Spice Blends

To make your blend, choose high-quality herbs dried whole, preferably home grown. Strip off the leaves and discard stems and any yellow or bug-eaten leaves. If the herb has gone to flower, be sure to include these because they contain a considerable amount of scent and therefore are rich in essential oils. Flowers of oregano and sage, for example, are not normally sold commercially because of the labor and expense involved in harvesting them, but they make fine seasoning. When the plant flowers, the lower leaves do lose some of their potency and should be left on the plant. There is another obvious advantage to letting herbs flower if you have bees —for the herbal honey that will result.

Grind the herbs in a flour mill, blender, or with a mortar and pestle (or the Mexican version—a stone matate). When powdered, put them through a sifter or in a large strainer and shake to remove any large pieces. The result should be a fine powder than can be put into doughs, soups, casseroles, sandwiches, salads, and almost any other dish. To make a truly instant spice blend, powdered garlic and/or onions may be added. You can even dry the onion or garlic yourself in the sun or in a dehydrator. Dry onions in individual layers, and dry garlic either sliced or whole; then powder in a grain grinder.

Middle Eastern Spice

3 ounces cumin
2 ounces parsley
½ ounce cayenne or black pepper
½ ounce garlic
½ ounce onion

These are the flavorings found in falafels—the sandwich of garbanzo beans in pita bread. Usually this spice blend is combined with tahini or ground sesame seeds and lemon juice.

Curry Spice

1 ounce cumin
1 ounce coriander
1 ounce turmeric
1 ounce whole black
mustard seed
½ ounce cayenne
½ ounce fenugreek

Originally, curries were made hot with black or white pepper instead of cayenne or chili peppers. Use either or both if desired. Garlic or yellow mustard powder are other hot herbs to substitute. Paprika offers a mellower warmth. To make a sweeter curry, try allspice. Star anise or saffron may also be added. Actually, any herbs you want can go into a curry, just be sure to include something hot, turmeric for the traditional yellow color, and usually cumin and coriander. There is a plant named "curry" (because of its similar fragrance) which some folks like to use in curry powder as well. If you really like curries, create selections so you will have hotter, sweeter, and spicier blends to choose from.

Winter Spice

1 ounce cinnamon
1 ounce orange peel
1 ounce star anise
½ ounce coriander
½ ounce allspice
½ ounce cardamom
¼ ounce ginger
¼ ounce cloves
¼ ounce nutmeg

This is a good seasoning for pies, cider, cakes, and other foods. My favorite use is in muffins and cookies.

Madras-Style Curry Powder

4 tablespoons turmeric
3 tablespoons coriander seed
3 tablespoons cumin seed
1 tablespoon dried ginger
20 black peppercorns
1 tablespoon whole cardamom pods
1 teaspoon fennel seeds
10 whole cloves
1 teaspoon cayenne pepper
1 teaspoon blades of mace (or substitute nutmeg if necessary)
1 teaspoon black mustard seed
1 teaspoon poppy seed
1 teaspoon fenugreek
½ stick cinnamon or 1 teaspoon ground cinnamon

Combine ingredients and crush in mortar and pestle, or grind in blender or food processor. Store in an airtight container. Two teaspoons of fragrant curry powder are sufficient to curry 6 cups of soup, 1 pound of vegetables, or 1–2 cups of dried grains. For extra flavor, sauté curry powder in a little oil or butter for 2–3 minutes before adding to other ingredients.

Yield: 1 cup

Italian Spice

2 ounces basil
1 ounce marjoram
1 ounce oregano
½ ounce garlic
½ ounce onion

These spices are famous for what they do to pizza, spaghetti, and almost any other tomato dish. Other herbs may be added in smaller amounts, but don't overpower the basil, for its sweet taste is part of the secret.

Ceylonese (Sri Lankan) Powder

**4 tablespoons
coriander seed
2 tablespoons cumin
seed
1 teaspoon fenugreek
1 teaspoon fennel
seeds
1 teaspoon black
mustard seeds
1 teaspoon cloves
1 teaspoon cardamom
pods
1 teaspoon cayenne
pepper
1 small cinnamon stick
1 teaspoon curry leaves
(optional)**

In a dry skillet over low heat, roast separately coriander, cumin, fenugreek, fennel, and mustard seeds until each becomes dark brown. (The mustard seeds will pop and crackle.) Combine remaining ingredients and crush in mortar and pestle, or grind in blender or food processor. Store in an airtight container.

Yield: about 1 cup

French Louisiana Spice

**2 ounces allspice
2 ounces black pepper
1 ounce thyme
½ ounce bay
½ ounce cayenne
½ ounce cloves**

This is another hot and spicy flavoring blending cayenne and bay from the New World with spices of the Far East.

Mexican Chili Spice

3 ounces paprika
2 ounces coriander
2 ounces oregano
½ ounce cayenne or
  other chili pepper
½ ounce garlic
½ ounce mustard seed

The hotter you like your chili, the more pepper it needs. It often includes black pepper. Cinnamon will sweeten it, and turmeric gives more color and its own subtle, unique flavor. There are many types of chili powder, each with a slightly different taste and pungency. Beans are the most common dish to season with this combination, but you don't have to stop there.

Spice Delight

1 ounce basil
1 ounce coriander
1 ounce cumin
1 ounce sage
1 ounce thyme
½ ounce celery seed
½ ounce nettle
½ ounce onion
½ ounce parsley
¼ ounce cayenne
¼ ounce garlic
¼ ounce kelp
¼ ounce mustard
¼ ounce paprika

This is a whopper of a formula. Eliminating some herbs or exchanging one for another will vary the flavor to your personal taste.

DESSERTS

It often comes as a surprise to new vegetarians that it is possible to have rich-tasting desserts that not only rival the commercial varieties but supply fine nutritional quality as well. The proof is in this prize collection of dessert recipes.

Carob, natural sweeteners such as sorghum and honey, peanut butter, a range of spices such as nutmeg, cinnamon, and cloves, raisins, fruits, nuts, and other good things guarantee flavor and high nutrition. Tofu, that all-purpose food, is also a fine mixer in dessert recipes, adding consistency and food value.

Try any of these tested cookies, cakes, toppings, sherbets, and see if you don't agree that there is nothing like them in store-shelf packages.

Note: The symbol **(L)** is used next to those recipe titles that include some form of dairy product. All other recipes are vegan in nature; that is, they contain no meat, eggs, or milk products.

CAROB DESSERTS

Caroballs I^(L)

1 cup carob
1 cup milk powder
   (noninstant)
1 cup natural liquid
   sweetener
2 cups natural peanut
   butter
Dash of vanilla extract
¼–½ cup safflower oil
Unsweetened raw
   coconut and/or
   toasted sesame seeds

In a large bowl, mix carob and milk powder. In a small bowl, mix sweetener, peanut butter, vanilla, and ¼ cup of oil. Mix well the ingredients of the smaller bowl with those of the larger bowl. If too dry to form into balls, add up to ¼ cup of oil. The consistency should be fudgy but not too wet. (Amount of oil needed may depend on brand of natural peanut butter.) Shape into balls and roll in coconut or sesame seeds.

Yield: about 30 caroballs, approximately 1½ inches in diameter

Caroballs II

½ cup carob powder
½ cup sunflower seeds
½ cup sesame seeds
½ cup wheat germ
½ cup honey
½ cup unhydrogenated
   peanut butter
⅔ cup grated
   unsweetened coconut
   (optional)

In a medium-size mixing bowl, combine first 4 ingredients. Add honey and peanut butter, and stir until mixture is well combined. Shape mixture into balls, using about 2 teaspoons of mixture for each. Roll in coconut if desired. Store, covered, in refrigerator.

Yield: 3½–4 dozen caroballs

Carobana Cupcakes

4 cups whole wheat flour or mixed flours
½ cup carob powder
1½ teaspoons baking powder
1 tablespoon allspice
½ cup safflower oil
½ cup natural liquid sweetener*
¼–½ teaspoon vanilla
2 ripe bananas plus ¾ to 1 cup water

Preheat oven to 350° F. In a large bowl combine dry ingredients. In blender combine wet ingredients or mix well by hand. When blended, yield will be approximately 2½ cups. Combine wet ingredients with dry and mix well. Scoop into oiled or paper-lined muffin tins with a lightly oiled ice cream scoop or large spoon. Bake about 20 minutes or until toothpick comes out clean.

Yield: 12 cupcakes

* Sorghum, honey, or barley corn malt—honey and sorghum tend to be sweeter than barley.

Carob Icing

11 pitted dates
4½ tablespoons + 2 tablespoons water
2 tablespoons soy powder
2 tablespoons sesame oil
1½ tablespoons carob powder, toasted

Finely chop dates and soak in 4½ tablespoons of water. Put in blender to make a smooth date paste.

Make soy butter by mixing soy powder with 2 tablespoons of water until smooth; stir in oil vigorously. Add carob powder to soy butter and stir. Combine date paste with soy butter and carob, mixing together until smooth. Pour icing over cupcakes (or cake) and spread. It will set when left to stand.

Yield: ¾ cup

Sugarless Carob Cookies^(L)

2 cups raw rolled oats
¾ cup whole wheat
flour
½ cup milk powder (soy
or noninstant skim)
½ cup chopped nuts
1½ cups wheat germ
½–¾ cup safflower oil
1¼ cups fruit-carob
whip*

Preheat oven to 350° F. Combine dry ingredients in a large bowl. Combine oil and fruit-carob whip in another bowl, then mix together well. Using your hands, make balls and press onto lightly greased cookie sheets. Bake in oven for 10–15 minutes.

Yield: about 2 dozen cookies

Variation: Add ½ cup of yogurt to 1 quart of fruit butter for creamy mixture.

* To make fruit-carob whip: Soak dried prunes or dried pitted dates in water overnight or cook them for 1–2 hours on a very low flame. Blend soaked fruit in soaking water—ratio is about 2:1 fruit to water. Mix fruit butter with carob (3–4 cups of dried fruit should yield close to 1 quart of fruit butter).

ICE CREAMS

Banana Honey Soymilk Ice Cream

2 gallons (32 cups) rich soymilk
12 bananas, frozen
2⅔ cups light vegetable oil (for example, safflower)
4–4½ cups honey
4 tablespoons slippery elm, guar gum, or carageenan (may omit with soft-serve)*
1 teaspoon vanilla extract
¾ cup powdered lecithin or ¼ cup liquid lecithin†
1 teaspoon salt
¼ cup agar
2 cups water
3 cups chopped walnuts

* Available in health-food stores.

† Available in drug stores.

Combine in large blender: 8 cups of soymilk, 6 frozen bananas, 1⅓ cups of oil, and next 5 ingredients; blend until smooth. Pour into a large pot together with 16 more cups of soymilk. Combine agar and water in a saucepan, bring to a boil, and simmer for 2 minutes. Pour into blender together with remaining 8 cups of soymilk and 1⅓ cups of oil. Blend until smooth, then pour into pot. Stir in chopped walnuts, then transfer mixture to ice cream freezer and freeze.

Yield: 4 gallons

Peach Frost

2 cups fresh peaches
2 cups orange juice

Blend peaches, then blend with orange juice. Pour mixture into shallow freezer trays. Freeze until solid. Cut frozen mixture into strips and put through a food grinder and blender. Serve at once.

Serves 4

Pineapple Sherbet

1 pineapple, sweet and ripe
1 pint fresh strawberries, sliced
Fresh mint sprigs

Blend pineapple until smooth. Pour it into a freezer container and freeze semi-hard. Then stir it well and fold in sliced fresh strawberries. Freeze overnight. When serving, garnish each dish with a single sprig of fresh mint.

Serves 4

Elizabeth's Double Dutch Chocolate Ice Cream

1¾ cups sugar
½ cup cocoa
Pinch of salt
½ teaspoon vanilla
3 cups soymilk
¼ cup oil

Put sugar in blender, cocoa on top, then salt and vanilla. Put in 1½ cups of milk and blend until cocoa is smooth. Add remaining milk and oil, and blend until mixed. Follow directions for freezing of your hand-crank or electric ice-cream machine.

Serves 4

Honey Banana Ice Cream

3 cups soymilk
1 large or 2 medium
    bananas
4–6 tablespoons oil
½ cup honey
Dash of salt

Blend all ingredients. Freeze mix in an ice-cream machine.

Serves 4

Rocky Banana Cream

10 medium-size ripe
    bananas
2 cups chopped dried
    apricots

Blend bananas until smooth. Fold in apricots. Turn mixture into a freezer container. Stir once when semifrozen, then freeze overnight to harden. Serve with slices of fresh fruit.

Variation: Substitute fresh strawberries, blueberries, or raspberries for apricots.

Serves 6

Carob Cream Swirl

10 medium-size ripe
    bananas
½ pound Mission figs,
    dried
1 cup carob powder
Water

Blend bananas alone until creamy. Turn into a freezer container and freeze until semihard. Blend Mission figs, adding enough water to make a thin paste. Mix in carob powder thoroughly. Fold carob-fig paste into the center of semifrozen banana mixture, using a swirling motion. Freeze hard before serving.

Serves 4–6

Avocado Sherbet

5–6 avocados
1⅓ cups honey
¼ cup fresh lime juice
4 tablespoons lemon juice
1 teaspoon grated lemon rind

Peel, pit, and mash avocados. Stir in honey, lime juice, lemon juice, and lemon rind. Mix or blend well. Pour mixture into a loaf pan and freeze about 2 hours or until mixture has become slushy. Then beat vigorously to aerate, return to freezer, and freeze overnight or until firm.

Yield: ½ gallon

Avocado Velvet

8 pureed avocados
2 teaspoons grated lemon peel
2 teaspoons grated lime peel
2 cups lime juice
¼ cup lemon juice
1⅓ cups light honey

Blend all ingredients. Pour mixture into a freezer container and freeze until firm, stirring once while mushy. Do not allow to stand at room temperature before serving because this is meant to have a slightly icy consistency.

Serves 6–8

Spumoni Sticks

4 ripe bananas
1½ cups carob powder
½ cup or more water
Grated peel of 2
 oranges

Peel bananas and set aside. In a shallow bowl, mix carob powder and water. Add more water or carob powder to make it a thinner or thicker paste. With a spoon or spatula, slather one banana at a time with carob paste and arrange on a flat pan or platter. Sprinkle with grated orange peel and freeze overnight or for several hours until hard. You may want to insert wooden sticks into each one before dipping and freezing.

Yield: 4 spumoni sticks

Fudgesicles

2½ cups water
½ cup sorghum
3 bananas, fresh,
 frozen, or sliced
½ tablespoon carob
 powder
1 tablespoon slippery
 elm powder*
1 tablespoon vanilla
5 tablespoons peanut
 butter

Blend all ingredients at medium speed for 1 minute until you have a smooth, medium-thick syrup. Pour into a plastic container or individual cups and freeze overnight.

Yield: 1 quart

 * Available in health-food stores.

Tofu Cheesecake with Fruit Topping [L]

Shell:
- ½ cup whole wheat flour
- 1 cup unbleached white flour
- ½ cup margarine or butter

Filling:
- 17 ounces tofu
- 2–4 tablespoons sesame tahini
- ½ cup pure maple syrup
- 2 tablespoons lemon juice
- ½ teaspoon sea salt
- 1½ teaspoons pure vanilla extract

Strawberry Topping:
- 1 cup strawberries, whole
- 10 tablespoons apple juice
- 3 tablespoons pure maple syrup
- ⅛ teaspoon salt
- 1½ tablespoons cornstarch

Sift together both flours. Cut in, then rub in margarine with fingertips until mixture resembles coarse sand. Wrap and chill for 1 hour or more. Then, using fingertips, press into an 8-inch pie tin to make a crust of even thickness. Prick bottom with a fork and bake at 450° F for 10 minutes.

Puree tofu in 2 batches in blender until smooth, then mix into a bowl with remaining filling ingredients. Spoon into prebaked shell and bake at 350° F for 30–35 minutes or until filling has set, maybe rises a little, and is golden yellow on top. Allow to cool to room temperature.

For topping, combine strawberries, ½ cup of apple juice, maple syrup, and salt in a small saucepan, and bring to a boil. Dissolve cornstarch in remaining juice, stir quickly into fruit mixture until thick and clear, then pour topping over cooled pie. Allow topping to cool and set. Serve cheesecake chilled.

Yield: 1 8-inch pie

Tofu-Fruit Whips or Puddings

½ pound fresh
  strawberries,
  peaches, or
  pineapple
12 ounces fresh or
  homemade tofu,
  chilled
1 tablespoon honey
Chopped nutmeats or
  sunflower seeds
  (optional)

Combine all ingredients except nut-meats in blender and puree until smooth. If desired, top with nutmeats. Serve immediately in small dessert dishes or use as a topping for pancakes, crepes, or waffles.

Variations: Tofu-Strawberry Pudding: Use 10½ ounces of tofu, 1¼ cups of chopped strawberries or raspberries, ½ banana, 1 teaspoon of vanilla, and 3 ta-blespoons of honey. Puree as above. Serve chilled.

Tofu-Frozen Banana: Use 6 ounces of silken tofu, ¼ cup or more of water, 1½ chopped frozen bananas, and a dash of nutmeg. Serve immediately.

Serves 2

Tofu Dessert Soufflé[L]

2 tablespoons oil
2½ tablespoons whole wheat flour
¾ cup soy or dairy milk
6 ounces tofu, mashed
½ cup chopped roasted soybeans or peanuts
¼ teaspoon salt
3 tablespoons honey
½ cup raisins
4 egg yolks
4 egg whites, beaten until stiff
½ teaspoon butter or margarine

Preheat oven to 350° F. Heat a skillet and coat with oil. Add 2 tablespoons of flour and cook until lightly browned and fragrant. Add milk gradually, stirring constantly, to form a thick sauce; turn off heat. Add next 6 ingredients and mix well. Carefully fold mixture into egg whites. Coat a soufflé dish lightly with butter, then dust with remaining flour. Place soufflé mixture into dish and bake for 30–40 minutes or until set.

Serves 4

Baroque Tofu Cheesecake

Crust:

1½ cups buckwheat
flour

1½ cups brown rice
flour

¾ cup whole wheat
pastry flour

¾ cup oil

1½ teaspoons
cinnamon

1 teaspoon salt

3 tablespoons crushed
seeds

¾ cup apple juice or 5
cups crushed granola

Filling:

5 cups apple juice

1½ cups currants

3 pounds tofu

3–4 tablespoons
sesame butter

1½ tablespoons vanilla

1 cup tahini

1 cup brown rice flour

½ cup arrowroot flour

½ teaspoon sea salt

Juice of 1 orange + 3
tablespoons grated
rind, or use 2 lemons
instead

Preheat oven to 350° F.

Mix flours for crust and blend in oil with a fork. Add remaining ingredients and blend well. Crust will be very crumbly. Press dough into two cake pans 9 inches by 15 inches. Bake crust for 10 minutes; remove from oven immediately. Meanwhile, bring 5 cups apple juice to a boil with currants. Simmer for 1 minute, remove from heat, and let cool. Combine 1 pound of tofu, a few tablespoons of sesame butter, and 1½ cups of apple juice in blender. Pour into a bowl when creamy. Repeat process, gradually adding remaining ingredients so the batter is uniformly creamy.

Pour into pie crust and bake about 40 minutes or until top is firm and faintly browned around the edges. Cool completely before serving. This pie is best when made the day before.

Serves 24

Country Life Tofu Cheesecake

Crust:

5 cups finely ground granola

¼ pound soy margarine

Filling:

1 cup soymilk or 1 cup dry Soyagen + 1 cup water

20 ounces tofu

½ cup dry fructose

½ cup refined soy oil

1 tablespoon vanilla extract

1 teaspoon almond extract

2 teaspoons arrowroot powder

Topping

¾ cup apple juice concentrate

3 tablespoons arrowroot powder

6 cups fresh strawberries

Blend granola and margarine together in a bowl. Spread in oiled pie plate and bake at 350° F for 5 minutes. Blend filling ingredients in blender until smooth. Pour into pie crust. Bake at 350° F for 20 minutes. Mix ½ cup of juice concentrate with arrowroot. Simmer strawberries with ¼ cup of juice concentrate. Add arrowroot mixture and simmer for 15 minutes more. Pour topping over cheesecake and cool before slicing.

Serves 8

Tofu Orange Soufflé(L)

3¼ ounces orange juice
3½ ounces tofu,
   mashed
3 egg yolks
1 teaspoon chopped
   orange rind
2 ounces Grand Marnier
2 tablespoons honey
2 egg whites

Reduce orange juice by half and add mashed tofu, egg yolks, orange rind, Grand Marnier, and honey. Blend ingredients together well and place bowl in a hot-water bath, stirring constantly until a golden cream forms. Beat egg whites until stiff but not dry, and fold carefully into tofu mixture. Pour into a greased 4-inch soufflé dish and bake at 375° F until golden brown.

Serves 1

OTHER SPECIAL DESSERTS

Sesame Halvah

4 cups sesame seeds
2 cups bulgur
3 cups water
1 tablespoon vanilla
  extract
¾ cup sorghum
  molasses

Wash sesame seeds. Dry-roast until they become tan and begin to dance around in the skillet. Shake the pan and stir with a wooden spoon—you have to watch seeds carefully. Grind in blender or grain mill to a fine meal. Grind bulgur so it resembles coarse flour. Combine all ingredients. Oil a baking pan about 12 inches by 16 inches and pour batter into it. Bake in a preheated 375° F oven about 25 minutes or until sides are nicely browned. Score into rectangles by dividing the lengthwise side into 4 sections and make 6 crosswise divisions.

Yield: 24 pieces

Carob-Pecan Squares (L)

1 egg, beaten
⅓ cup oil
⅓ cup honey
¼ teaspoon salt
1 teaspoon vanilla
¾ cup whole wheat
  flour
½ cup broken pecans
½ cup carob chips

In a medium-size mixing bowl, blend together first 5 ingredients. Add flour and mix well. Stir in pecans and carob chips. Pour mixture into a greased baking pan 8 inches by 8 inches by 2 inches, spreading evenly. Bake at 400° F about 15 minutes or until lightly browned and mixture pulls away from sides of pan. Remove from oven and immediately cut into 16 squares. Cool in pan.

Yield: 16 squares

Oatmeal Bars^(L)

1 cup honey
1 cup butter or
  margarine, melted
2 eggs
2 teaspoons vanilla
1 cup whole wheat flour
4 cups rolled oats

In a medium-size mixing bowl, blend together first 4 ingredients. Stir in flour and oats, and mix well.

Spread mixture evenly in a greased baking pan 13 inches by 9¼ inches by 2 inches. Bake at 350° F for 25–30 minutes or until lightly browned. Remove from oven and immediately cut into 24 bars. Cool in pan.

Yield: 24 bars

Ginger-Coconut Drops^(L)

2 cups whole wheat
  flour
½ teaspoon salt
1 teaspoon ground
  ginger
1 cup grated
  unsweetened coconut
½ cup honey
½ cup oil
2 eggs, beaten
1 teaspoon vanilla

In a medium-size mixing bowl, mix together flour, salt, ginger, and coconut. Add remaining ingredients and mix well. Drop mixture by rounded teaspoonfuls onto oiled cookie sheets. Bake at 375° F about 10 minutes or until bottoms of cookies are golden brown. Immediately remove from cookie sheets and cool on wire rack.

Yield: about 3½ dozen

Gingerbread[(L)]

⅓ cup butter or
  margarine, softened
  to room temperature
1 cup molasses
1 egg
½ cup buttermilk
2 cups whole wheat
  flour
½ teaspoon salt
1½ teaspoons baking
  soda
1½ teaspoons ground
  ginger
¼ teaspoon ground
  cloves

In a medium-size mixing bowl, blend together butter and molasses. Add egg and buttermilk. Stir in half the flour, the remaining ingredients, then the other half of the flour until well combined. Pour mixture into a well-buttered baking pan 8 inches by 8 inches by 2 inches and bake at 350° F for 30–35 minutes or until a toothpick inserted in the center comes out clean. Cool in pan.

Serves 6

Baked Honey Custard[(L)]

2 cups milk
¼ cup honey
4 eggs
⅛ teaspoon salt
½ teaspoon nutmeg

Put all ingredients into a medium-size mixing bowl and beat with an electric or rotary beater until mixture is frothy and thoroughly combined. Divide mixture evenly among 6 buttered custard cups. Place cups on a cookie sheet. Bake at 300° F about 45 minutes or until a knife inserted in the center of custard comes out clean. Do not overbake. Serve hot, warm, or cold. Custard may be topped with fresh fruit if desired.

Serves 6

Cinnamon-Raisin Rice Pudding[(L)]

1 quart milk
½ cup uncooked brown
  rice
⅓ cup honey
¼ teaspoon salt
½ cup raisins
¼ teaspoon ground
  cinnamon
1 tablespoon butter or
  margarine

In a large saucepan, mix together first
4 ingredients. Cook, uncovered, over
medium-low heat, stirring occasionally,
about 2½ hours. About 20 minutes before pudding is done, add remaining ingredients. Continue cooking until milk
is absorbed and pudding is creamy.
Serve hot, warm, or cold.

Serves 6

Sprouted Wheat-Nut Cookies[(L)]

2 eggs
½ cup oil
½ cup honey
½ cup dry milk
½ cup wheat germ
2 tablespoons vanilla
1 cup chopped nuts
1 cup sesame seeds,
  unhulled
2 cups 5–6-day-old
  chopped wheat
  sprouts
2 cups whole wheat
  flour

Combine all ingredients in mixing
bowl. Mix thoroughly and drop onto an
oiled baking sheet with a teaspoon. Bake
at 350° F about 12–15 minutes.

Yield: 4 dozen

Indian Pudding (L)

1 quart fresh dairy or
  soy milk
1 cup yellow cornmeal
4 tablespoons butter or
  margarine
½ cup honey
⅓ cup molasses
¾ teaspoon salt
1 teaspoon ginger
½ teaspoon nutmeg
½ teaspoon cinnamon
½ cup raisins (optional)
3 eggs or 3
  tablespoons egg
  substitute

Bring milk to a boil and slowly sprinkle in cornmeal, stirring with a wire whisk to keep it smooth. Lower heat and cook until mixture thickens (about 10 minutes), then remove from heat. Add remaining ingredients except eggs and allow mixture to cool slightly. Blend in lightly beaten eggs and pour pudding into a buttered 2-quart baking dish. Bake in a preheated 325° F oven about 45 minutes to 1 hour or until pudding is firm. Serve warm or cold with yogurt, sour cream, or ice cream.

Serves 6

Corn Pudding (L)

3 cups fresh corn
  kernels
1 tablespoon cornstarch
1 teaspoon salt
Dash of mace
  (optional)
1 teaspoon honey or
  sugar
3 tablespoons butter or
  margarine, melted
1 cup milk
3 large eggs

In a bowl, combine corn, cornstarch, salt, mace, honey, and melted butter. For a lighter pudding, separate eggs, beat yolks with the milk, and add to corn mixture; then beat egg whites until stiff and fold them into corn mixture. Alternately, simply mix lightly beaten eggs into corn mixture. Turn mixture into a buttered 1½-quart baking dish and bake in a preheated 350° F oven about 30 minutes or until a knife inserted in the center comes out clean.

Serves 6

Applesauce Soufflé^(L)

1 ¼ cups unsweetened
  applesauce
1 tablespoon honey
½ teaspoon cinnamon
2 teaspoons raisins
3 egg whites

Preheat oven to 350° F. Blend apple-sauce with honey and cinnamon. Spoon 1 tablespoon of applesauce into bottom of each of 4 (6-ounce) custard cups. Top with raisins. Beat egg whites until stiff but not dry. Fold half into remaining applesauce and blend well. Fold remaining whites into applesauce very gently. Spoon into custard cups and sprinkle tops with cinnamon. Bake about 15–20 minutes, until puffed and browned. Serve immediately.

Serves 4

Poached Pear

2 pears, halved and
  cored but not peeled
½ cup apple juice
½ cup water
1 cinnamon stick
6 cloves, whole
2 pitted dates, thinly
  sliced
4 teaspoons plain low-
  fat yogurt
Cinnamon or nutmeg

Trim a small slice from the round side of pear halves so they will lie flat, cut side up. Place pears in a small skillet or saucepan. Add apple juice, water, cinnamon stick, and cloves. Cover, bring to a boil, reduce heat, and simmer gently about 5–10 minutes until pears are fork tender but not mushy or overcooked. Remove pears from pan to serving dishes. Keep warm. Add dates to pan juices and boil 5 minutes, uncovered. Spoon yogurt into pear core holes and spoon sauce over all. Sprinkle with cinnamon or nutmeg if desired. Serve warm or chilled.

Serves 4

Honey-Nut-Popcorn Crunch^(L)

½ cup butter or
  margarine, melted
½ cup honey
3 quarts corn, popped
1 cup chopped nuts

Preheat oven to 350° F. Blend butter and honey together and heat gently on the stove. Mix popcorn with nuts and pour the honey-butter mixture over all. Mix well. Spread on a cookie sheet in a thin layer. Bake for 10–15 minutes or until crisp. Wrap in small bundles when cool.

Yield: about 3 quarts broken nut crunch

Raisin-Nut Twigs

¼ cup raisins
⅓ cup apple juice
¼ cup dates
1 cup ground almonds
1 cup ground cashews
Finely grated
  unsweetened coconut

Place raisins in a small bowl and add apple juice to cover. Let soak overnight. The next day, blend raisins, juice, and dates in blender until well mixed. Add a bit more juice if needed. Mix fruit with ground nuts and form into sticks 2 inches long by ½ inch in diameter. Roll in coconut.

Yield: 1 dozen twigs

Carrot Halvah(L)

3 pounds carrots,
  grated
1 quart dairy or soy
  milk
10 cardamom seeds,
  ground
2 sticks cinnamon,
  broken in half
8 ounces honey
1 cup sweet butter or
  margarine
½ cup sliced almonds

Place grated carrots and milk in a saucepan. Add cardamom seeds, cinnamon sticks, and honey, and bring to a boil. Boil over low heat, stirring often, until mixture is very thick. Remove cinnamon sticks. Add sweet butter and simmer about 25 minutes more. Pour into a buttered pan. Cool to room temperature. Sprinkle with almonds. Cut into small squares and wrap.

Yield: about 4 pounds

Peanut Butter Cookies

¾ cup peanut butter
½ cup sorghum
¼ cup date sugar
⅓ cup oil
¼ teaspoon sea salt
1 teaspoon vanilla
1 cup whole wheat
  pastry flour

Preheat oven to 350° F. In a large bowl, combine all ingredients except flour; gradually mix flour in. Drop batter by teaspoonfuls onto a greased cookie sheet. Flatten each cookie with a fork. Bake 8–10 minutes.

Variation: Add chopped nuts or raisins to the batter.

Yield: 2 dozen

Carob Apple Brownies

1 cup finely chopped
  dates
1 cup grated apple
¾ cup oil
½ cup sunflower seeds
2 cups rolled oats
¾ cup carob powder

Combine dates, apple, and oil, mixing well. Add other ingredients and mix. Let stand 10 minutes for oats to absorb moisture. Press mix into an oiled pan; it should be 1 inch thick. Bake at 375° F about 25–30 minutes. Cut into squares when cool.

Yield: 2 dozen

Flan(L)

2 eggs
1 ¼ cups nonfat milk
1 tablespoon honey
1 teaspoon vanilla
Nutmeg to taste

Beat eggs. Add milk, honey, and vanilla, and blend well. Pour into 4 (6-ounce) custard cups. Sprinkle with nutmeg. Place in a baking pan with deep sides. Add hot water to ½ inch depth. Bake at 350° F about 40 minutes or until knife inserted in the center comes out clean.

Serves 4

Honey-Seed Mounds

⅓ cup honey
⅛ teaspoon salt
2 cups lightly toasted
  nuts, seeds, or
  coconut

Boil honey and salt until a drop forms a soft ball in cold water. Add nuts and mix well. Drop by tablespoons onto a platter.

Yield: 16–20 mounds

Fruit Cookies

1 whole coconut
1 cup raisins
1 cup dried apple
1 cup dried figs
1 cup prunes
2 bananas

Shred coconut and spread in pan. Grind dried fruits together and mix with banana. Pour into a pan and sprinkle with grated coconut. Refrigerate for several hours, then cut into pieces of desired size. Will keep in refrigerator for weeks.

Yield: 20–30 cookies

Soy Coffee Cake[L]

1 yeast cake dissolved in 4 tablespoons lukewarm water
1 cup soymilk
3 tablespoons oil
3 tablespoons sugar or honey
½ teaspoon salt
1 cup soy flour
3 cups whole wheat flour
1 egg, lightly beaten, or 1 tablespoon liquid lecithin
3 tablespoons brown sugar mixed with chopped nuts

Break yeast cake into water and let stand a few minutes. Heat milk until lukewarm, pour into a mixing bowl, and add oil, sugar, and salt. Stir and add dissolved yeast, ½ cup of soy flour, and 1 cup of whole wheat flour. Cover mixture and let stand until it bubbles, then add beaten egg, ½ cup of soy flour, and about 2 cups of whole wheat flour. Mix well and knead as for bread. Place dough in oiled bowl and let rise until double in bulk. Remove from bowl and knead slightly. Flatten with rolling pin and shape into 1-inch-thick loaf. Place in well-oiled cake pan, cover, and let rise until double in bulk. Brush top with melted butter, and sprinkle with brown sugar and nuts. Bake in a 350° oven for 30 minutes.

Yield: 1 loaf

Raisin-Carob-Peanut Cookies[(L)]

½ cup butter or
   margarine
¾ cup honey
½ cup peanut butter
1 egg
1 cup whole wheat flour
1 teaspoon salt
½ teaspoon soda
½ teaspoon baking
   powder
¼ cup milk
1 teaspoon vanilla
3 cups rolled oats
1½ cups peanuts
1 cup raisins and 1
   teaspoon cinnamon
   or 1 cup carob chips

Cream together butter and honey, then mix in peanut butter and egg. In a separate bowl, combine flour, salt, soda, and baking powder. Add flour mixture to butter mixture along with milk and vanilla. Stir in rolled oats and peanuts. Add raisins and cinnamon, or add carob chips. Drop by spoonfuls on a greased cookie sheet and bake at 325° F for 15 minutes.

Yield: 20–30 cookies

Fruit Kabobs with Strawberry Dip[(L)]

Kabobs:
12 (1 cup) fresh
   strawberries or
   watermelon balls
12 (1 cup) fresh
   pineapple chunks
½ honeydew melon

Dip:
½ cup fresh strawberries
   (or frozen with no
   sugar)
½ cup plain low-fat
   yogurt
1 teaspoon honey

Place strawberries and pineapple chunks on picks. To make dip, combine ½ cup of strawberries with yogurt and honey in blender. Whirl until smooth. Use half of honeydew melon as serving dish. Place fruit kabobs around cut edge and fill center with strawberry dip.

Serves 4

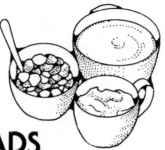

LUNCH SPREADS

Make It Simple and Quick

Very few people have either the time or the inclination to spend hours in the kitchen preparing lunches for themselves or their family. This fact becomes increasingly clear as you grope around the kitchen at 6:00 A.M. on Monday morning. Who wants to think about lunch? Thinking about breakfast can be an effort.

The keys to portable lunchtime meals without chaos are planning and quantity preparation. Know what your family enjoys, and focus your planning accordingly. Spice can add zest to many spreads and dips. Experiment!

Many people make spreads and dressings in advance and store them until needed. Some families make it a practice to set aside an hour one evening a week or on a Sunday afternoon to make spreads and prepare lunches. It makes sense to spend the time one evening rather than use four mornings gathering items for the blender and cleaning up four separate times.

Since lunchtime planning and preparation is a family affair, children should always be welcome in the kitchen. Even younger children can help with simple tasks.

Note: The symbol **(L)** is used next to those recipe titles that include some form of dairy product. All other recipes are vegan in nature; that is, they contain no meat, eggs, or milk products.

In addition to spreads and freshly made bottled juices, keep cut, wrapped pieces of cheese, carrot sticks, and celery stalks in the refrigerator's crisper. Morning commotion and tension are often alleviated when the prepared brown bag components are in the refrigerator the night before.

For more lunchtime ideas, don't neglect *Laurel's Kitchen* and *The Book of Tofu,* which offer recipes for making bread, tofu, and many other lunchtime goodies. Look at your favorite cookbooks, and let them inspire you.

Often, however, you won't need a cookbook to devise a tasty lunchtime treat—the blender, some vegetables in the refrigerator and a pinch of spice and you're off to a galloping gourmet meal. The recipes that follow are simple; few require cooking. They serve as a starting point for your own epicurean delights.

Chick-Pea Spread

2 pounds chick-peas (garbanzo beans)
1 teaspoon crushed cumin seeds
1 large onion, chopped
3 large scallions, chopped
1 teaspoon paprika
1 teaspoon salt
Dash of cayenne pepper
1–2 tablespoons matzo meal (optional)

Cook chick-peas and reserve water. In blender or food processor, blend all ingredients until smooth. If you find that the spread is too thick, add a small amount of reserved water. If the spread is too thin, add matzo meal. Refrigerate until ready to use. To serve, spread mixture on whole-grain bread, pita, or bagel. Garnish with tomato, cucumber, squash, or cheese slices, or sprouts.

Serves 6

Avocado Spread or Dressing [L]

1 large avocado,
  peeled and chopped
1 cup cottage cheese
3 large scallions,
  chopped
3 fresh parsley sprigs
Dash of cayenne
  pepper
Salt and pepper to taste

In blender or food processor, blend all ingredients until smooth. Refrigerate until ready to use. To serve, spread mixture on whole-grain bread, pita, or bagel. Garnish with tomatoes, lettuce, cucumber, or squash slices, or sprouts. For the calorie conscious, this can be eaten minus the bread.
Serves 4

Tofu-Tahini Spread

8 ounces tofu,
  squeezed
3 ounces tahini
1 teaspoon Miso Instant
  Cup of Soup Mix
Salt and pepper to taste

In blender or food processor, blend all ingredients until smooth. Refrigerate until ready to use. To serve, spread thickly on whole-grain bread, pita, or bagel. Garnish with tomatoes, sprouts, cucumber, cheese, or squash slices. This can also be used with a jam or jelly sandwich, a special favorite of children.
Serves 4–5

Spicy Tofu-Banana-Apple Spread

8 ounces tofu,
  squeezed
2 large bananas,
  peeled and sliced
2 Granny Smith apples
  or other variety, sliced
½ teaspoon cinnamon
Dash of nutmeg
Dash of cloves

In blender or food processor, blend all ingredients until smooth. Refrigerate until ready to use. To serve, spread tofu-banana-apple mixture on whole-grain bread, pita, or bagel. Garnish with sprouts or use with jam or jelly. For the calorie conscious, this can be eaten minus the bread.
Serves 4

Curried Tofu Spread or Dressing (L)

8 ounces tofu, squeezed
8 ounces cottage cheese
1 tablespoon curry blend
1 teaspoon paprika
3 large scallions, chopped
½ teaspoon ground black pepper
1 teaspoon snipped chives

In blender or food processor, blend all ingredients until smooth. Refrigerate until ready to use. To serve, spread mixture on whole-grain bread, pita, or bagel. Garnish with tomato, cheese, cucumber, or squash slices and sprouts.

Serves 5–6

The Devil's Egg Salad (L)

8 hard-cooked eggs, shelled and sliced
Salt to taste
5 tablespoons mayonnaise
1 teaspoon paprika
1 teaspoon curry
1 teaspoon ground black pepper
½ teaspoon dry mustard powder
3 fresh parsley sprigs

In blender or food processor, blend eggs and seasonings until smooth. Keep refrigerated until ready to use. To serve, spread egg salad thickly on whole-grain bread, pita, or bagel. This can also be eaten as an open-face sandwich. Garnish with tomato slices, sprouts, and lettuce. For the calorie conscious, omit the bread and serve on beds of lettuce with sprouts and tomato.

Serves 4

Tofu Eggless "Egg Salad"

2 pounds tofu
½ cup mayonnaise
2 tablespoons prepared
  mustard
1 teaspoon natural soy
  sauce
½ teaspoon salt
½ teaspoon garlic
  powder
¼ teaspoon turmeric
½ teaspoon celery
  seeds
Pinch of black pepper
2 stalks celery, minced
½ cup scallions, minced
1 green pepper,
  minced (optional)
1 carrot, minced or
  grated (optional)

Press water out of tofu and place in bowl. Break up with fork. Add other ingredients. Chill.

Whipped Spread for Toast, Muffin, or Bread(L)

¼ cup spring water
¼ cup cold-pressed
  vegetable oil
2 sticks (½ pound)
  butter, at room
  temperature

In blender or food processor, blend all ingredients until smooth. When mixture is whipped smooth, store in a refrigerator container. The spread maintains its soft, margarinelike consistency but without all the hydrogenated fat of margarine.

Yield: 1 cup

Broccoli-Tofu Spread

8 ounces broccoli, chopped (florets and stems)
1 large onion, chopped
1 large scallion, chopped
8 ounces tofu, squeezed
½ teaspoon ground black pepper
½ teaspoon paprika
½ cup Miso Instant Cup of Soup Mix
Salt to taste

In blender or food processor, blend all ingredients until smooth. Add 1–2 tablespoons of water if mixture becomes too thick. Refrigerate until ready to use. To serve, spread on whole-grain bread, pita, or bagel. Garnish with tomatoes, sprouts, cheese, cucumber, or squash slices.

Serves 5–6

Peanut Butter Spread

1 cup natural peanut butter
¼ cup roasted sunflower seeds
½ cup chopped dried fruit
1 teaspoon orange juice
2 tablespoons unsweetened applesauce
1 tablespoon brewer's yeast
1 tablespoon dolomite or calcium lactate powder

Mix all ingredients in blender until desired consistency is reached. Refrigerate.

Serves 4

Vegetable-Spread Sandwiches[L]

1 pound cream cheese,
  softened to room
  temperature
2 tablespoons onion
  powder
½ cup shredded
  cucumber, with
  moisture squeezed
  out after measuring
½ cup shredded carrot
2 tablespoons milk
¼ teaspoon salt
16 slices whole wheat
  bread (not thick-
  sliced)

Put all ingredients except bread in a medium-size mixing bowl and blend well. Cover and chill several (up to 48) hours. Spread mixture on half the bread slices, being sure to spread all the way to the edges. Top with remaining slices.

Serves 8

Pimiento-Soy Spread

2 cups water
2 cups soy flour
1 teaspoon salt
2 tablespoons lemon
  juice
1 4-ounce jar pimientos
Soy oil to thicken
2–3 tablespoons yeast
  flakes (optional)

Liquify and double boil water, soy flour, and salt for 1 hour. Put 1 cup of mixture in blender. Add lemon juice and pimientos. Blend until smooth, then add soy oil to thicken or yeast flakes if stiffer spread is desired. Put in shallow cups and store in refrigerator to set. Good on crackers or as sandwich spread.

Serves 4

Clubhouse Sandwich with Fried Tofu

1 7-ounce cake firm tofu
3 tablespoons oil
¼ cup whole wheat flour
Butter or margarine
3 slices whole wheat toast
⅓ cup ketchup
½ teaspoon mustard
3 small lettuce leaves, cut into halves, or 1 cup alfalfa sprouts
6 tomato slices and/or dill pickle slices

Cut tofu horizontally into thirds, then crosswise into halves to make 6 slices. Place tofu slices between double layers of dish toweling and allow to stand for 5 minutes while texture firms. Heat a skillet and coat with oil. Dust tofu slices with flour, then fry for 2–3 minutes on each side or until golden brown. Butter whole wheat toast and cut crosswise into halves. Combine ketchup and mustard in a small bowl, mixing well, then spread half of the mixture on each of the 6 slices of buttered toast. Top each slice with lettuce (or sprouts) and a slice of fried tofu, spreading remainder of ketchup-mustard mixture on top of tofu. Serve open-faced, each portion topped with a tomato slice.

Serves 2

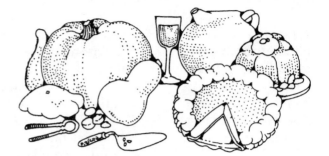

HOLIDAY MENUS

The fall and winter holidays are times for festive entertaining. We have included menus and recipes that cover the important ones, as well as a fine section on beverages and snacks in order to make these occasions something special.

Since these are busy days, it is helpful to keep on hand foods that can be prepared ahead of time to serve when needed and foods that can be produced at the last minute.

Staples for entertaining that you might want to stock up on include: whole-grain crackers and breads, raw nuts and seeds, nut butters, homemade spreads and dips (or the ingredients for them), fresh raw vegetables to be served with them, fresh and dried fruits, and a variety of juices and herb teas.

Peggy Crump, a veteran author for *Vegetarian Times,* suggests that dips be made the day before to save entertaining time. Almost all of them (except the hot ones) taste better if they are chilled and given a little time to allow the flavors to blend. And dips can double as spreads or fondues.

Nuts and seeds can be served raw or toasted alone or in combi-

Note: The symbol (L) is used next to those recipe titles that include some form of dairy product. All other recipes are vegan in nature; that is, they contain no meat, eggs, or milk products.

nation. Dried fruits are especially handy now in making breads, desserts, and candies, and of course are delicious served just as they are.

With a little planning you can spend less time in the kitchen and more time enjoying your guests. The following recipes are designed to help you do that.

SEDER MENU

Vegetable Broth with Matzo Balls
Stuffed Lettuce with Tomato Sauce
Potato-Almond Loaf with White Sauce
Linzer Torte
Fruit and Nuts

Vegetable Broth

(See recipe on page 73.)

Matzo Balls(L)

3 tablespoons butter or margarine, melted
1 cup matzo meal*
½ cup boiling water
1 egg, beaten

Add melted butter to matzo meal. Stir in boiling water. Allow to cool. Stir in eggs, mixing completely. Chill thoroughly in refrigerator. Dip hands in cold water and form mixture into 1-inch balls. Drop into boiling soup and simmer 15 minutes before serving.
Serves 4

* To make whole wheat matzo meal, grind one of the available brands of kosher whole wheat matzo in blender.

Stuffed Lettuce

1 head romaine lettuce
1 medium onion
12 tablespoons
  vegetable oil
4 large carrots, grated
½ cup chopped walnuts
½ cup matzo farfel
1 8-ounce can tomato
  sauce

Wash about 20 large outer leaves of lettuce and place in freezer. When frozen, remove from freezer and rinse quickly under hot tap water; this renders them pliable for stuffing. Meanwhile, slice onion thinly and sauté in oil until transparent; combine with carrots, nuts, and farfel. Place 1 tablespoon of mixture at base of leaf and roll up, tucking in edges. Place rolls in oiled baking pan as you finish them. Pour tomato sauce over stuffed leaves and bake at 375° F for 30 minutes.

Serves 4

Potato-Almond Loaf (L)

1 medium onion
1 cup thinly sliced
  mushrooms
4 tablespoons
  margarine or butter
4 medium potatoes
1 cup sliced almonds
1 egg
1 cup milk powder
1 cup slivered almonds

Slice onion thinly and sauté with mushrooms in margarine until transparent. Wash and grate potatoes. Mix all ingredients thoroughly and turn into greased loaf pan 9 inches by 5 inches. Bake at 375° F for 1 hour.

Serves 4

Linzer Torte[(L)]

½ cup margarine or
  butter
1 cup matzo meal
1 cup ground almonds
⅜ cup sugar
1 egg
Strawberry jam

Cut margarine into matzo meal. Add remaining ingredients except strawberry jam and work with fingers to form a stiff dough. Reserve a ball of dough, about ⅕ of total. Press larger part of dough into 8-inch-round flan dish or cake pan, covering bottom and forming edges ½-inch high. Spoon strawberry jam into crust, covering bottom evenly. Roll reserved dough into pencil-thin strips and use to form a latticework over jam. Bake at 350° F for 45 minutes.

Serves 4

THANKSGIVING MENU I

Noodle Soup
Stuffed Squash with Gluten Gravy
Cranberry Applesauce
Candied Sweet Potatoes
Tossed Salad
Marinated Beets
Pumpkin Pie

Noodle Soup

8 cups gluten stock or water
1 piece kombu seaweed (about 6 inches by 3 inches)
2 onions, thinly sliced
2 carrots, thinly sliced
1 parsley root with top
2 teaspoons salt
4 ounces whole wheat ribbon noodles

Bring stock to a boil. Drop in seaweed and simmer for 10 minutes. Remove seaweed and add vegetables and salt. Simmer for 40 minutes in a covered pot. Add noodles and cook until tender. Remove parsley root. Season to taste with soy sauce or miso if desired.

Serves 4–6

Stuffed Squash

1 large squash
(hubbard, buttercup,
or 2–3 acorn squash)
2 tablespoons olive oil
3 onions, minced
6 celery stalks (with
leaves)
1 teaspoon salt
1 cup soup stock or
water
1 cup chestnuts, cooked
and mashed*
3 cups cooked brown
rice, millet, or bulgur†
Cayenne pepper to
taste
1 teaspoon paprika
1 teaspoon crushed
sage
½ cup toasted and
chopped almonds

* *Pureed Chestnuts*
1 cup dried chestnuts

Split squash in half and scoop out seeds and membrane. (These can be used in other recipes; they are quite delicious roasted.) Heat 1 tablespoon oil in a skillet and sauté onion. When it is lightly browned, add celery and sauté a few minutes more. Add salt and ½ cup of water. Simmer for 10 minutes. Combine with remaining stuffing ingredients. Fill squash cavities and brush sides with remaining oil. Place in a roasting pan and cover the whole pan with foil. Bake at 350° F for 1–2 hours. (Hubbard squash usually takes much longer to bake than acorn.)

Variation: Tamari soy sauce can be used to season squash.

Serves 6

Soak chestnuts overnight in several cups of water. Cook chestnuts until soft. If pressure cooking, allow about 30 minutes; regular cooking will take about 1 hour. Chestnuts can be prepared a day or two ahead of time if necessary. Drain and puree in blender, adding cooking liquid as needed, or put through food mill or grinder.

† If desired, you can cook rice and chestnuts together. Pressure-cook 1¼ cups of rice with ½ cup of dried chestnuts and 3½ cups of water for 45 minutes. Or boil for 50 minutes, increasing water to 4 cups.

Gluten Gravy with Seitan

8 cups starch water from first kneading of gluten (see recipe on page 192)
2 tablespoons sesame oil
2 onions, chopped
½ pound mushrooms, thinly sliced
2 tablespoons minced fresh parsley
1 teaspoon crushed basil
¼ teaspoon ground coriander
2 cups chopped seitan (recipe follows)
Tamari soy sauce

Heat gluten water in a large pot and let simmer, stirring occasionally. Meanwhile, heat sesame oil in a separate pan and sauté onions until golden. Add mushrooms and sauté until well browned. Add vegetables to gluten stock. Bring to a boil, then lower flame and simmer for 45 minutes. Add remaining ingredients. Simmer for 30–40 minutes more. For a thick gravy, blend ¼ cup of arrowroot or unbleached flour in some cooled stock, return to pan, and cook a few minutes more. Season to taste with additional soy sauce.

Yield: 2½ quarts

Seitan

1 tablespoon sesame oil
1 tablespoon minced fresh ginger root
1 cup soy sauce
1 cup water
1 small piece kombu seaweed
5 cups cold gluten

Heat oil in a large skillet or heavy saucepan. Add ginger and sauté. Add soy sauce, water, and seaweed, bring to a boil. Drop in pieces of gluten and simmer over low heat in a covered pot about 2–3 hours or until gluten is dark and soft. Stir frequently to prevent sticking.

Seitan is a perfect sandwich filling— try it with a touch of mustard, a generous bed of alfalfa sprouts, and a pickle or two. You can put the seitan hunks in stews and casseroles.

Serves 4–6

Cranberry Applesauce

1 pound fresh
   cranberries
1 cup apple cider
⅛ teaspoon sea salt
3 pounds small red
   apples, cored and
   chopped
½ cup currants or raisins
1 tablespoon lemon
   juice
Grated lemon or
   orange rind

Rinse cranberries in cold water and sort out spoiled fruit. Bring apple cider to a boil in a deep, heavy saucepan or pressure cooker and add salt and cranberries. Boil until cranberries begin to pop. Add remaining ingredients and cover. Simmer for 20 minutes; if pressure cooking, 10 minutes. Puree sauce if desired.

Yield: 7 cups

Candied Sweet Potatoes

6 good-size sweet
   potatoes
1 tablespoon oil
½ pound dates, pitted
   and mashed
1 cup water or orange
   juice
Ground cloves to taste
Grated orange rind

Bake sweet potatoes in an oiled casserole until soft. Split and place faceup in pan. Combine dates and remaining ingredients in a heavy saucepan and cook until thick, stirring occasionally. Spread date mixture over potatoes. Place pan under broiler and cook until top is bubbly and beginning to caramelize.

Serves 6

Tossed Salad

1 head romaine lettuce
4 ounces fresh alfalfa
 sprouts
½ cup black olives or
 Greek-style olives
1 green pepper, cut into
 rings
1 cup cherry tomatoes
 or small bunch red
 radishes, sliced
¼ head red cabbage,
 thinly sliced or
 shredded
Several handfuls of
 toasted sesame or
 sunflower seeds or ¼
 pound feta cheese,
 crumbled, or 8
 ounces tofu, baked
 and cubed

Instead of serving a cooked vegetable with this rather rich meal, a crisp salad really compliments everything much better. A light lemon-and-oil dressing is recommended.

Serves 4–6

Marinated Beets

1 pound small red
 beets
3 medium onions
2 sprigs fresh dill or 1
 teaspoon dill seed
1 bay leaf
3 tablespoons rice or
 apple cider vinegar
 (good quality, 4–6
 percent acidity)
3 tablespoons oil
2 tablespoons salt
Water

Scrub beets and thinly slice. Thinly slice onions. Place all ingredients into a large jar and pour in enough water so that the vegetables are completely submerged. Let marinate at least 48 hours.

Serves 6

Pumpkin Pie

Crust:
- 1½ cups rolled oats (not the thick type)
- ¾ cup brown rice flour
- ½ teaspoon sea salt
- ⅓ cup safflower or sesame oil
- 3 tablespoons apple juice, approximately
- 2 tablespoons crushed sesame or sunflower seeds

Filling:
- 5–6 pounds sweet fall buttercup or butternut squash*
- 1 tablespoon sesame oil
- ½ teaspoon sea salt
- 2 cups apple juice
- 1 cup chestnuts, pureed
- 2 tablespoons arrowroot flour
- ¼ cup tahini
- ½ teaspoon cinnamon
- ½ teaspoon ground cloves
- ½ teaspoon ginger
- ¼ teaspoon nutmeg (optional)

For crust, mix together first 4 ingredients. Dough should be crumbly. Add juice and seeds. The dough will be soft and does not require rolling. Simply spread crust into a pie pan and press edges firmly with your fingers to smooth it out. Bake in a 375° F oven about 10 minutes or until lightly browned.

For filling, scrub squash thoroughly. Using a heavy knife, cut in half and scoop out seeds, then quarter and cut into chunks. (The seeds are good to eat; simply wash, spread on a cookie sheet, and bake when you make the pie.)

Heat oil in a large, heavy skillet and sauté squash over a high flame for 10 minutes. Add salt and juice. Bring to a boil, then cover, lower flame, and steam for 45 minutes or until tender. (If pressure cooking, 15 minutes is enough time.)

Drain liquid and reserve. Mash pulp and mix in remaining ingredients and enough cooking liquid to make a puddinglike consistency. Cook a few more minutes to blend flavors.

Pour filling into crust and bake in a 350° F oven for 25 minutes. This pie is delicious served hot or cold and can be frozen.

Yield: 1 pie

* Regular pumpkin is too watery for pie filling; commerical canned pumpkin is actually made from squash.

THANKSGIVING MENU II

Carrot Soup

Vegetable Key with Brown Gravy

Walnut-Pecan Mold

Yams in Pineapple Sauce

Mincemeatless Pie

Holiday Pudding

Carrot Soup (L)

1 pound carrots
6 cups water
Nutmeg and pepper to taste
2 tablespoons butter or margarine

Wash carrots and remove tops and ends. Slice into medium to thin rounds. Add just enough water to cover plus ½ inch and cook over low to medium heat until soft (test by seeing if fork can easily be inserted and withdrawn). Remove from heat and let cool slightly. In 2 or 3 batches, puree carrots in blender or food processor, or push through a large strainer, using water they were cooked in. Return pureed carrots to pot, add water until desired thinness is reached, and heat. (Milk or cream can be substituted for water for a richer taste. If using milk or cream, be careful not to let soup come to a boil.) Add nutmeg and pepper (fresh-grated if possible). Add butter just in time for it to melt before serving.

Serves 6

Vegetable Key^(L)

Group I—Beans and Grain Mixture:

3 cups lentils, cooked (retain excess cooking water)
3 cups brown rice, cooked (slightly overcooked)
1 cup whole wheat bread, crumbled
½ cup rolled oats or cornmeal, uncooked
¼ pound butter, melted
1 cup walnuts, finely ground
½ cup sunflower seeds, finely ground
⅓ cup tamari

Group II—Garbanzo Beans:

2 cups garbanzo beans, cooked (optional)

Group III—Stuffing Mixture:

4 tablespoons butter or margarine
1 tablespoon mustard seeds
1 bunch celery, coarsely chopped
6 cups whole wheat bread crumbs
1 teaspoon thyme
½ teaspoon savory
1 tablespoon sage

1. Retain cooking water from cooked lentils to use as instructed later. Combine all ingredients in Group I. Make sure all are well mixed together. Use your hands or a large mixing spoon. You could use blender or food processor, but it might make mixture too liquid. Set mixture aside.

2. In a separate bowl, mash garbanzo beans into a thick, mushy consistency. (This can be done in blender or food processor with a minimum amount of liquid; use some bean cooking water.)

3. Assemble Group III ingredients as follows: Melt butter and sauté mustard seeds until they pop. Add celery and sauté until soft. Add bread crumbs and enough water to moisten. (Use lentil or bean cooking water. Be careful to add it slowly, and check a minute or so later to see if enough has been added, since bread will take a brief time to absorb the liquid.) Cook for 5 minutes more, then add seasonings. Remove from heat and add water chestnuts and bean sprouts if desired.

4. Put a thin layer, about ½ inch thick of beans-grain mixture on a greased baking pan. Mound handfuls of stuffing mixture on top, patting into a rounded mound or any other desired shape. Take handfuls of remainder of beans-grain mixture and pat between hands until flat. Place over stuffing, sealing it in entirely. Take garbanzo bean mixture and, in a similar fashion, place over beans-grain mixture.

Black pepper to taste
2 teaspoons tamari
8 ounces water
   chestnuts, thickly
   sliced (optional)
1 cup mung bean
   sprouts (optional)

Group IV—Tofu
   Covering:
8 pieces fairly firm tofu
¼ pound butter or
   margarine, melted
Paprika

5. Cut tofu pieces thinly widthwise and place on top and all around mounded ingredients, using toothpicks to hold in place. Pour melted butter onto tofu (or spread with pastry brush) and sprinkle with paprika. Cover with aluminum foil, bake at 350° F for 15 minutes so that tofu can slightly crisp. Serve with gravy and all fixings.

Serves 8–10

Brown Gravy(L)

¼ pound (1 stick) butter
   or margarine
1 cup whole wheat flour
4 cups water, bean
   liquid, or vegetable
   broth
½ cup tamari
2 tablespoons basil

Melt butter in a double boiler over medium flame or in a heavy saucepan over low flame. Stir in flour and let cook for 5 minutes, stirring so it won't burn. Add liquid very slowly. Make sure gravy stays smooth and well combined at all times; stirring with a whisk helps. Add tamari and basil. Cook for 10 minutes more. Serve hot.

Yield: 4 cups

Walnut-Pecan Mold[(L)]

2 celery stalks, finely chopped
½ onion, finely chopped
1 carrot, finely chopped
2 tablespoons parsley, finely chopped
1 cup coarsely ground walnuts
1 cup coarsely ground pecans
1½ cups bread crumbs
2 tablespoons soy sauce
1½ cups plain yogurt
3 eggs, lightly beaten

Preheat oven to 375° F and oil a 2-quart mold. Mix vegetables, nuts and bread crumbs. Mix soy sauce, yogurt, and eggs. Add soy mixture to nuts mixture, stirring well. Spread in mold and bake for 1 hour or until loaf pulls away from mold. Allow to cool in mold for 10 minutes. Loosen and unmold onto bed of greens. Serve with sauce.

Serves 6–8

Yams in Pineapple Sauce[(L)]

8 large yams or sweet potatoes
4 tablespoons butter or margarine
½ cup honey
1 can crushed pineapple
2 teaspoons arrowroot or cornstarch

Scrub yams and bake until soft. Allow to cool and remove skins, then mash and set aside. Melt butter and stir in honey and pineapple. Dissolve arrowroot in 2 tablespoons of water and stir into pineapple mixture. Cook over low flame, stirring constantly, until mixture thickens. Stir into mashed yams. Bake at 250° F about 20 minutes.

Serves 6

Mincemeatless Pie

½ cup adzukis beans
2 tablespoons oil
2½ cups chopped
  apples
1 teaspoon salt
½ teaspoon cinnamon
1 cup strong molasses
2 cups water
1½ cup raisins
1 tablespoon minced
  lemon rind
¼ teaspoon ground
  cloves
¼ teaspoon ground
  nutmeg

Soak beans in water overnight, then simmer in same water for 1 or 2 hours until tender. In a large pot, stir oil and apples until apples are coated, then add remaining ingredients except beans. Heat and simmer, covered, for 15–20 minutes, boiling off any remaining liquid. Pour into baked whole wheat pie crust and bake for 15–20 minutes in a preheated 350° F oven.

Serves 8

Holiday Pudding

½ cup raisins
½ pound prunes
½ cup Sultana raisins
½ cup currants
Juice and rind of 1
  lemon
½ cup grape juice
Agar-agar flakes to
  thicken
½ cup blanched sweet
  almonds

Soak all fruit for 24 hours. Cook prunes in water in which fruit has soaked to make 1 cup of prune pulp. Bring fruit juice and grape juice to a boil while adding agar-agar flakes to thicken. Add fruit and almonds. Set in a mold. Chill. Serve with whipped cream.

Serves 4–6

Elegant Stuffed Pumpkin(L)

1 5-pound pumpkin
2–3 cups brown rice, cooked
2 cups crumbled dry whole wheat bread (or part corn bread, et cetera)
1 onion, chopped
½–1 cup chopped celery and leaves
2 apples (tart and unpeeled), chopped
1 cup roasted chestnuts or a handful of cashew nuts, cut in half
Sage, savory, marjoram, oregano, and paprika to taste
1–2 cups vegetable stock
¼–½ cup butter, melted, or safflower oil
Soy sauce or salt to taste

Cut off top of pumpkin to make a lid. Remove seeds and scrape out any stringy pulp. Combine dry ingredients in a large mixing bowl and mix well with hands. Add stock and butter, and mix well, adding soy sauce or salt if desired. Stuffing should be moist but not wet. Pack loosely into pumpkin, replace lid, and bake on an oiled cookie sheet for 1½ hours or more at 325° F. It is done when a fork pushes easily through the pumpkin. Transfer to a casserole dish and serve at the table, scooping out some of the tender pumpkin flesh with each serving of stuffing. If the pumpkin is organically grown, you may eat the skin too. (If you have too much stuffing for your pumpkin, place extra in an oiled casserole, cover, and bake for 1 hour.)

Serves 5–6

Cream of Pumpkin Soup^(L)

1½ pounds fresh pumpkin
½ cup chopped onion
1½ tablespoons soy sauce or miso
¼–½ teaspoon nutmeg or fresh grated ginger (optional)
Chopped parsley, yogurt, or whole wheat croutons (garnish)

Cut pumpkin into large chunks and steam in a vegetable steamer until tender, about 15 minutes. Reserve cooking water. Scoop pumpkin from its skin and puree with cooking water in blender or food mill. Return puree to pot. Add chopped onion and additional water if necessary. Bring soup to a boil, then simmer for 15 minutes. Just before serving, stir in soy sauce or miso; if you use miso, cream with a few tablespoons of water before adding, and remember not to boil it or its healthy enzymes will be destroyed. Add nutmeg or ginger if desired. This soup can also be made with any winter squash.

Serves 4–6

Pumpkin Sauce^(L)

Reheat leftover Cream of Pumpkin Soup and serve as a sauce for brown rice, millet, noodles, a nut loaf, et cetera.

Pumpkin Butter

4 cups pureed
   pumpkin*
½–1 cup honey
1 tablespoon cinnamon
¼ teaspoon ginger
½ teaspoon ground
   cloves
2–3 tablespoons lemon
   juice

Combine pureed pumpkin with remaining ingredients in a heavy saucepan and cook over low heat for 45–60 minutes, stirring often. Taste and adjust seasonings. Mixture should be thick and smooth. Pour simmering butter into hot, sterilized canning jars and seal immediately. You can skip the canning procedure if you make a small amount; it will keep in the refrigerator several weeks. This is a delicious spread for toast or muffins.

Serves 12

* For puree, simmer about 1½ pounds of peeled and diced pumpkin in a little water or steam in a vegetable steamer until tender. Puree in blender with a small amount of cooking water.

Tofu Pumpkin Pie

½ pound tofu
2 cups pureed pumpkin
   (preferably fresh)
6 tablespoons honey
2 tablespoons molasses
½ teaspoon powdered
   ginger
1 teaspoon cinnamon
¼ teaspoon cloves or
   nutmeg
1 tablespoon whole
   wheat flour
1 prebaked 9-inch
   whole wheat pie crust

Preheat oven to 350° F. Process all ingredients in blender or food processor until very smooth. Pour into prebaked pie shell and bake for 35–40 minutes. Chill for 2 hours before serving. Serve pie topped with Tofu Creme (see recipe that follows).

Serves 8

Tofu Creme

1 pound firm or pressed tofu
2–4 tablespoons cashews
½ cup water
4–6 tablespoons honey or maple syrup
1½ teaspoons vanilla
¼ teaspoon cinnamon (optional)

Steam tofu for 3–4 minutes in a vegetable steamer, then cool. Whirl nuts in blender until finely powdered; add water to make cashew milk. Reserve half of the milk. Add remaining ingredients to blender and process until very smooth, adding more cashew milk if necessary.

Yield: 2½ cups

Tofu-Pumpkin Tart (L)

Filling:
3 eggs
8¾ ounces tofu, pressed
3¼ ounces honey
3 tablespoons lemon juice
1 vanilla bean
5¼ ounces cooked pumpkin puree

Crust:
7 ounces carob coconut granola
1¾ ounces soy margarine, melted
1 tablespoon honey

Whip eggs in food processor until foamy. While processor is running, add tofu in small pieces, as well as pumpkin puree, honey, lemon juice, and vanilla. Blend until smooth.

To make the crust, put carob coconut granola into food processor and blend until coarse. Mix with melted margarine and honey, and press into an 8-inch tart pan. Pour filling into prepared crust and bake at 350° F for 40–45 minutes.

When tart is completely baked, allow to cool for at least 1 hour before serving.

Serves 8

Pumpkin Seed Snacks

1 cup pumpkin seeds
1 teaspoon safflower oil
½ teaspoon soy sauce
** or salt**
¼ teaspoon garlic
** powder**
Paprika to taste

Clean pulp from seeds, and wash seeds if necessary. Brush oil on a cookie sheet, place seeds on sheet, and roast in a 350° F oven until they begin to turn golden, about 10 minutes. Add remaining ingredients and stir to coat seeds. Bake until crispy, about 10–15 minutes more. You may roast any squash seeds in this manner.

Serves 4–6

Pumpkin-Rice Pudding (L)

2 cups pumpkin or
** winter squash,**
** cooked**
1 cup milk or water
3–5 tablespoons honey
1 tablespoon tahini
1½ teaspoons pumpkin
** pie spice**
1–2 eggs
2 cups brown rice,
** cooked**
½ cup raisins

Blend pumpkin, milk, honey, tahini, pumpkin pie spice, and eggs until smooth. Combine with rice and raisins. Pour into a greased casserole and place in a pan of hot water. Bake at 350° F for 1 hour or until an inserted knife comes out clean. Serve warm or chilled, with yogurt if desired. This makes a great breakfast as well as a satisfying dessert.

Serves 6

HOLIDAY SNACKS

Citrus Punch

2 cups orange juice
2 cups grapefruit juice
2 tablespoons lemon
  juice
¼ cup honey (optional)

Stir all ingredients together until thoroughly combined. Serve over ice in tall glasses.

Yield: slightly more than 1 quart

Roasted Almonds

2 cups almonds, whole
  and unblanched
1 tablespoon cold-
  pressed oil
2 tablespoons tamari
  soy sauce
¼ teaspoon garlic
  powder

Put almonds in a baking pan 8 inches by 8 inches by 2 inches. Add oil, soy sauce, and garlic powder, and stir until almonds are evenly coated. Shake almonds into a single layer and bake at 350° F for 25–30 minutes or until roasted to taste. Stir nuts 2 or 3 times during roasting, shaking back into a single layer after each stirring.

Yield: 2 cups

Toasted Sunflower Seeds

1 cup shelled sunflower
  seeds

Spread seeds in a shallow pan and toast at 350° F for 15–20 minutes or until seeds brown. Shake seeds occasionally during toasting.

Yield: 1 cup

Bean Dip or Fondue

1 ⅓ cups dried pinto
  beans
½ cup chopped green
  pepper
2 cups chopped fresh
  tomatoes
1 cup water
1 ½ teaspoons sea salt
  or to taste
1 teaspoon ground
  cumin
1 teaspoon ground
  coriander
1 teaspoon garlic
  powder
½ teaspoon chili
  powder
2 tablespoons cold-
  pressed oil

Cook beans until tender and drain. Mash beans well, then stir in remaining ingredients. Simmer, covered, for 1 hour or until mixture is thick. Serve with natural potato or corn chips or whole grain crackers. This dish may be served either hot in a fondue pot or cold.

Yield: 1½ quarts

Yogurt Olive Dip⁽ᴸ⁾

1 cup plain yogurt
1 cup mayonnaise
½ cup pimiento-stuffed
  olives, sliced
½ cup broken pecans
½ teaspoon sea salt
2 tablespoons dried
  chives
½ teaspoon dried
  oregano leaves

With a fork, blend yogurt and mayonnaise together until smooth. Stir in remaining ingredients and chill for at least 1 hour to allow flavors to blend. This dip is especially good with raw vegetables.

Yield: about 2¾ cups

Mustard Dip[L]

1 cup mayonnaise
2 teaspoons apple cider
  vinegar
3 tablespoons
  buttermilk
1 teaspoon herb
  seasoning salt (Spike)
Sea salt to taste
Black pepper to taste
¼ teaspoon ground
  cumin
2–3 teaspoons dry
  mustard

Combine mayonnaise, vinegar, and buttermilk, whipping with a fork until smooth. Mix together remaining ingredients, making sure there are no lumps. Stir into mayonnaise mixture until well combined. Chill.

Yield: about 1¼ cups

Caraway-Cheese Spread[L]

8 ounces cream cheese,
  softened to room
  temperature
¼ cup yogurt or sour
  cream
2 tablespoons milk
2 tablespoons caraway
  seeds
¼ teaspoon garlic
  powder
Sea salt to taste

Combine cream cheese with yogurt and milk until smooth. Stir in caraway seeds, garlic powder, and salt. Chill. Serve on whole-grain crackers.

Yield: about 1¼ cups

Alfalfa Sprout Cheese Spread[L]

4 ounces cream cheese,
  softened to room
  temperature
½ cup milk
2 tablespoons
  mayonnaise
½ teaspoon garlic
  powder
2½ cups shredded
  cheddar cheese
½–1 cup alfalfa sprouts

Beat together cream cheese, milk, mayonnaise, garlic powder, and half of the cheddar cheese until mixture is reasonably smooth. Beat in remaining cheddar cheese, half of it at a time. Continue beating until mixture is thoroughly combined. Chill. Just before serving, stir in alfalfa sprouts.

Yield: about 2 cups

Sesame Crackers

1 cup yellow cornmeal
3 cups whole wheat
  flour
1 cup sesame seeds
1 teaspoon sea salt
¾ cup cold-pressed oil
1 cup water,
  approximately

Stir together cornmeal, flour, sesame seeds, and salt. Add oil and enough water to make a dough that is soft enough to roll but not too soft. Turn dough out onto a floured sheet of wax paper and knead just enough to work into a ball. Cover with another sheet of wax paper and roll out thin. Cut into desired shapes with knife or cookie cutters. Repeat until all dough is used. Bake on ungreased cookie sheets at 375° F for 25–35 minutes depending on shapes; rounds, for example, take longer than diamonds.

Yield: about 5 dozen medium-size crackers

Cheese-Oat Balls[(L)]

1 cup rolled oats
1 cup cheddar cheese,
   shredded and
   softened to room
   temperature
1 cup whole wheat flour
½ cup butter or
   margarine, softened
   to room temperature
⅛ teaspoon sea salt
½ teaspoon chili
   powder
¼ cup milk

Spread oats in shallow pan and toast at 350° F until a pale, golden brown. Combine oats well with remaining ingredients. Pinch off pieces a little larger than marbles and roll into balls. Place balls on ungreased baking sheet and bake at 350° F for 15–20 minutes or until bottoms are lightly browned. Store in an airtight container.

Yield: about 5 dozen balls

Fruit 'n' Nut Balls

¾ cup ground pitted
   prunes
½ cup finely chopped
   pecans or cashews
¼ cup honey
½ cup raisins
¼ cup sunflower seeds
Unsweetened coconut,
   grated

Mix together all ingredients except the coconut. Shape into small balls using a scant teaspoonful for each. Roll in coconut and chill.

Yield: about 3 dozen

Spicy Apple Bread(L)

1 cup dried apples or ½ cup each dried apples and apricots, chopped

6 tablespoons water

2 teaspoons active dry yeast

¼ cup warm water (105° F to 115° F)

2 eggs

½ cup honey

2 tablespoons cold-pressed oil

1⅓ cups rye flour

⅔ cup whole wheat flour

1 teaspoon sea salt

¼ teaspoon ground nutmeg

¼ teaspoon ground cloves

½ teaspoon ground cinnamon

Stir dried fruit with 6 tablespoons of water and set aside. Stir yeast into ¼ cup of warm water and let sit 5 minutes. Meanwhile, beat eggs with honey and oil. When yeast has dissolved, stir well and add to egg mixture. Stir in flours, salt, and then spices. Beat well. Fold in fruit along with any of the soaking water that may not have been absorbed.

Pour batter into a well-oiled loaf pan 9 inches by 5 inches by 3 inches. Cover with a clean towel or cloth and let rise in a warm, draft-free place for about 1 hour. Bake at 325° F about 45 minutes or until nicely browned and a toothpick inserted in center comes out clean.

Yield: 1 loaf

Hot Spiced Apple Juice

Apple juice
Stick of cinnamon
Whole cloves
Orange or lemon slices
  (optional)

For every cup of apple juice, use 1 stick of cinnamon and 6 whole cloves. Put all ingredients in a saucepan, bring to a boil, reduce heat and simmer for 5 minutes. Strain into mugs. Garnish with orange or lemon slices if desired.

Dried Fruit Platter

Pitted dates
Turkish apricots
Dried pineapple slices,
  cut in half
Raisins

On a serving platter, arrange dates, apricots, and pineapple slices. Garnish with a sprinkling of raisins.

MAIL-ORDER SOURCES

FOR VEGETARIAN PRODUCTS

Dairy Products

American Supply House, Box 1114, Columbia, MO 65205 (cultures)

Countryside General Store, 103 N. Monroe Street, Waterloo, WI 53594 (general)

Homecraft, 111 Stratford Center, Winston-Salem, NC 27104 (cheese-making)

International Yogurt, 628 North Doheny Drive, Los Angeles, CA 90069 (cultures)

Grain and Flour, Nuts and Seeds, Soyfood Products, Sea Vegetables, Beans, Seeds for Sprouting, Citrus and Sweeteners, Herbs and Spices

Arrowhead Mills, Inc., Box 866, Hereford, TX 79045 (seeds, nuts, beans, grains)

Attar Herbs & Spices, Playground Road, New Ipswich, NH 03071 (herbs, spices)

Butte Creek Mill, 402 Royal Ave. N., Eagle Point, OR 97524 (flours, cereal, beans)

Calloway Gardens Country Store, Highway 27, Pine Mt., GA 31822 (whole grains)

Caprilands Herb Farm, 534 Silver Street, Coventry, CT 06238 (spices, herbs, seeds)

Country Herbs, 3 Maple Street, Stockbridge, MA 01262 (herbs, spices, plants, seeds)

Eden Foods, 701 Tecumseh Road, Clinton, MI 49236 (fruit butters, jams, grains, soy products, baking supplies)

Erewhon Trading Co., 236 Washington St., Brookline, MA 02146 (grains, flours, sea vegetables, nuts, seeds, beans, soyfoods)

Fantastic Foods, 106 Galli Drive, Novato, CA 94947 (confections, meat substitutes, crackers, tofu mix)

Flintridge Herbs, R. R. 1, Sister Bay, WI 54234 (herbs, spices, plants)

Great Valley Mills, Box 260, Quakertown, PA 18451 (flours, grains)

Hilltop Herb Farm, P.O. Box 1734, Cleveland, TN 77327 (herbs, spices, seeds, plants)

Katagiri Co., 224 E. 59th St., New York, NY 10022 (sea vegetables)

Lee's Fruits, Box 450, Leesburg, FL 32748 (honey, citrus)

Letoba Farm Foods, Box 180, R. R. 3, Lyons, KS 67554 (beans, sea vegetables, spices, herbs, grains, oils, flours)

Mountain Ark Trading Co., 120 S. E. Street, Fayetteville, AR 72701 (whole grains, organic beans, sea vegetables, condiments)

Nature's Way, P. O. Box 2233, Provo, UT 84603 (herbal capsules and tablets)

Nichols Garden Nursery, 1190 N. Pacific, Albany, OR 97321 (seeds, plants, herbs, spices)

Park Seed Co., Greenwood, SC 29647 (seeds)

Shiloh Farms, Box 97, Highway 59, Sulphur Springs, AR 72768 (natural sweeteners)

Thousand Island Apiaries, Clayton, NY 13624 (honey)

Wide World of Herbs, 11 St. Catherine St. E., Montreal, PQ H2X 1K3, Canada (herbs, spices)

Yankee Peddler Herb Farm, R. R. 1, Box 251, Burton, TX 77835 (herbs, spices, teas, seeds)

INDEX

grape leaves stuffed with rice, 45
gravies:
    brown, 287
    cashew milk, 227
    gluten, with seitan, 281
    nutritional yeast, 227
green bean almondine, 145
guacamole, tofu, 44

halvah:
    carrot, 262
    sesame, 255
harvest punch, 68
herbs, 9–10
    dip for fresh vegetables, 218
    how to use, 10–12
    -onion bread, 209
    rice, 155
    rice, bell peppers with, 157
    spinach pesto cream, 226
holiday menus, 274–289
    for Seder, 276–278
    for Thanksgiving, 279–289
holidays, pumpkin treats for, 290–294
holiday snacks, 295–301
    alfalfa sprout cheese spread, 298
    bean dip or fondue, 296
    caraway-cheese spread, 297
    cheese-oat balls, 299
    citrus punch, 295
    dried fruit platter, 301
    fruit 'n' nut balls, 299
    hot spiced apple juice, 301
    mustard dip, 297
    pumpkin seed, 294
    roasted almonds, 295
    sesame crackers, 298
    spicy apple bread, 300
    toasted sunflower seeds, 295
    yogurt olive dip, 296
honey, 7
    banana ice cream, 246
    banana soymilk ice cream, 244
    custard, baked, 257
    -nut-popcorn crunch, 261
    -seed mounds, 263
    and walnut scones, 208

horseradish:
    chestnut sauce, 221
    and nut dip, 216
hot-and-sour cucumbers, 43
hummus, 46

ice creams, 244–248
    avocado sherbet, 247
    avocado velvet, 247
    banana honey soymilk, 244
    carob cream swirl, 246
    Elizabeth's double Dutch chocolate,
        245
    fudgesicles, 248
    honey banana, 246
    peach frost, 245
    pineapple sherbet, 245
    rocky banana, 246
    spumoni sticks, 248
icing, carob, 242
Indian pudding, 259
Irish potato bread, 203
Italian:
    dressing, 102
    no-oil dressing, 102
    spice, 237
    tofu meatballs, 167
    zucchini, 123

Jarlsberg rice, 153
juicers, 25, 59
juices:
    carrot-apple, 61
    frozen concentrates, 8
    pineapple-cucumber, 61

kabobs, fruit:
    lemonade delight with, 60
    with strawberry dip, 265
ketchup:
    homemade, 229
    tomato, 231
kitchen equipment, 23–27
    accessories and gadgets, 26–27
    helpful appliances, 25–26
    pots and pans, 24–25
knives, 26

stir-frying, 31
strawberry dip, fruit kabobs with, 265
Stroganoff:
    mushroom with tofu, 178
    tofu, 120
sunflower seeds:
    ginger bread, 198
    sauce, curried, 222
    toasted, 295
sweet-and-sour:
    lentils with brown rice, 135
    tofu soup, cold, 79
sweeteners, 7–8
sweet potatoes, candied, 282
Szechuan tofu, spicy, 177

tabouli salad, 16, 104–105
tacos, tofu with, 170
tahini-tofu spread, 268
taratoor sauce, 45
tart, tofu-pumpkin, 293
tartar sauce, 230
tea:
    cranberry punch, 70
    -fruit punch, Clare's hot, 67
teriyaki tofu, 166
Thanksgiving menus, 279–289
tiropite, 124
tofu (bean curd), 16–17, 158–178
    in American diet, 163
    asparagus sauce, 162
    -banana-apple spread, 268
    and bean sprout salad, 99
    -broccoli spread, 271
    brochettes with vegetables, 161
    burgers, 165
    cheesecake, baroque, 252
    cheesecake, country life, 253
    cheesecake with fruit topping, 249
    creamy dip or dressing, 214
    creme, 293
    and curried rice salad, 171
    cutlets, 164
    dessert soufflé, 251
    dill dip, 217
    dressing, creamy, 104
    eggless "egg salad," 270

firm vs. soft forms, 158
foo young, 169
fried, clubhouse sandwich with, 273
fried, with vegetables, 173
-fruit whips or puddings, 250
-garlic dip, 48
with ginger, 168
guacamole, 44
Italian meatballs, 167
marinade, spiced, 53
mayonnaise, 230
mushroom Stroganoff with, 178
orange soufflé, 254
pan-fried, 174
pumpkin pie, 292
-pumpkin tart, 293
rainbow sandwich, 163
sauce, white, 161
scrambled, 170
-sesame dressing, 110
settling boxes, 26
soup, cold sweet-and-sour, 79
sour cream, 219
spicy Szechuan, 177
spread or dressing, curried, 269
squash soup with, 78
Stroganoff, 120
stuffed mushroom caps, 164
-stuffed mushrooms, 121
-stuffed peppers, 160
stuffing, baked potatoes with, 169
with tacos, 170
-tahini spread, 268
teriyaki, 166
terrine, 162
timely, 116
vegetables, simple, 160
and vegetable salad, California, 99
tomatoes:
    curry of zucchini and, 118
    fresh, soup, 76
    ketchup, 231
    -nut mélange sauce, 224
    -onion vinaigrette, 105
    -peanut sauce, spicy, 221